He was the greatest soldier the world would ever know.
When a devastating Civil War divided the super heroes,
he surrendered to end the conflict.
Despite his noble sacrifice, he was assassinated.

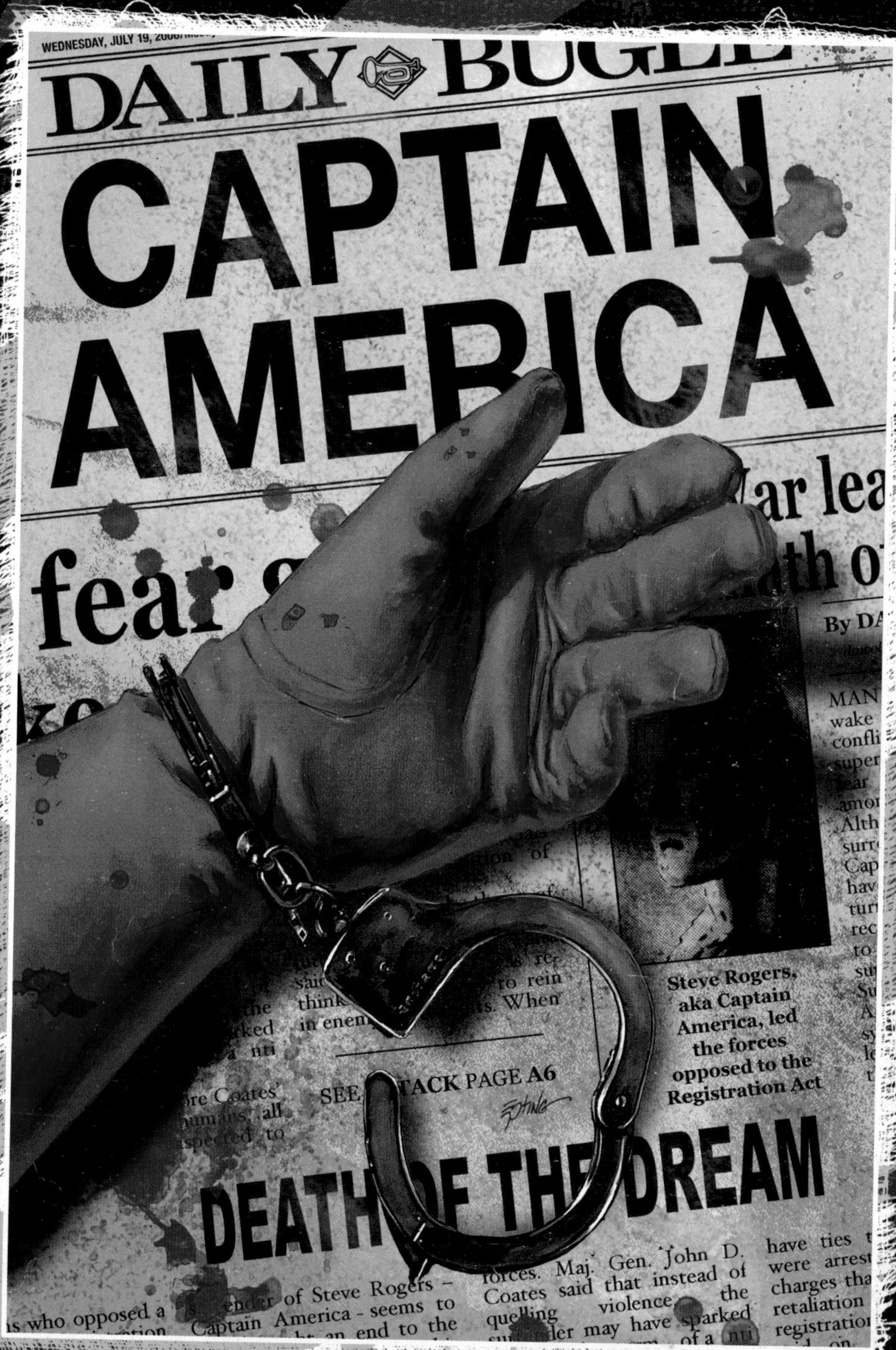
DAILY BUGLE
CAPTAIN AMERICA
Steve Rogers, aka Captain America, led the forces opposed to the Registration Act
DEATH OF THE DREAM

Captain America is dead.

This is what happens next.

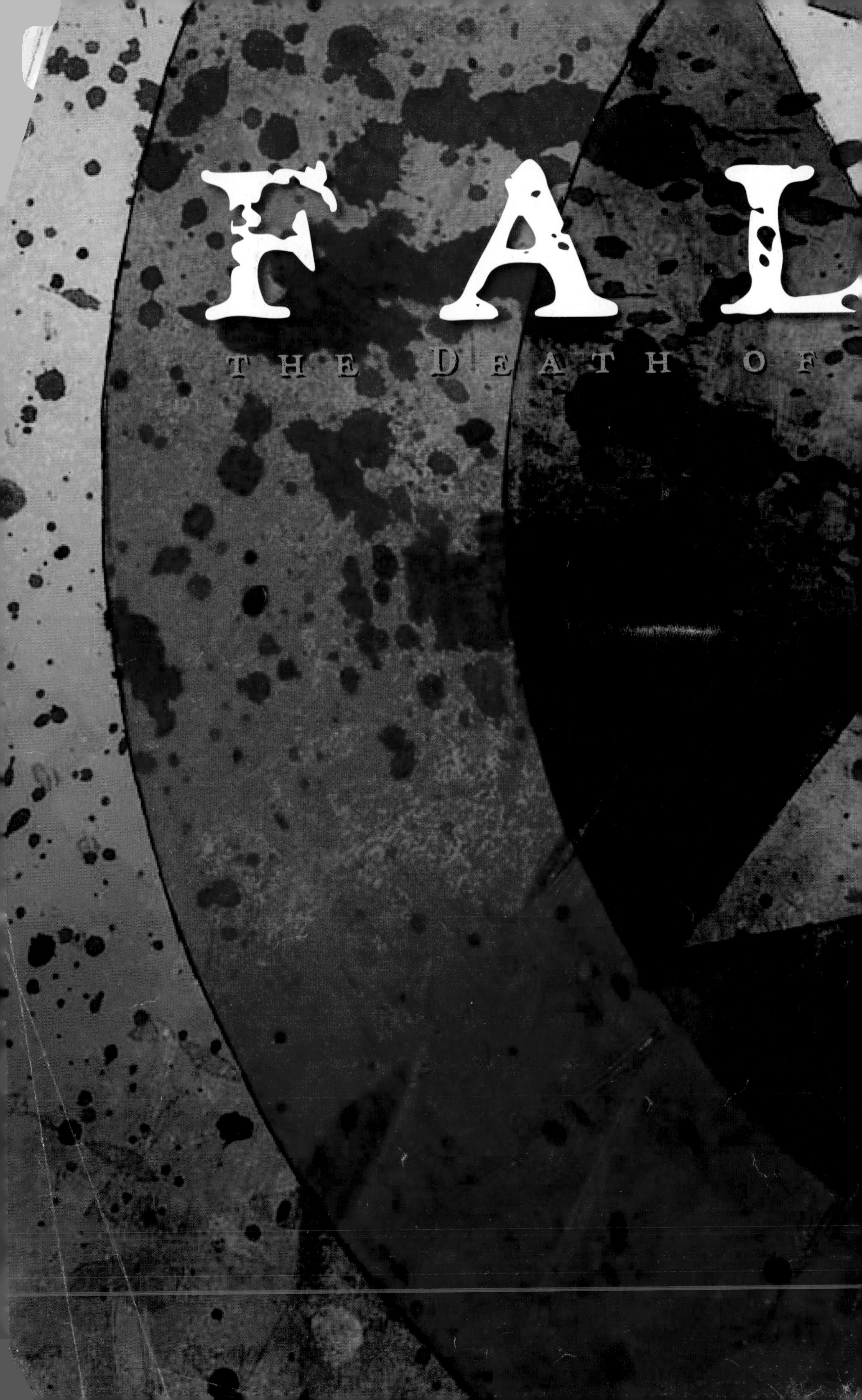
FAL
THE DEATH OF

LEN
CAPTAIN AMERICA
SON

Writer JEPH LOEB
From an idea by J. MICHAEL STRACZYNSKI

Artist LEINIL YU
Colors/Digital Inks DAVE McCAIG

Pencils ED McGUINNESS
Inks DEXTER VINES
Colors JASON KEITH

Pencils JOHN ROMITA JR.
Inks KLAUS JANSON
Colors MORRY HOLLOWELL

Pencils DAVID FINCH
Inks DANNY MIKI
Colors FRANK D'ARMATA

Artist JOHN CASSADAY
Colors LAURA MARTIN

Lettering RICHARD STARKINGS
AND COMICRAFT'S
ALBERT DESCHESNE &
JIMMY BETANCOURT

Assistant Editor ALEJANDRO ARBONA
Editor BILL ROSEMANN

Variant Cover Art MICHAEL TURNER
WITH MARK ROSLAN
& PETER STEIGERWALD

Book Cover Art JOHN CASSADAY

Collection Editor JENNIFER GRÜNWALD
Assistant Editors CORY LEVINE & JOHN DENNING
Editor, Special Projects MARK D. BEAZLEY
Senior Editor, Special Projects JEFF YOUNGQUIST
Senior Vice President of Sales DAVID GABRIEL
Production JERRY KALINOWSKI
Book Design JOHN ROSHELL OF COMICRAFT

Editor in Chief JOE QUESADA
Publisher DAN BUCKLEY

FALLEN 1 SON

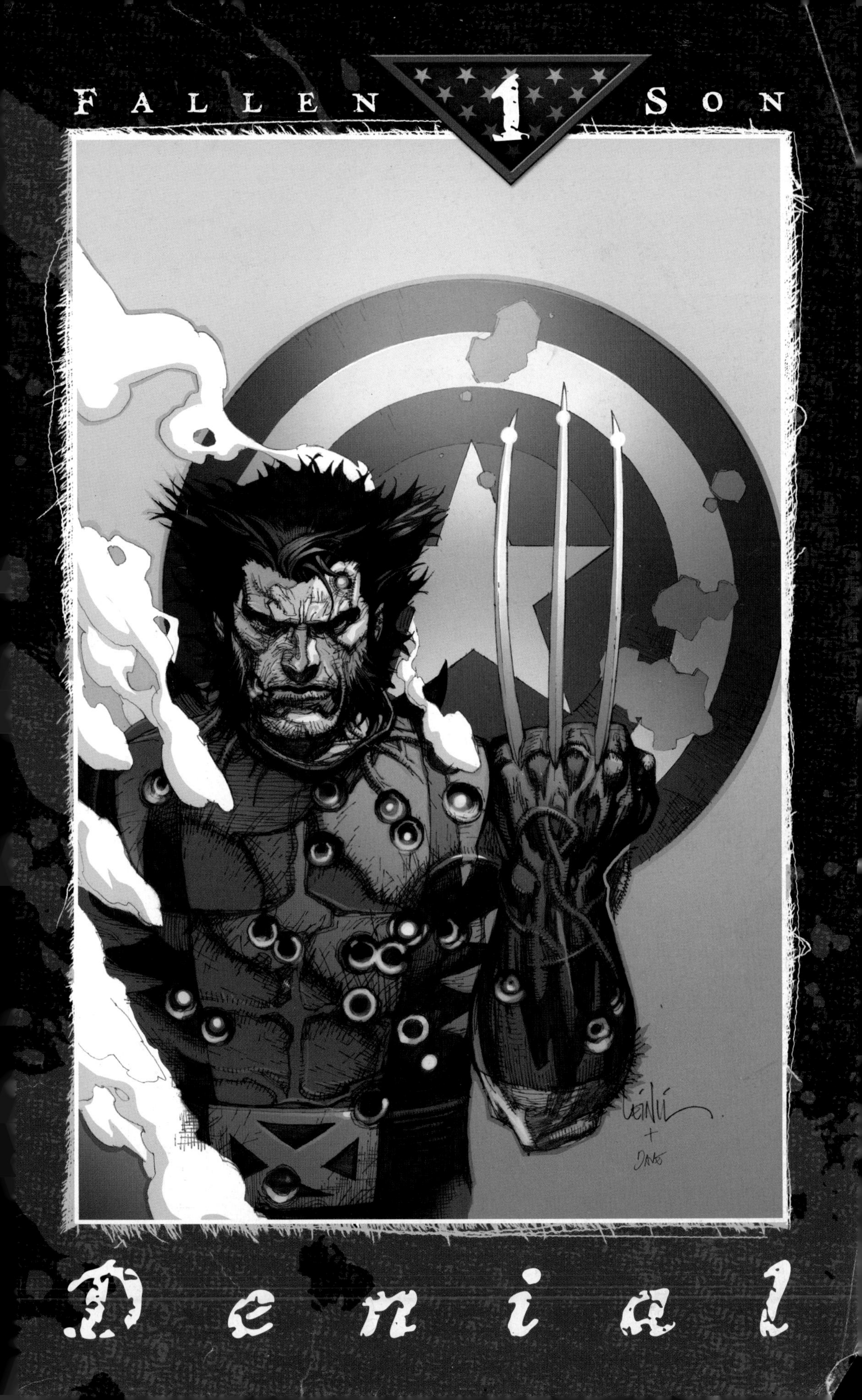

Denial

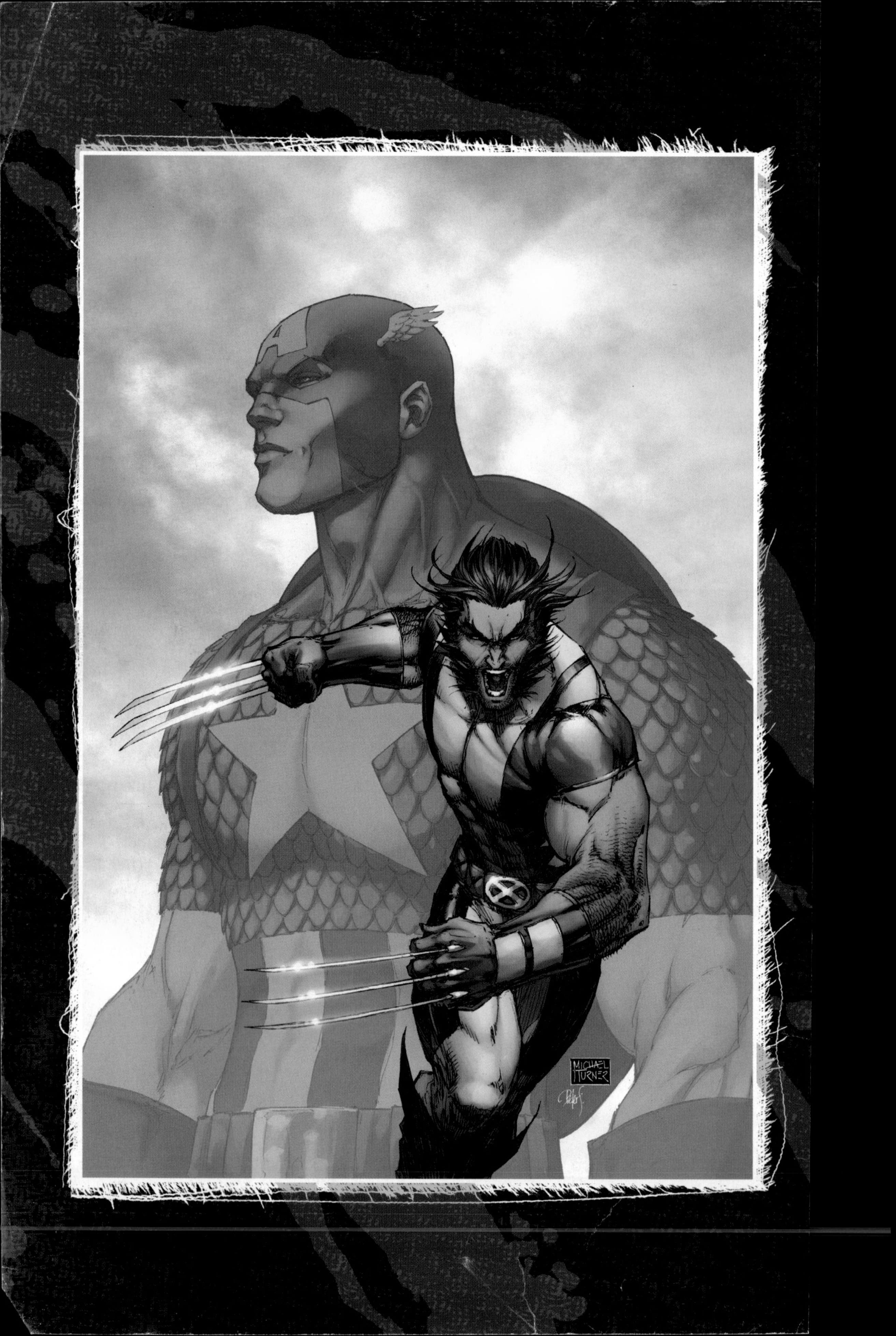
MICHAEL TURNER

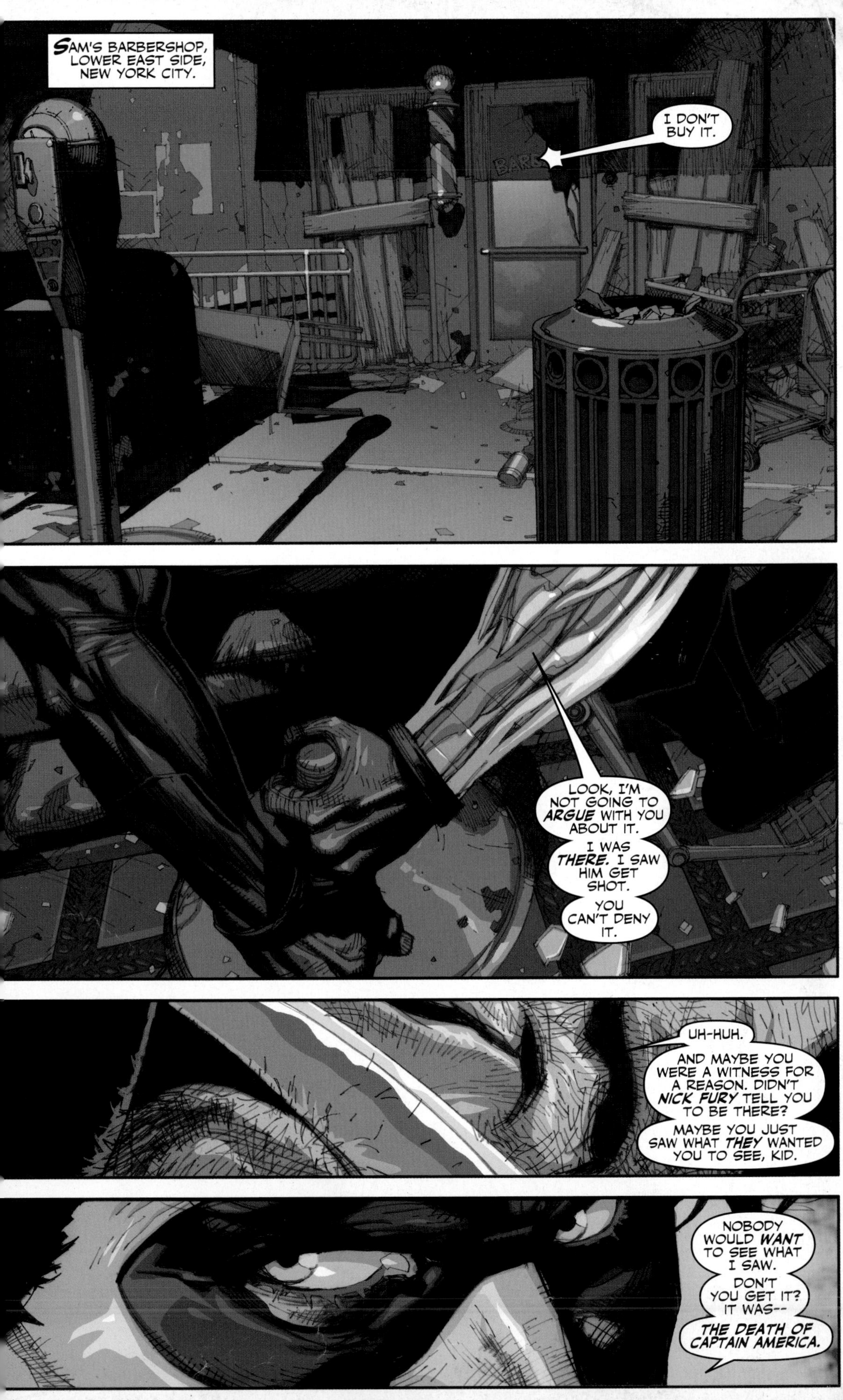
SAM'S BARBERSHOP, LOWER EAST SIDE, NEW YORK CITY.
I DON'T BUY IT.
LOOK, I'M NOT GOING TO ARGUE WITH YOU ABOUT IT.
I WAS THERE. I SAW HIM GET SHOT.
YOU CAN'T DENY IT.
UH-HUH.
AND MAYBE YOU WERE A WITNESS FOR A REASON. DIDN'T NICK FURY TELL YOU TO BE THERE?
MAYBE YOU JUST SAW WHAT THEY WANTED YOU TO SEE, KID.
NOBODY WOULD WANT TO SEE WHAT I SAW.
DON'T YOU GET IT? IT WAS--
THE DEATH OF CAPTAIN AMERICA.

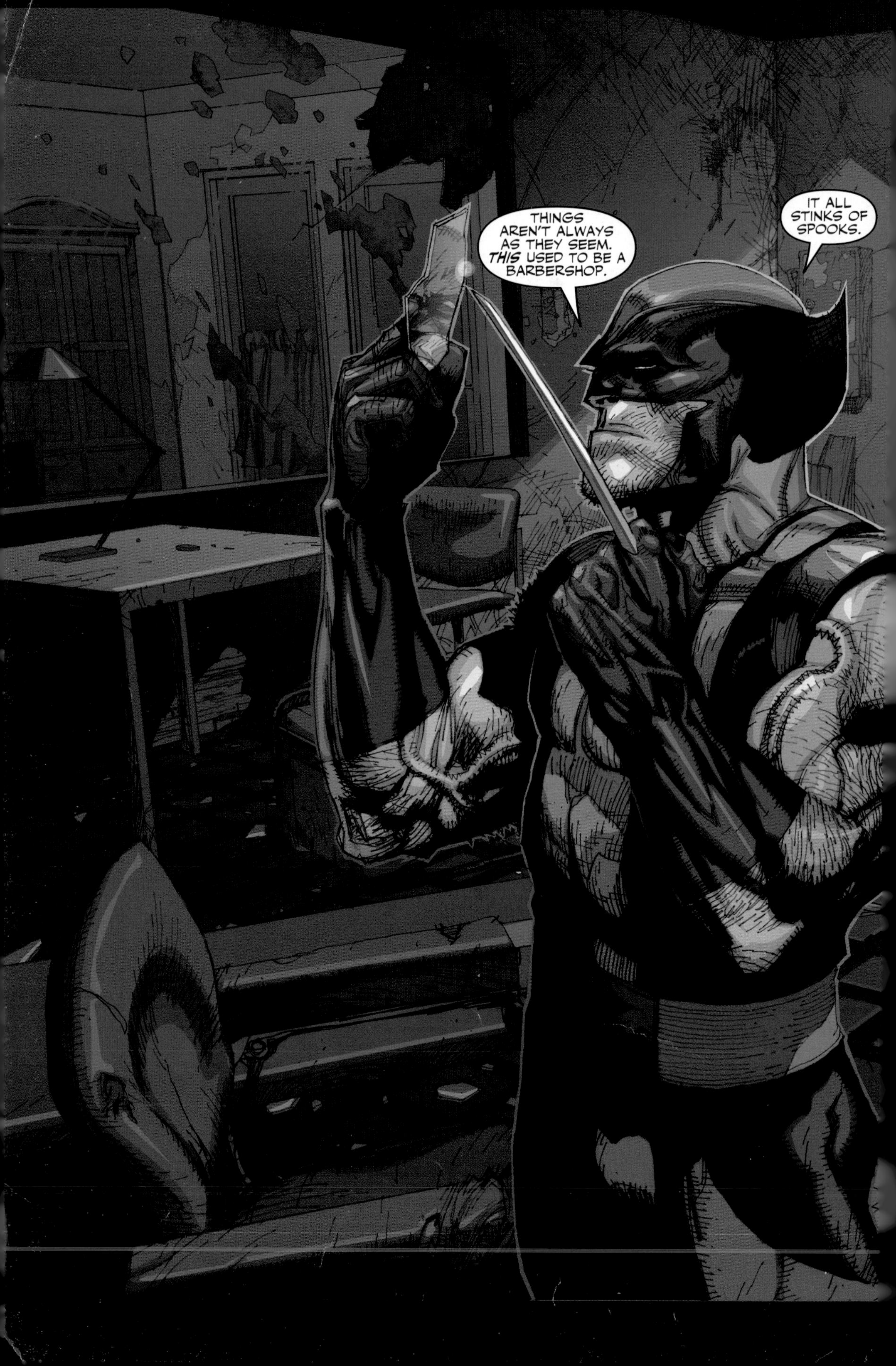
THINGS AREN'T ALWAYS AS THEY SEEM. *THIS* USED TO BE A BARBERSHOP.
IT ALL STINKS OF SPOOKS.

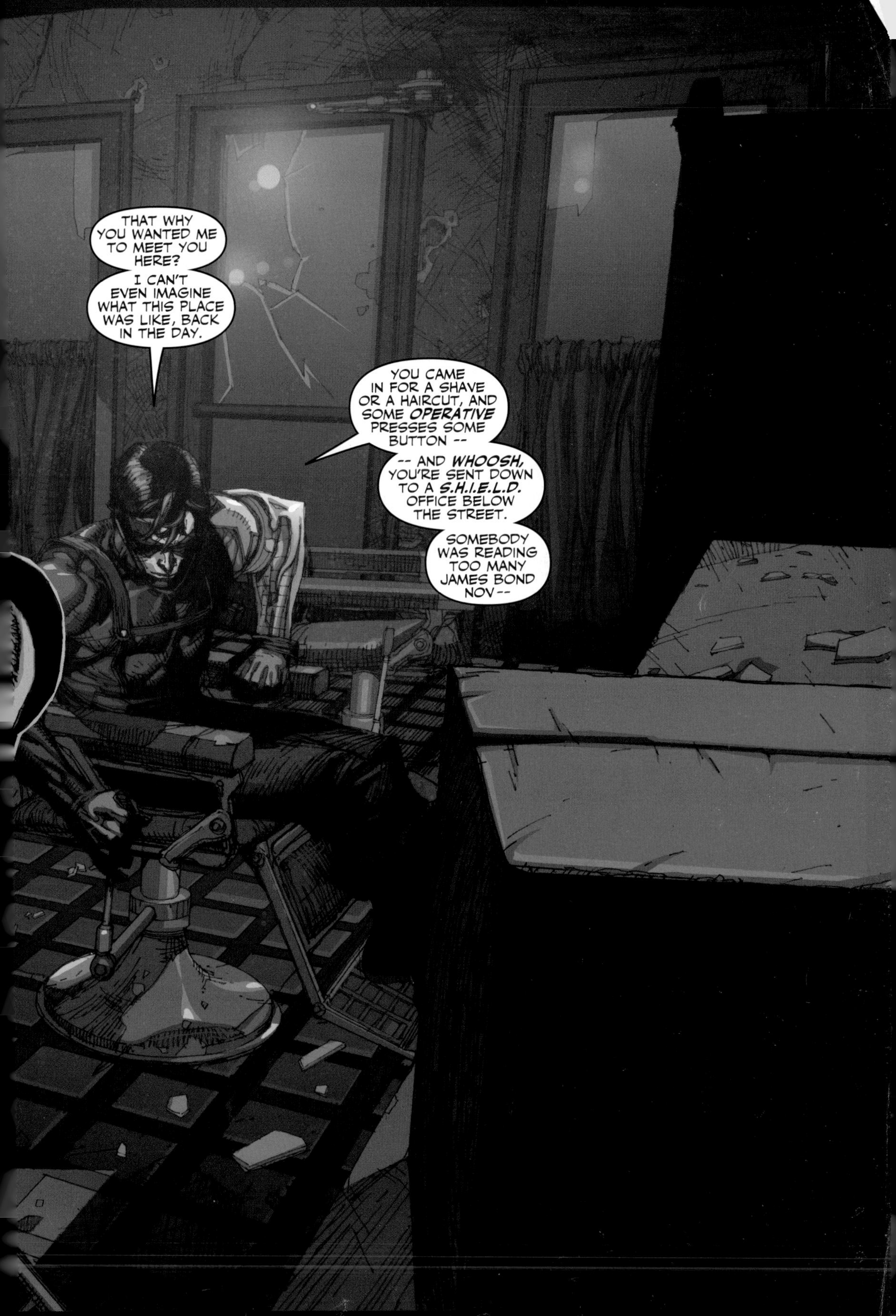
THAT WHY YOU WANTED ME TO MEET YOU HERE?
I CAN'T EVEN IMAGINE WHAT THIS PLACE WAS LIKE, BACK IN THE DAY.
YOU CAME IN FOR A SHAVE OR A HAIRCUT, AND SOME *OPERATIVE* PRESSES SOME BUTTON --
-- AND ***WHOOSH,*** YOU'RE SENT DOWN TO A ***S.H.I.E.L.D.*** OFFICE BELOW THE STREET.
SOMEBODY WAS READING TOO MANY JAMES BOND NOV--

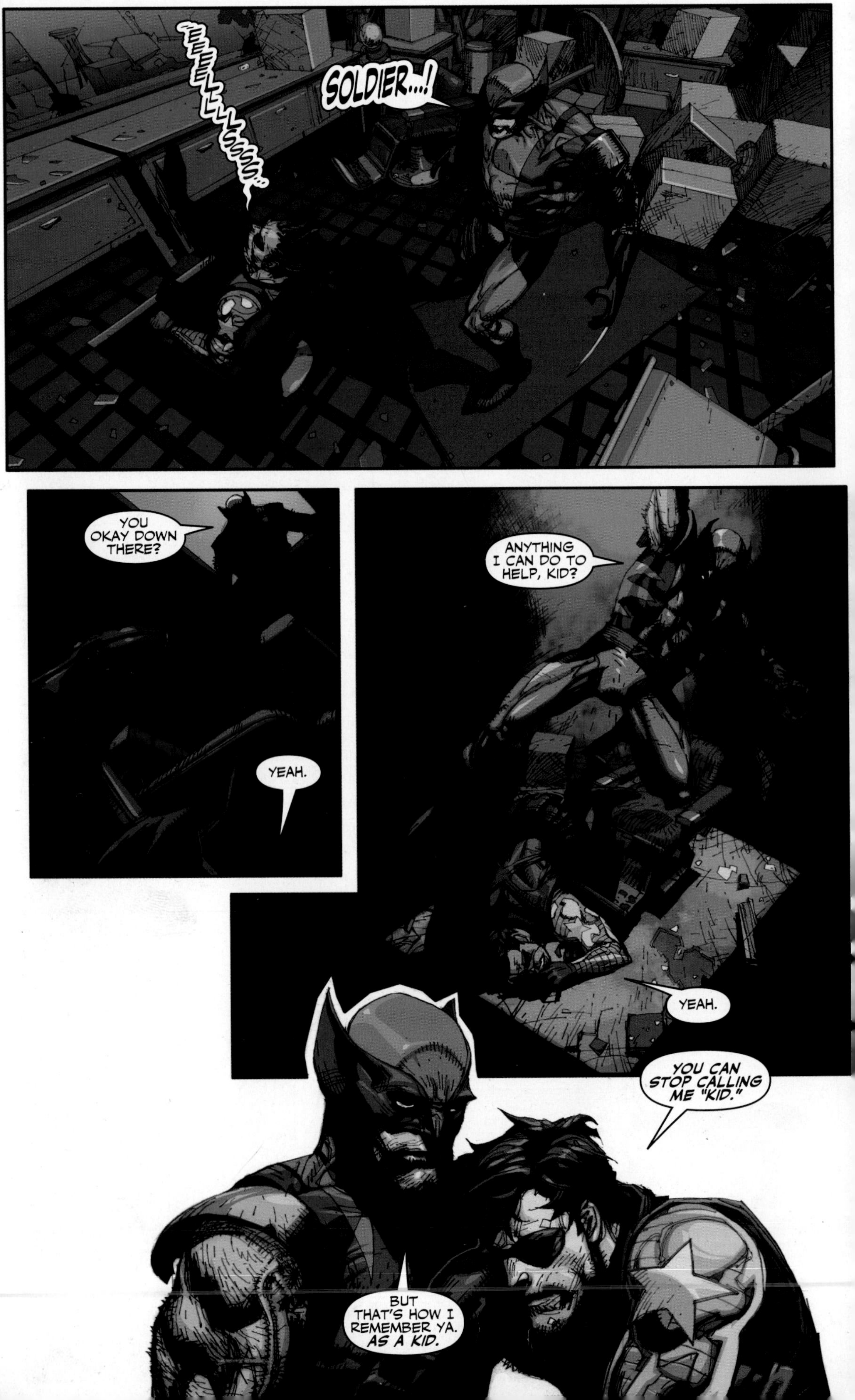
"EEELLLSSSS..."
SOLDIER...!
YOU OKAY DOWN THERE?
YEAH.
ANYTHING I CAN DO TO HELP, KID?
YEAH.
YOU CAN STOP CALLING ME "KID."
BUT THAT'S HOW I REMEMBER YA. AS A KID.

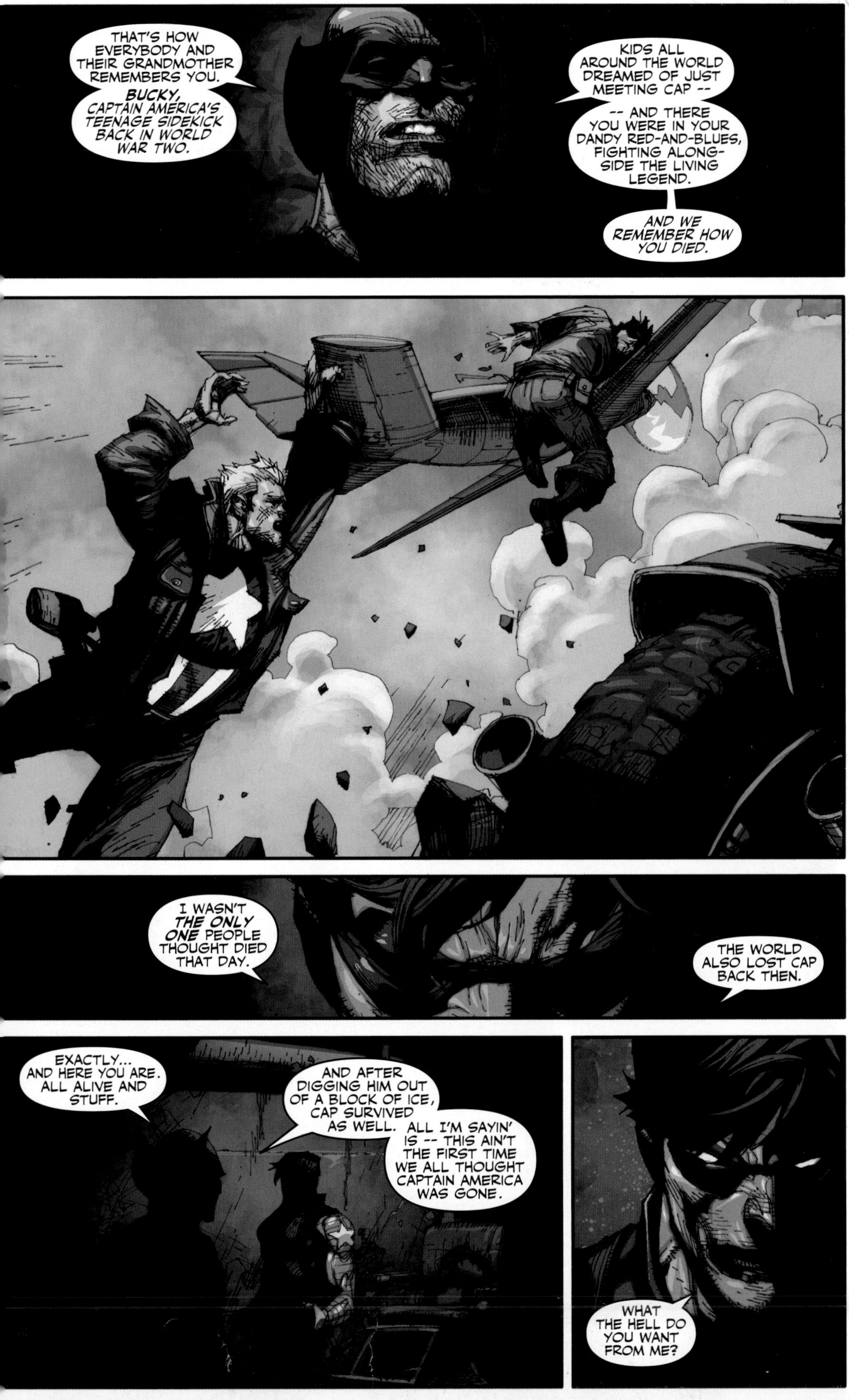
THAT'S HOW EVERYBODY AND THEIR GRANDMOTHER REMEMBERS YOU.
BUCKY, CAPTAIN AMERICA'S TEENAGE SIDEKICK BACK IN WORLD WAR TWO.
KIDS ALL AROUND THE WORLD DREAMED OF JUST MEETING CAP --
-- AND THERE YOU WERE IN YOUR DANDY RED-AND-BLUES, FIGHTING ALONG-SIDE THE LIVING LEGEND.
AND WE REMEMBER HOW YOU DIED.
I WASN'T *THE ONLY ONE* PEOPLE THOUGHT DIED THAT DAY.
THE WORLD ALSO LOST CAP BACK THEN.
EXACTLY... AND HERE YOU ARE. ALL ALIVE AND STUFF.
AND AFTER DIGGING HIM OUT OF A BLOCK OF ICE, CAP SURVIVED AS WELL.
ALL I'M SAYIN' IS -- THIS AIN'T THE FIRST TIME WE ALL THOUGHT CAPTAIN AMERICA WAS GONE.
WHAT THE HELL DO YOU WANT FROM ME?

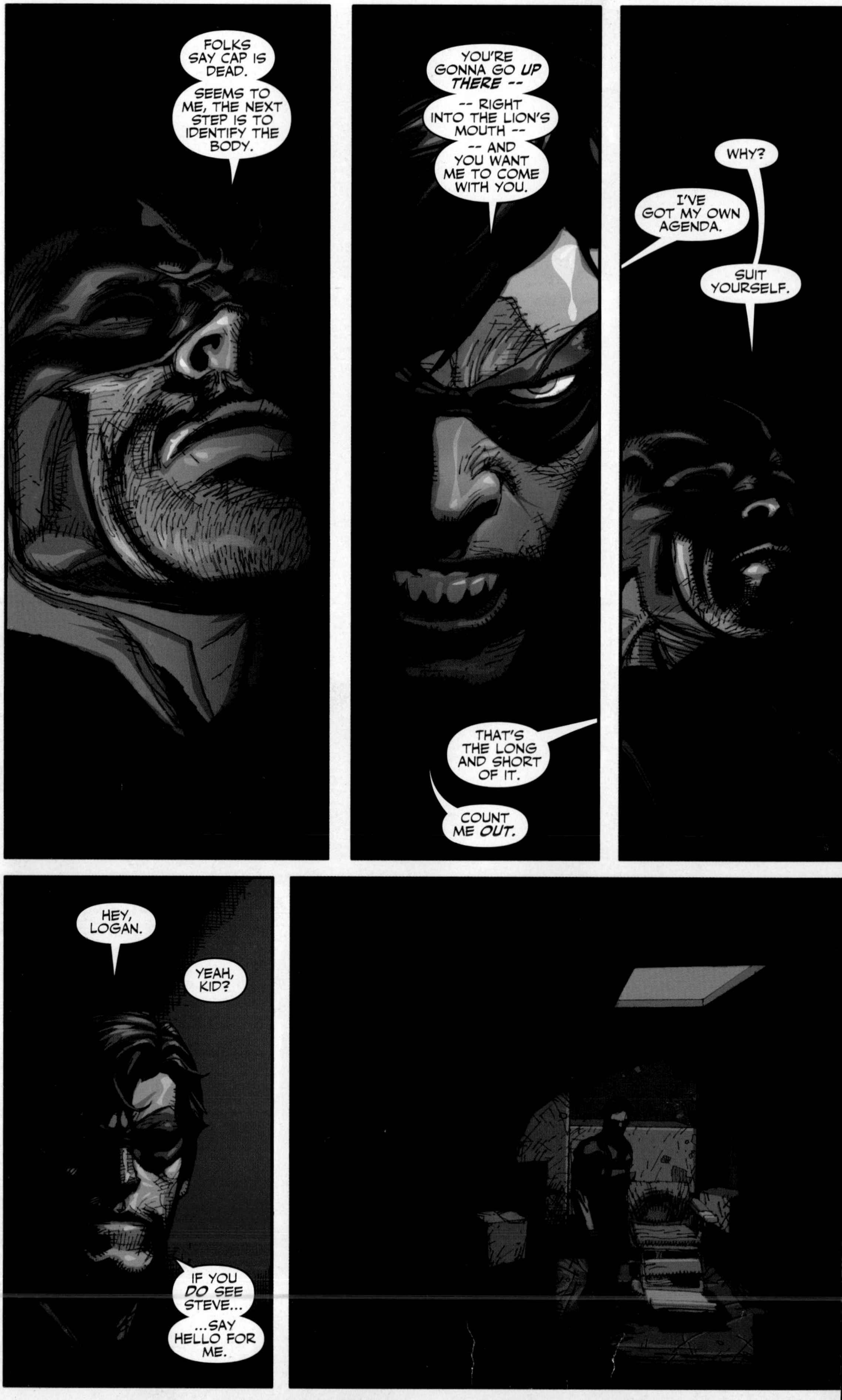
FOLKS SAY CAP IS DEAD.
SEEMS TO ME, THE NEXT STEP IS TO IDENTIFY THE BODY.
YOU'RE GONNA GO *UP THERE --*
-- RIGHT INTO THE LION'S MOUTH --
-- AND YOU WANT ME TO COME WITH YOU.
THAT'S THE LONG AND SHORT OF IT.
COUNT ME *OUT.*
WHY?
I'VE GOT MY OWN AGENDA.
SUIT YOURSELF.
HEY, LOGAN.
YEAH, KID?
IF YOU *DO* SEE STEVE...
...SAY HELLO FOR ME.

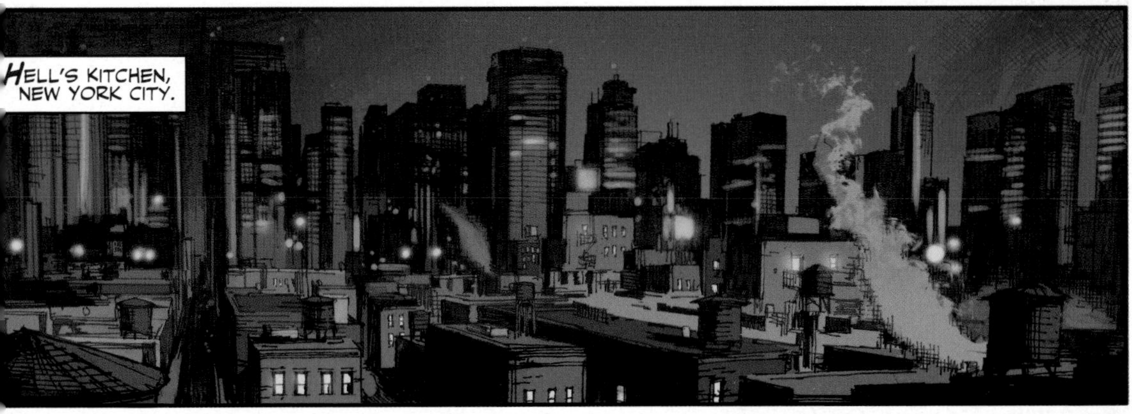
HELL'S KITCHEN, NEW YORK CITY.

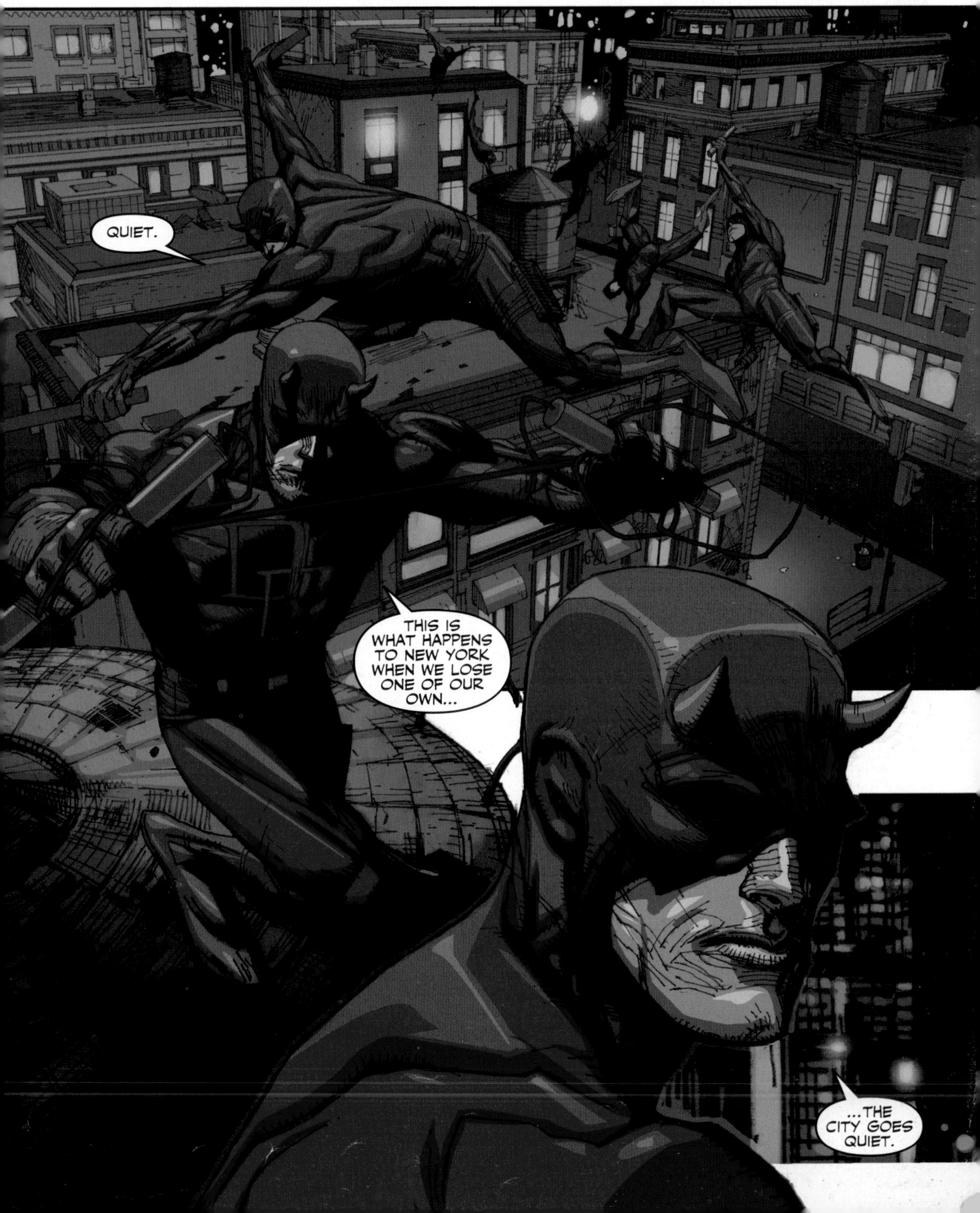
QUIET.
THIS IS WHAT HAPPENS TO NEW YORK WHEN WE LOSE ONE OF OUR OWN...
...THE CITY GOES QUIET.

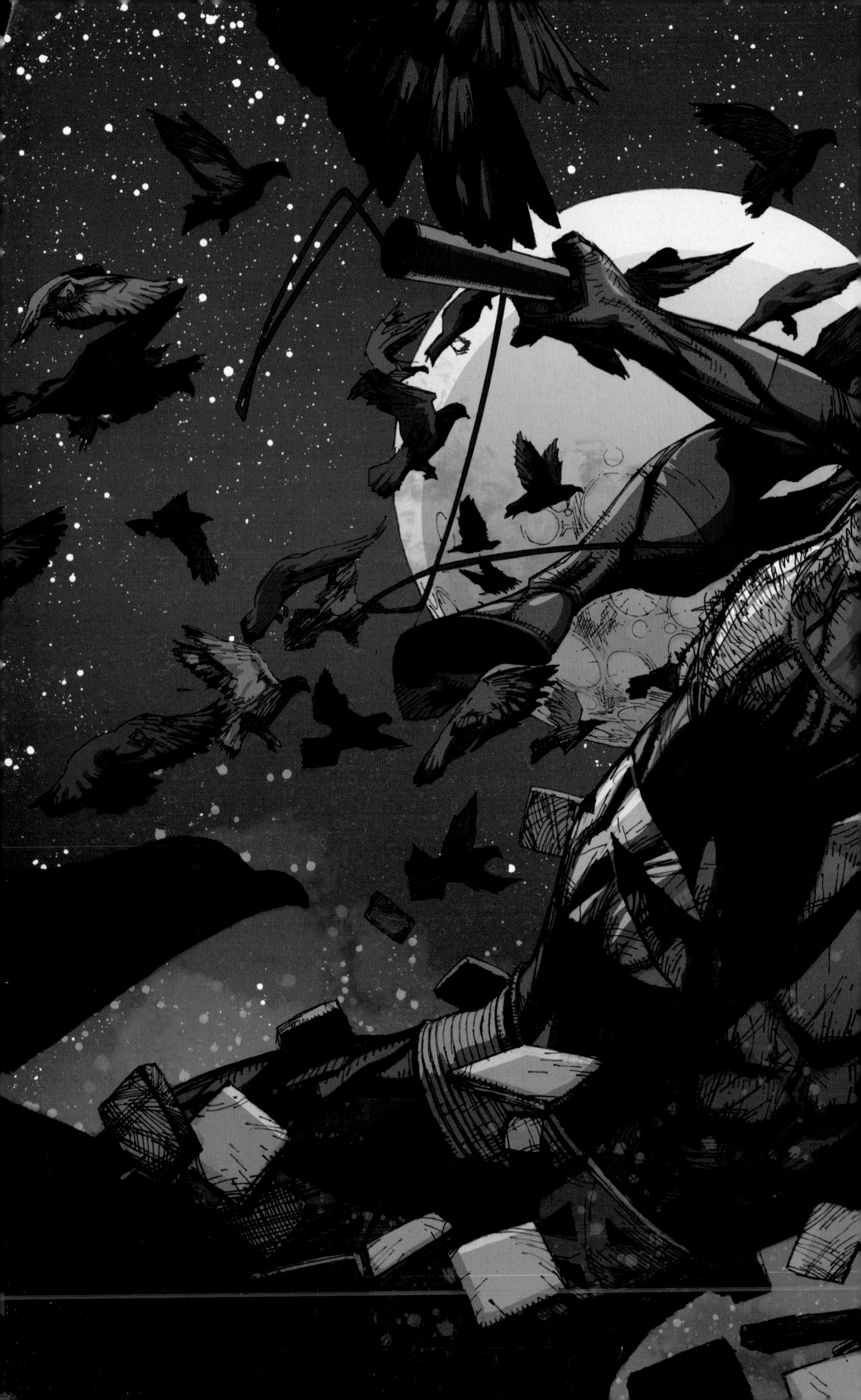

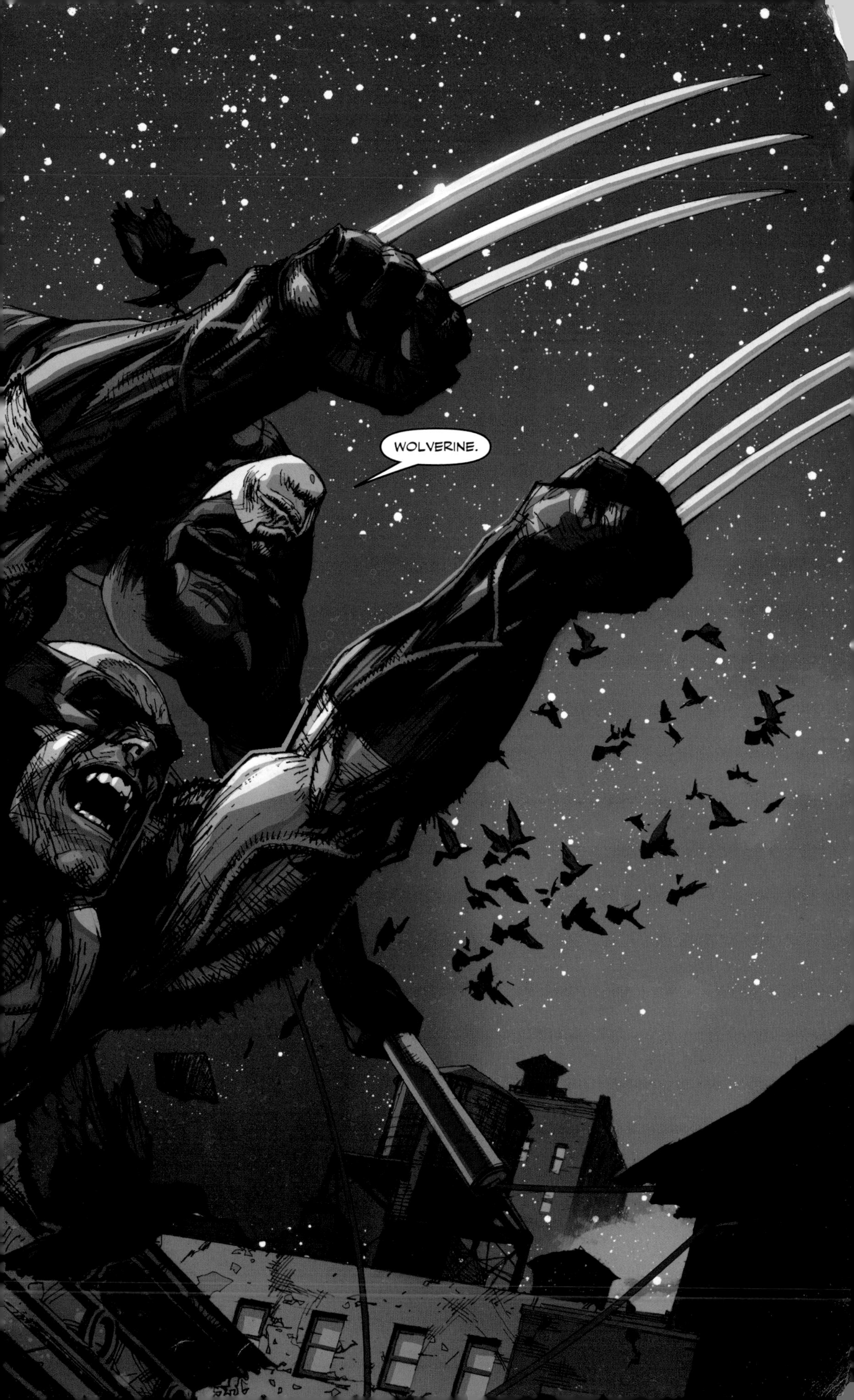
WOLVERINE.

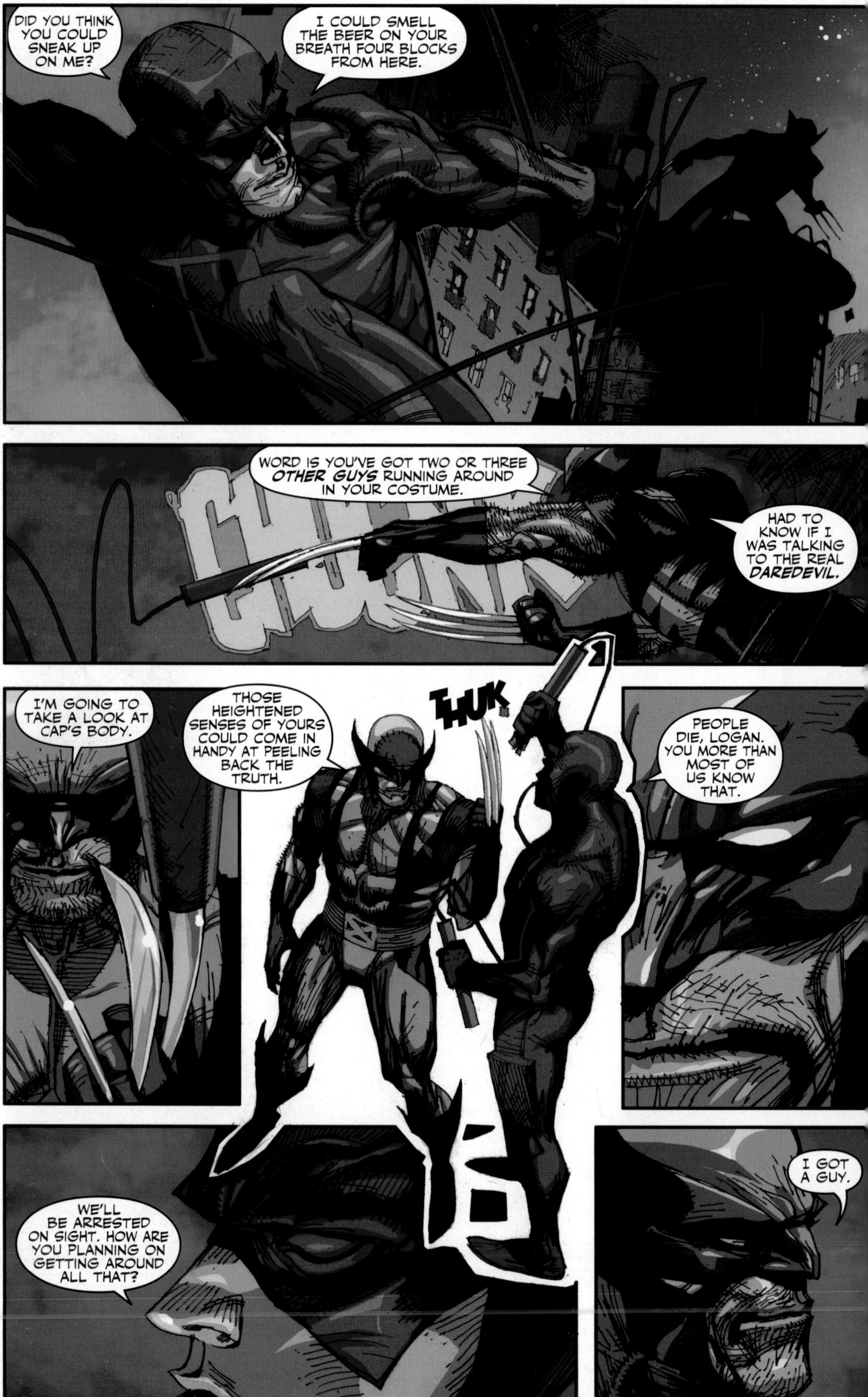
DID YOU THINK YOU COULD SNEAK UP ON ME?
I COULD SMELL THE BEER ON YOUR BREATH FOUR BLOCKS FROM HERE.
WORD IS YOU'VE GOT TWO OR THREE OTHER GUYS RUNNING AROUND IN YOUR COSTUME.
HAD TO KNOW IF I WAS TALKING TO THE REAL DAREDEVIL.
I'M GOING TO TAKE A LOOK AT CAP'S BODY.
THOSE HEIGHTENED SENSES OF YOURS COULD COME IN HANDY AT PEELING BACK THE TRUTH.
THUK
PEOPLE DIE, LOGAN. YOU MORE THAN MOST OF US KNOW THAT.
WE'LL BE ARRESTED ON SIGHT. HOW ARE YOU PLANNING ON GETTING AROUND ALL THAT?
I GOT A GUY.

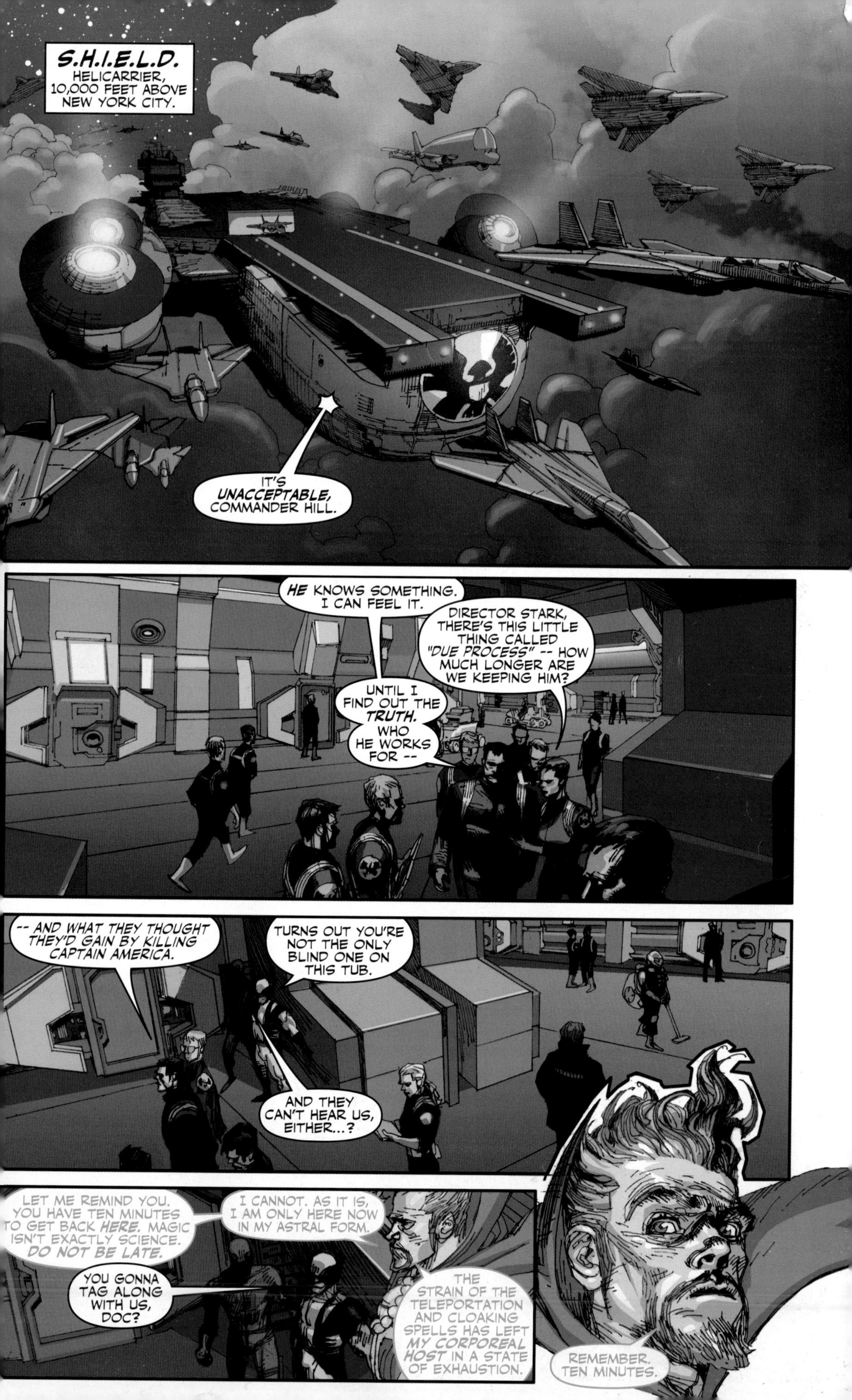
S.H.I.E.L.D. HELICARRIER, 10,000 FEET ABOVE NEW YORK CITY.
IT'S *UNACCEPTABLE,* COMMANDER HILL.
HE KNOWS SOMETHING. I CAN FEEL IT.
DIRECTOR STARK, THERE'S THIS LITTLE THING CALLED *"DUE PROCESS"* -- HOW MUCH LONGER ARE WE KEEPING HIM?
UNTIL I FIND OUT THE *TRUTH.* WHO HE WORKS FOR --
-- AND WHAT THEY THOUGHT THEY'D GAIN BY KILLING CAPTAIN AMERICA.
TURNS OUT YOU'RE NOT THE ONLY BLIND ONE ON THIS TUB.
AND THEY CAN'T HEAR US, EITHER...?
LET ME REMIND YOU. YOU HAVE TEN MINUTES TO GET BACK *HERE.* MAGIC ISN'T EXACTLY SCIENCE. *DO NOT BE LATE.*
YOU GONNA TAG ALONG WITH US, DOC?
I CANNOT. AS IT IS, I AM ONLY HERE NOW IN MY ASTRAL FORM.
THE STRAIN OF THE TELEPORTATION AND CLOAKING SPELLS HAS LEFT *MY CORPOREAL HOST* IN A STATE OF EXHAUSTION.
REMEMBER. TEN MINUTES.

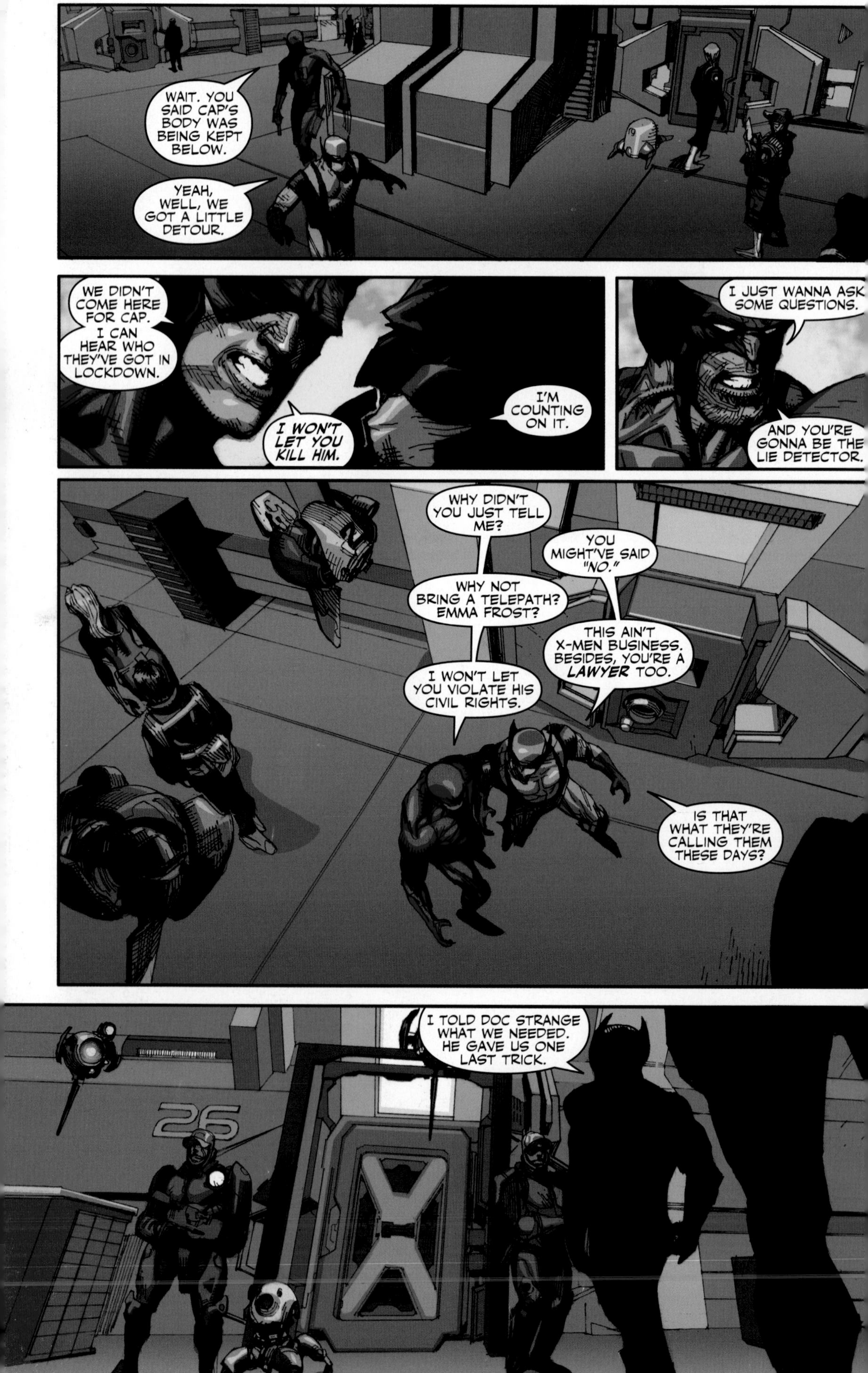
WAIT. YOU SAID CAP'S BODY WAS BEING KEPT BELOW.
YEAH, WELL, WE GOT A LITTLE DETOUR.
WE DIDN'T COME HERE FOR CAP. I CAN HEAR WHO THEY'VE GOT IN LOCKDOWN.
I WON'T LET YOU KILL HIM.
I'M COUNTING ON IT.
I JUST WANNA ASK SOME QUESTIONS.
AND YOU'RE GONNA BE THE LIE DETECTOR.
WHY DIDN'T YOU JUST TELL ME?
YOU MIGHT'VE SAID "NO."
WHY NOT BRING A TELEPATH? EMMA FROST?
THIS AIN'T X-MEN BUSINESS. BESIDES, YOU'RE A LAWYER TOO.
I WON'T LET YOU VIOLATE HIS CIVIL RIGHTS.
IS THAT WHAT THEY'RE CALLING THEM THESE DAYS?
I TOLD DOC STRANGE WHAT WE NEEDED. HE GAVE US ONE LAST TRICK.
26

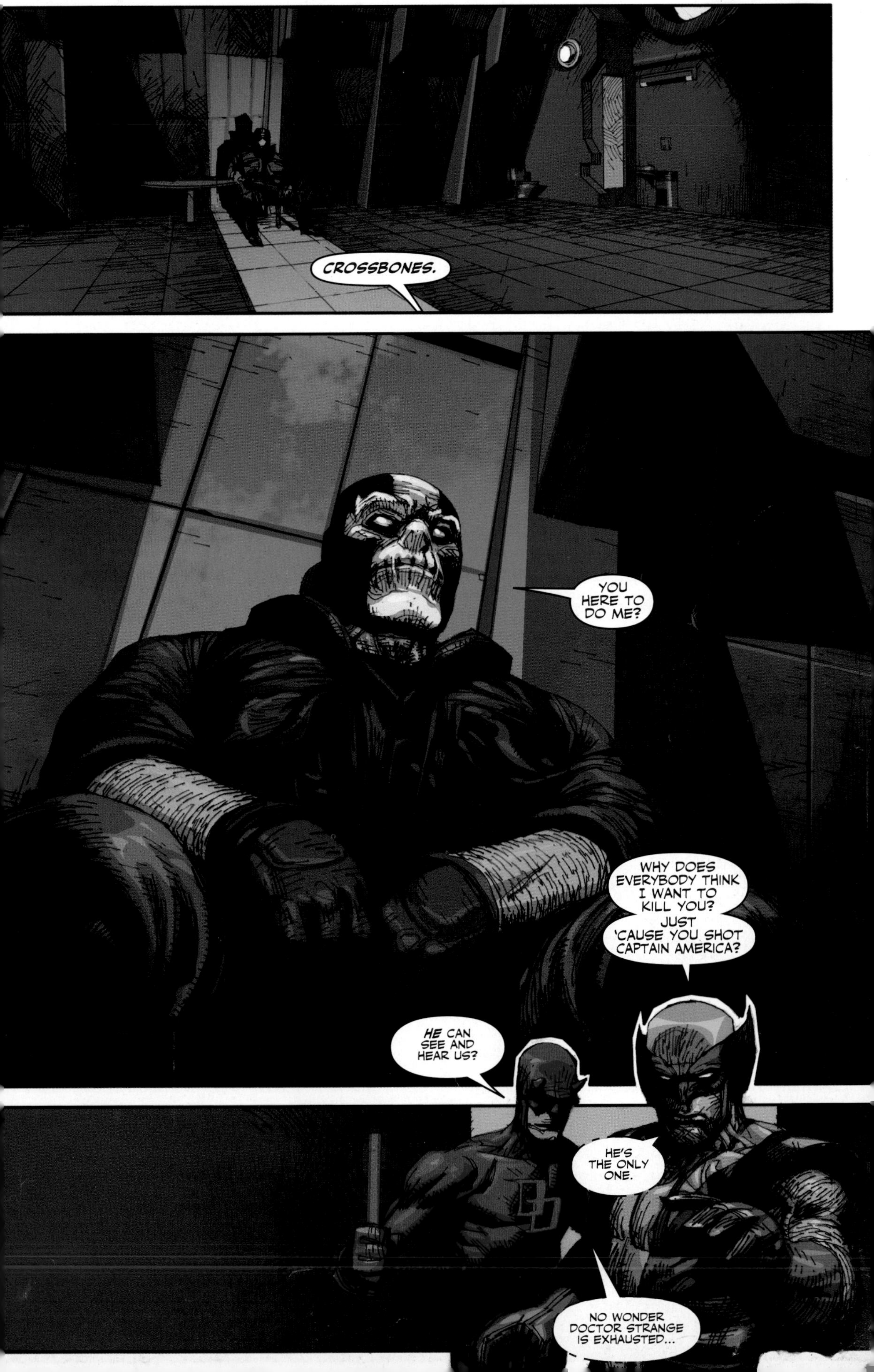
CROSSBONES.
YOU HERE TO DO ME?
WHY DOES EVERYBODY THINK I WANT TO KILL YOU?
JUST 'CAUSE YOU SHOT CAPTAIN AMERICA?
HE CAN SEE AND HEAR US?
HE'S THE ONLY ONE.
NO WONDER DOCTOR STRANGE IS EXHAUSTED...

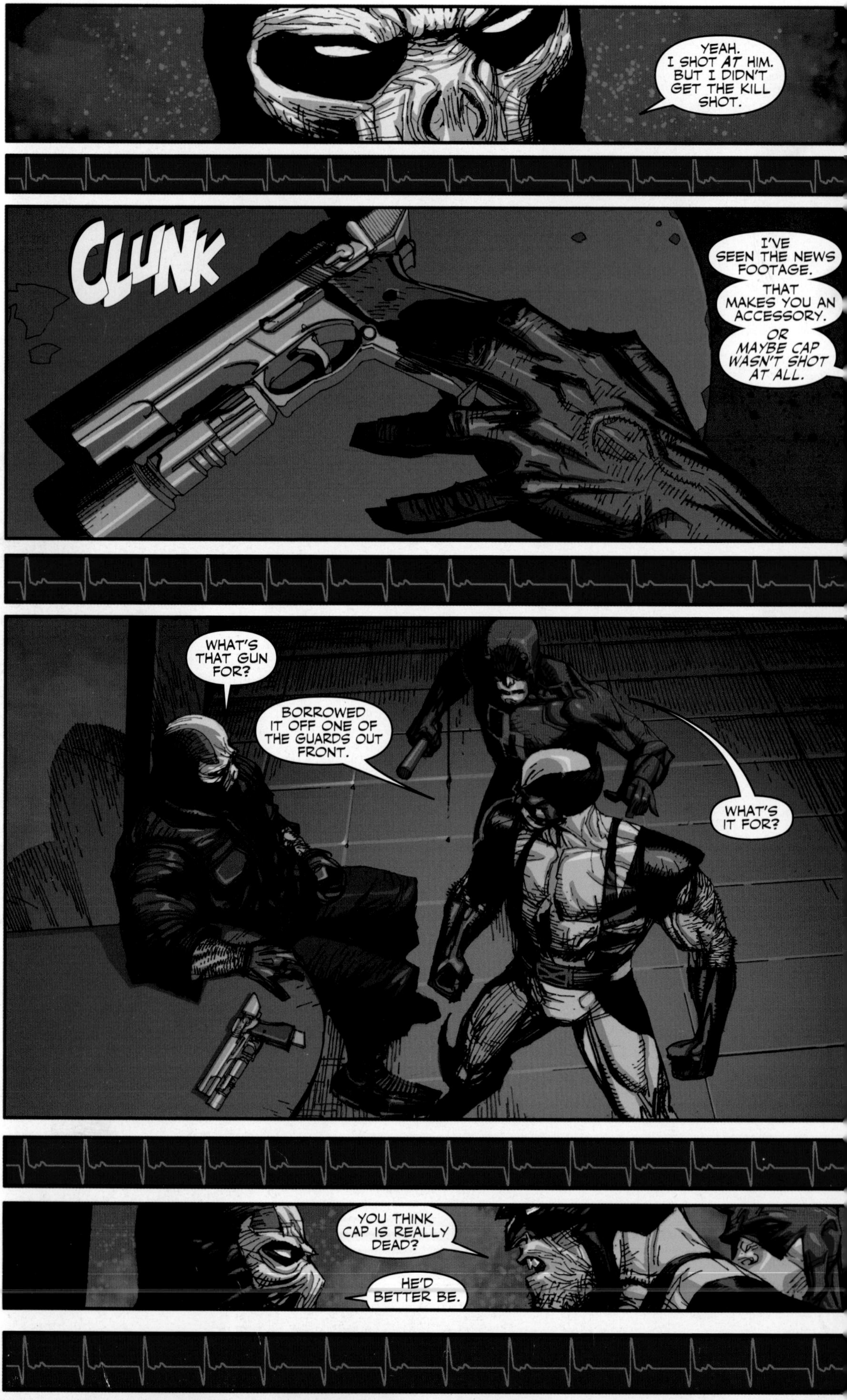
YEAH. I SHOT AT HIM. BUT I DIDN'T GET THE KILL SHOT.
CLUNK
I'VE SEEN THE NEWS FOOTAGE.
THAT MAKES YOU AN ACCESSORY.
OR MAYBE CAP WASN'T SHOT AT ALL.
WHAT'S THAT GUN FOR?
BORROWED IT OFF ONE OF THE GUARDS OUT FRONT.
WHAT'S IT FOR?
YOU THINK CAP IS REALLY DEAD?
HE'D BETTER BE.

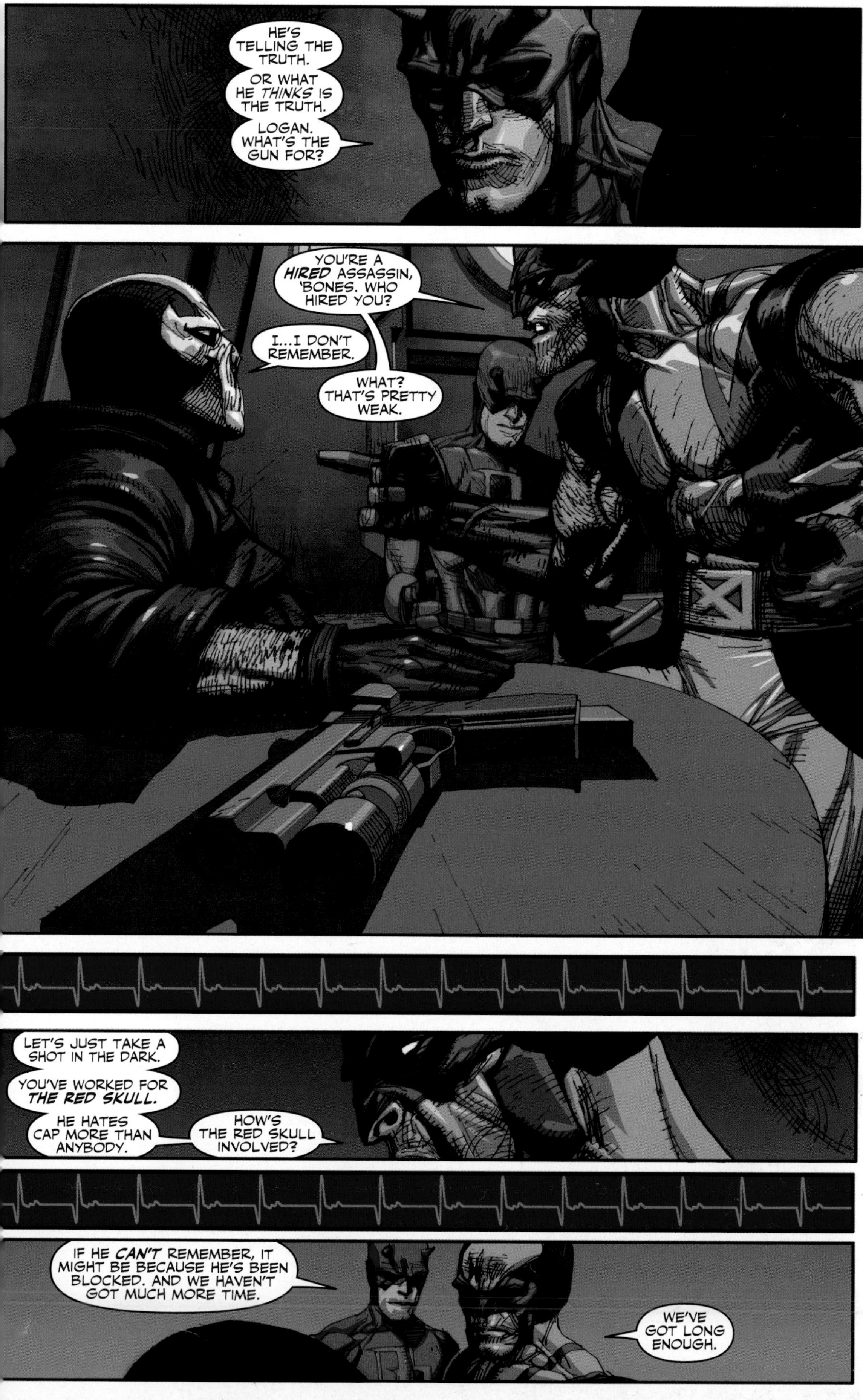
HE'S TELLING THE TRUTH.
OR WHAT HE *THINKS* IS THE TRUTH.
LOGAN. WHAT'S THE GUN FOR?
YOU'RE A ***HIRED*** ASSASSIN, 'BONES. WHO HIRED YOU?
I...I DON'T REMEMBER.
WHAT? THAT'S PRETTY WEAK.
LET'S JUST TAKE A SHOT IN THE DARK.
YOU'VE WORKED FOR ***THE RED SKULL.***
HE HATES CAP MORE THAN ANYBODY.
HOW'S THE RED SKULL INVOLVED?
IF HE ***CAN'T*** REMEMBER, IT MIGHT BE BECAUSE HE'S BEEN BLOCKED. AND WE HAVEN'T GOT MUCH MORE TIME.
WE'VE GOT LONG ENOUGH.

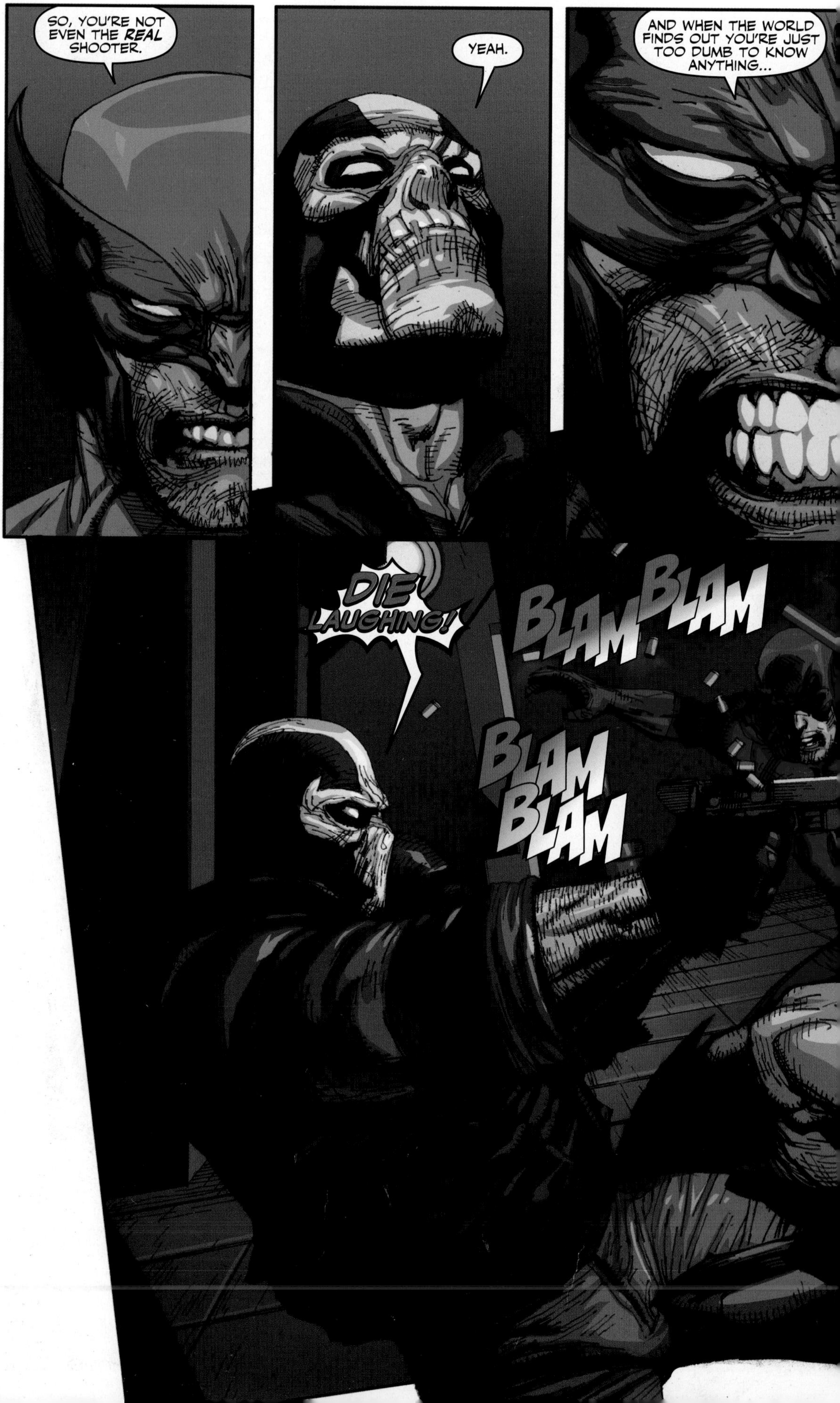
SO, YOU'RE NOT EVEN THE *REAL* SHOOTER.
YEAH.
AND WHEN THE WORLD FINDS OUT YOU'RE JUST TOO DUMB TO KNOW ANYTHING...
DIE LAUGHING!
BLAM BLAM
BLAM BLAM

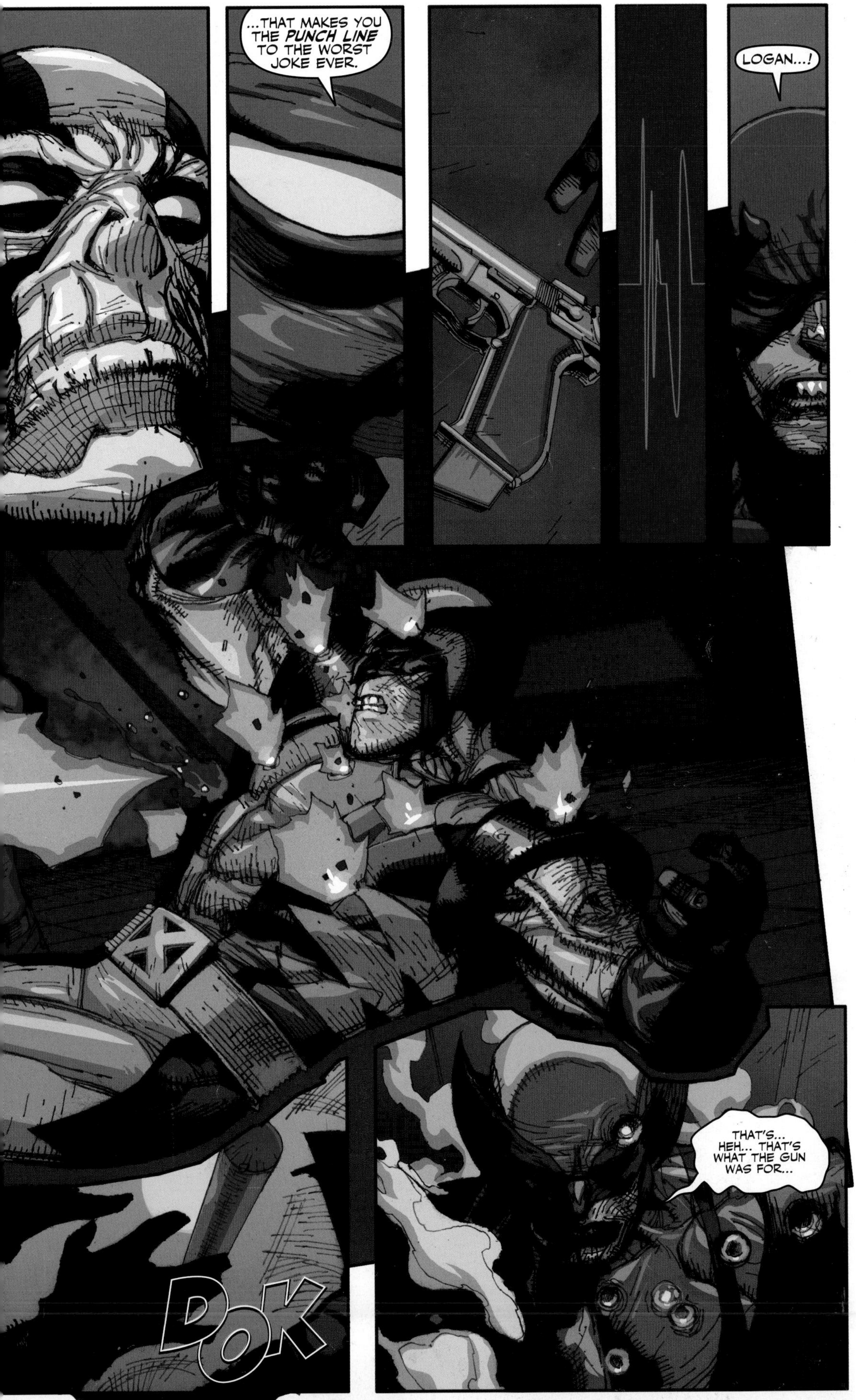
...THAT MAKES YOU THE *PUNCH LINE* TO THE WORST JOKE EVER.
LOGAN...!
DOK
THAT'S... HEH... THAT'S WHAT THE GUN WAS FOR...

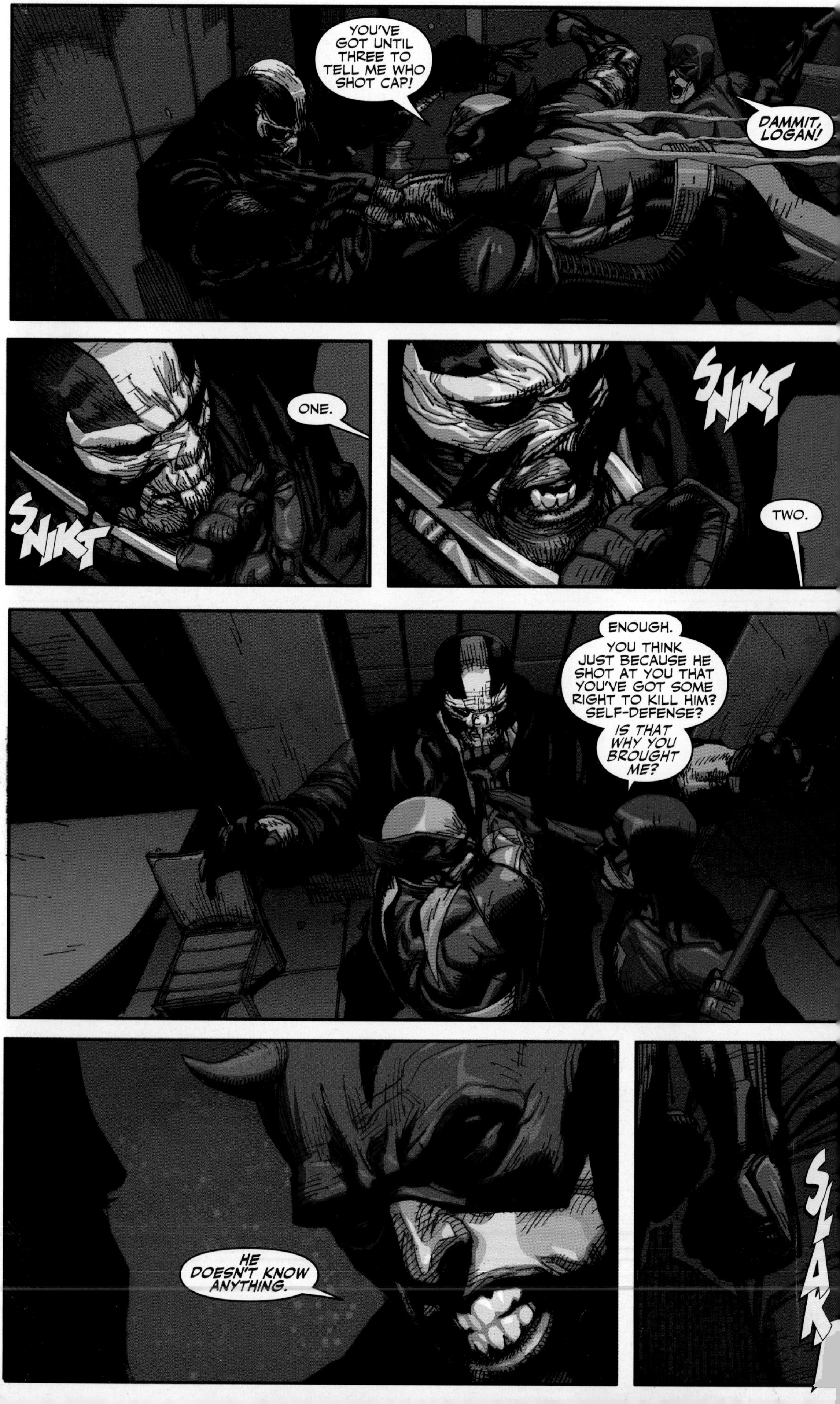
YOU'VE GOT UNTIL THREE TO TELL ME WHO SHOT CAP!
DAMMIT, LOGAN!
ONE.
SNIKT
SNIKT
TWO.
ENOUGH.
YOU THINK JUST BECAUSE HE SHOT AT YOU THAT YOU'VE GOT SOME RIGHT TO KILL HIM? SELF-DEFENSE?
IS THAT WHY YOU BROUGHT ME?
HE DOESN'T KNOW ANYTHING.
SLAK!

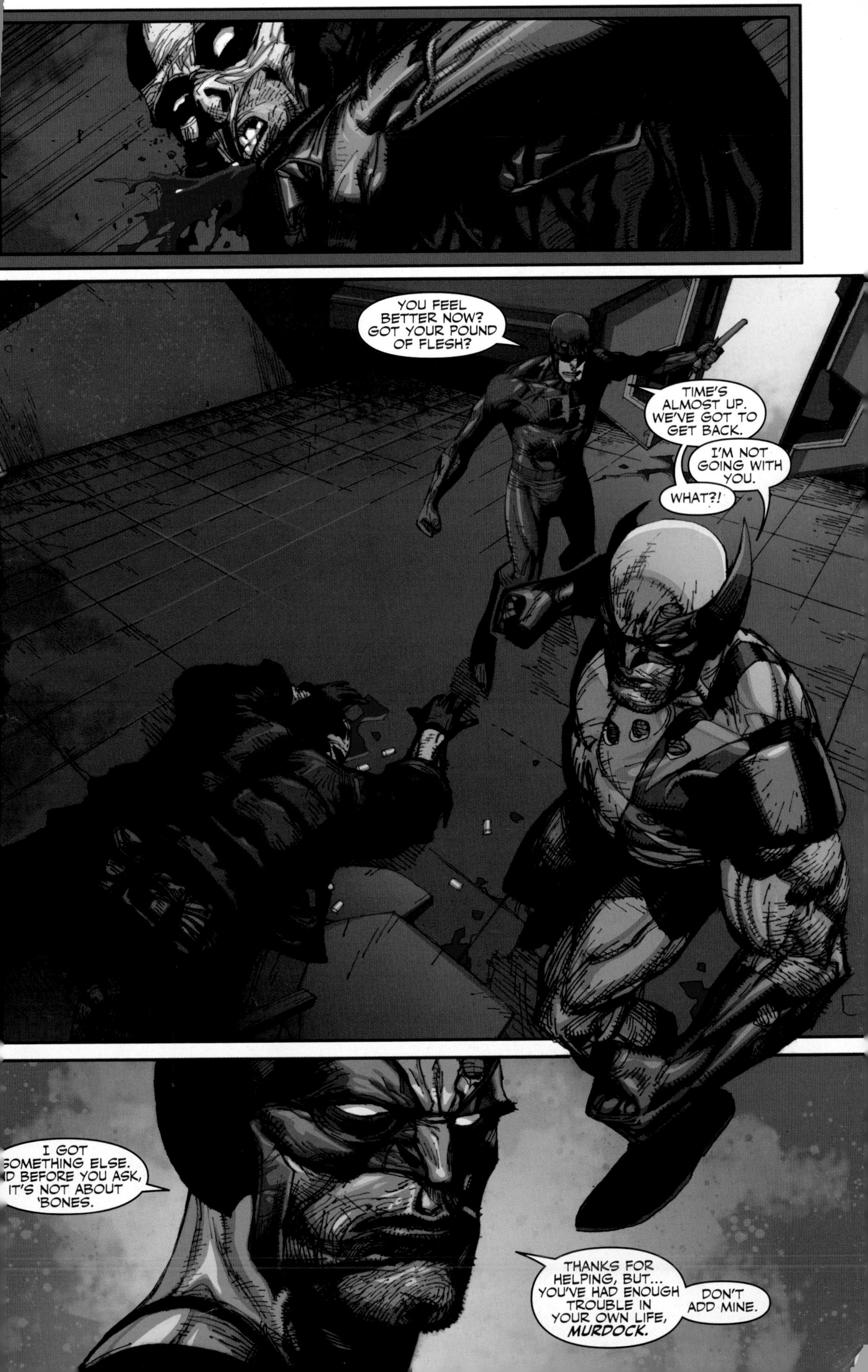

YOU FEEL BETTER NOW? GOT YOUR POUND OF FLESH?
TIME'S ALMOST UP. WE'VE GOT TO GET BACK.
I'M NOT GOING WITH YOU.
WHAT?!
I GOT SOMETHING ELSE. D BEFORE YOU ASK, IT'S NOT ABOUT 'BONES.
THANKS FOR HELPING, BUT... YOU'VE HAD ENOUGH TROUBLE IN YOUR OWN LIFE, MURDOCK.
DON'T ADD MINE.

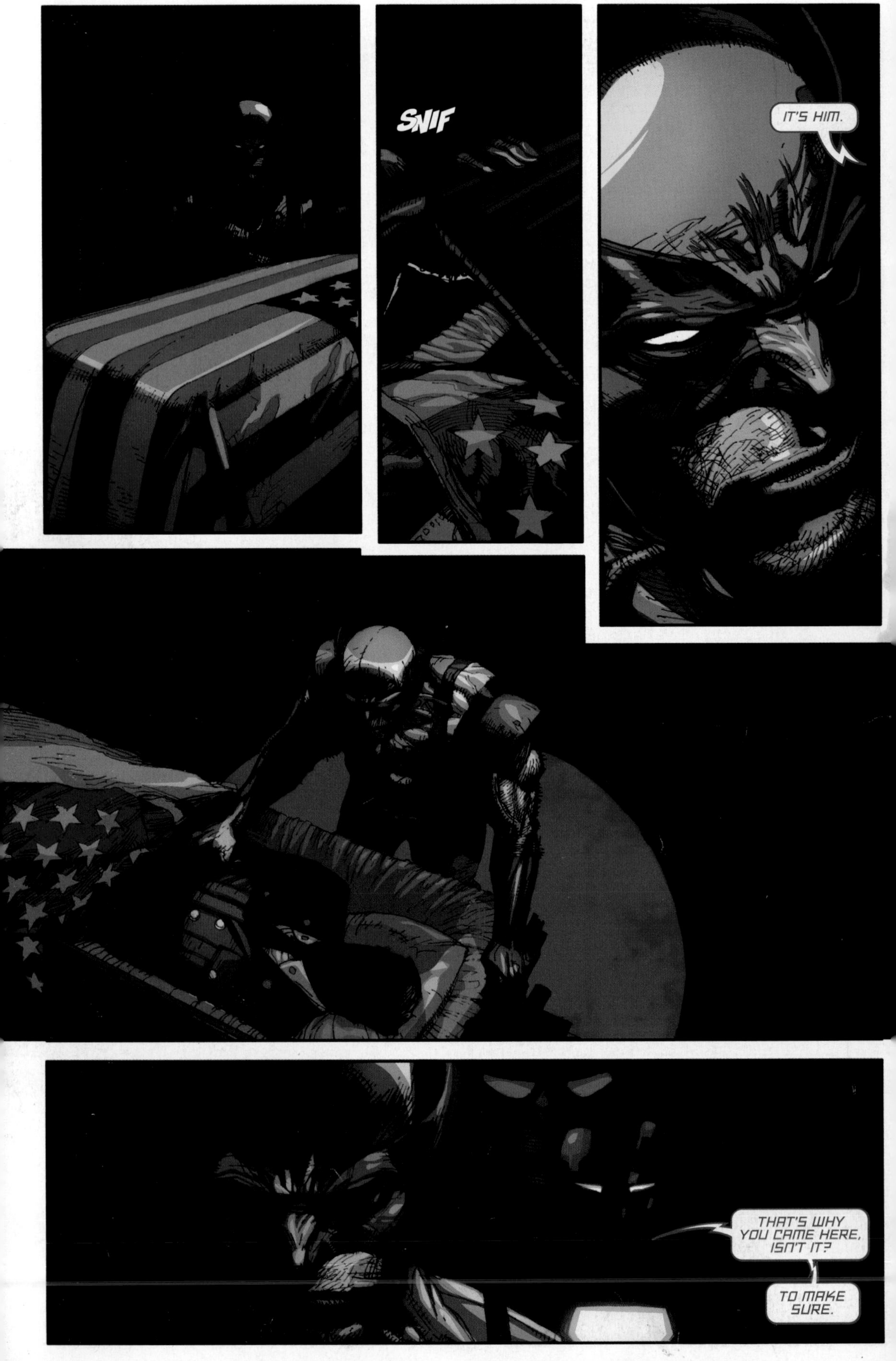
SNIF
IT'S HIM.
THAT'S WHY YOU CAME HERE, ISN'T IT?
TO MAKE SURE.

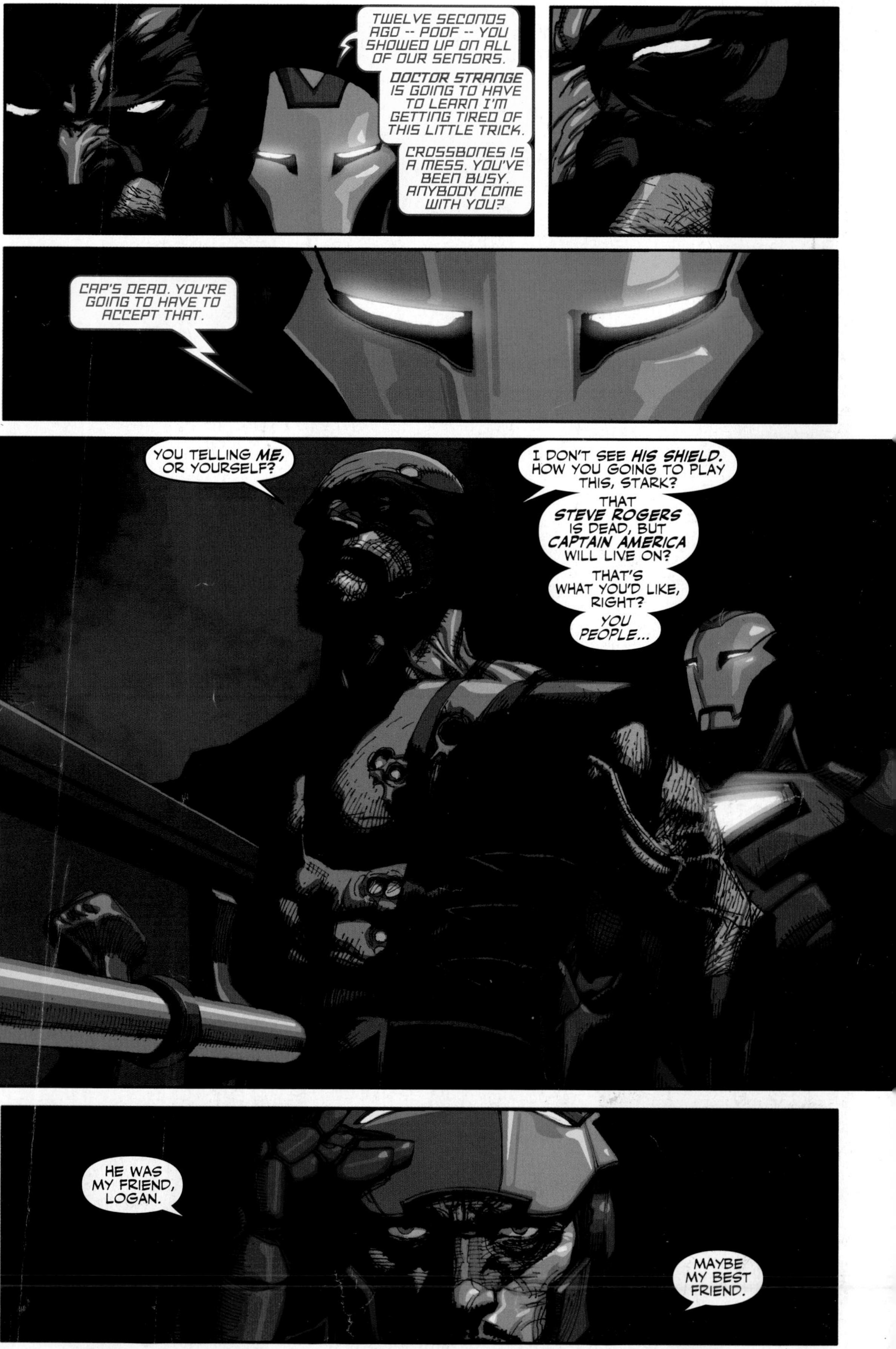
TWELVE SECONDS AGO -- POOF -- YOU SHOWED UP ON ALL OF OUR SENSORS.
DOCTOR STRANGE IS GOING TO HAVE TO LEARN I'M GETTING TIRED OF THIS LITTLE TRICK.
CROSSBONES IS A MESS. YOU'VE BEEN BUSY. ANYBODY COME WITH YOU?
CAP'S DEAD. YOU'RE GOING TO HAVE TO ACCEPT THAT.
YOU TELLING ME, OR YOURSELF?
I DON'T SEE HIS SHIELD. HOW YOU GOING TO PLAY THIS, STARK?
THAT STEVE ROGERS IS DEAD, BUT CAPTAIN AMERICA WILL LIVE ON?
THAT'S WHAT YOU'D LIKE, RIGHT?
YOU PEOPLE...
HE WAS MY FRIEND, LOGAN.
MAYBE MY BEST FRIEND.

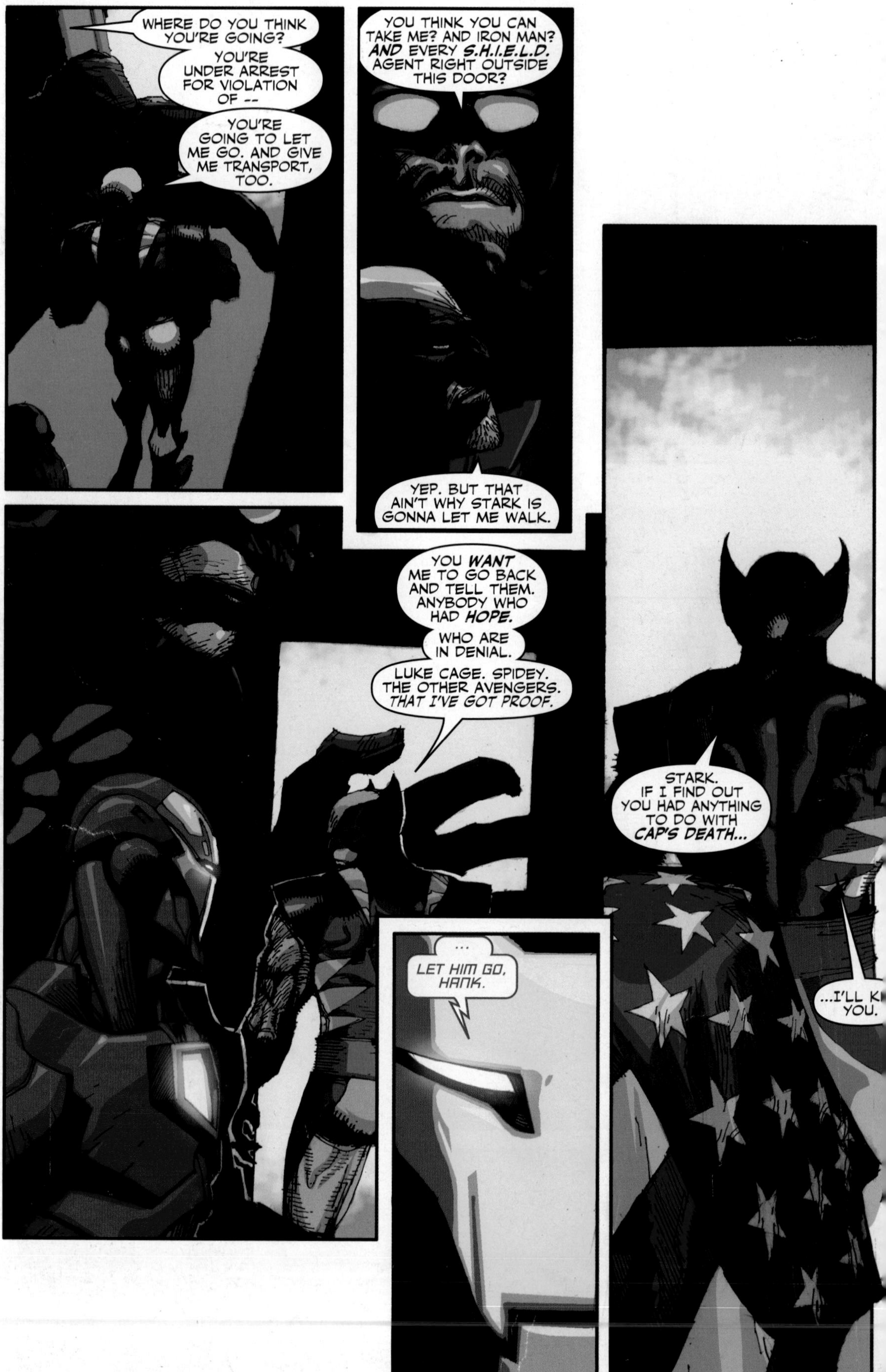
WHERE DO YOU THINK YOU'RE GOING?
YOU'RE UNDER ARREST FOR VIOLATION OF --
YOU'RE GOING TO LET ME GO. AND GIVE ME TRANSPORT, TOO.
YOU THINK YOU CAN TAKE ME? AND IRON MAN? AND EVERY S.H.I.E.L.D. AGENT RIGHT OUTSIDE THIS DOOR?
YEP. BUT THAT AIN'T WHY STARK IS GONNA LET ME WALK.
YOU WANT ME TO GO BACK AND TELL THEM. ANYBODY WHO HAD HOPE.
WHO ARE IN DENIAL.
LUKE CAGE. SPIDEY. THE OTHER AVENGERS. THAT I'VE GOT PROOF.
...
LET HIM GO, HANK.
STARK. IF I FIND OUT YOU HAD ANYTHING TO DO WITH CAP'S DEATH...
...I'LL K
YOU.
THE END

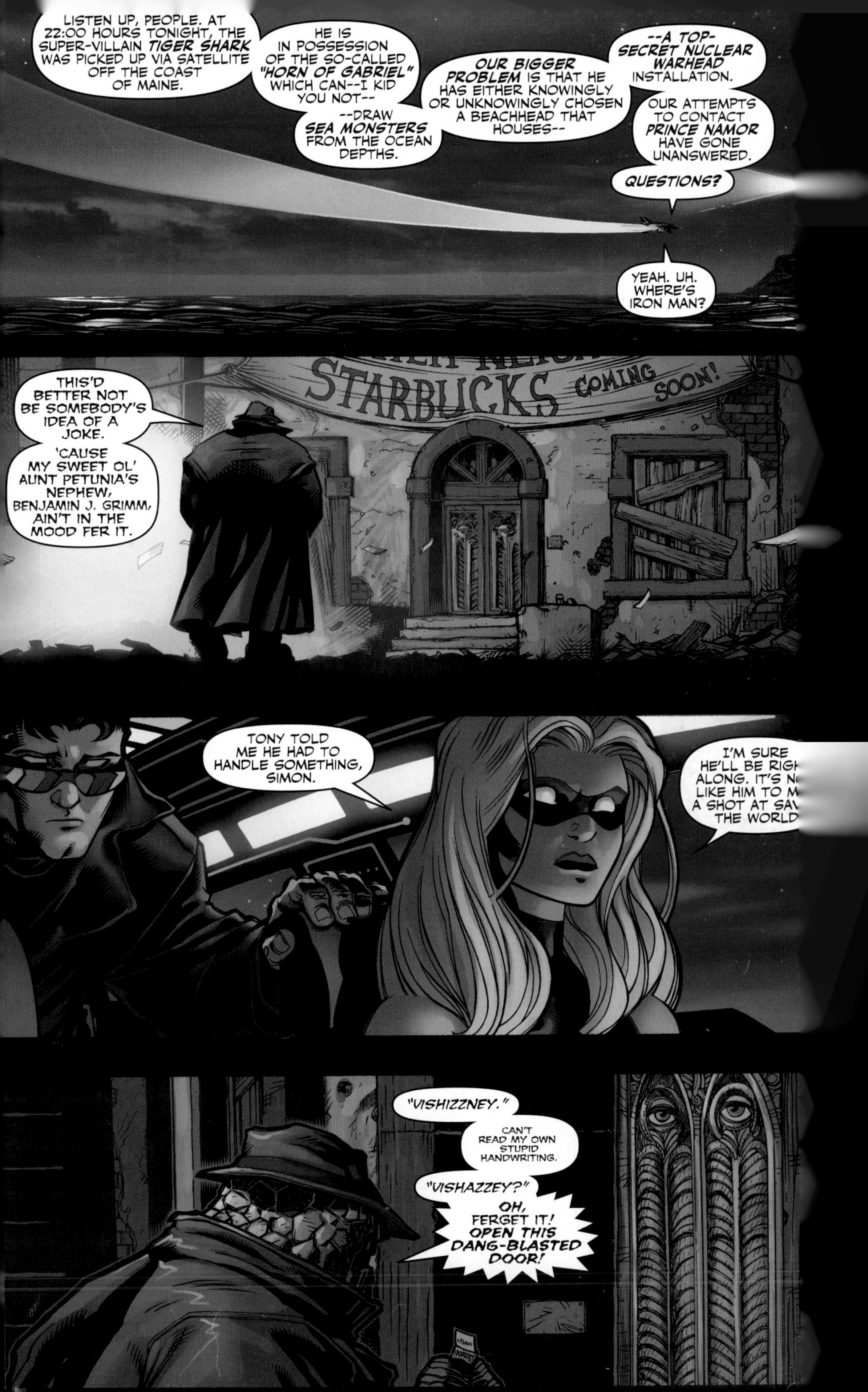
LISTEN UP, PEOPLE. AT 22:00 HOURS TONIGHT, THE SUPER-VILLAIN TIGER SHARK WAS PICKED UP VIA SATELLITE OFF THE COAST OF MAINE.
HE IS IN POSSESSION OF THE SO-CALLED "HORN OF GABRIEL" WHICH CAN--I KID YOU NOT--
--DRAW SEA MONSTERS FROM THE OCEAN DEPTHS.
OUR BIGGER PROBLEM IS THAT HE HAS EITHER KNOWINGLY OR UNKNOWINGLY CHOSEN A BEACHHEAD THAT HOUSES--
--A TOP-SECRET NUCLEAR WARHEAD INSTALLATION.
OUR ATTEMPTS TO CONTACT PRINCE NAMOR HAVE GONE UNANSWERED.
QUESTIONS?
YEAH. UH. WHERE'S IRON MAN?
STARBUCKS COMING SOON!
THIS'D BETTER NOT BE SOMEBODY'S IDEA OF A JOKE.
'CAUSE MY SWEET OL' AUNT PETUNIA'S NEPHEW, BENJAMIN J. GRIMM, AIN'T IN THE MOOD FER IT.
TONY TOLD ME HE HAD TO HANDLE SOMETHING, SIMON.
I'M SURE HE'LL BE RIGH ALONG. IT'S N LIKE HIM TO M A SHOT AT SAV THE WORLD
"VISHIZZNEY."
CAN'T READ MY OWN STUPID HANDWRITING.
"VISHAZZEY?"
OH, FERGET IT! OPEN THIS DANG-BLASTED DOOR!

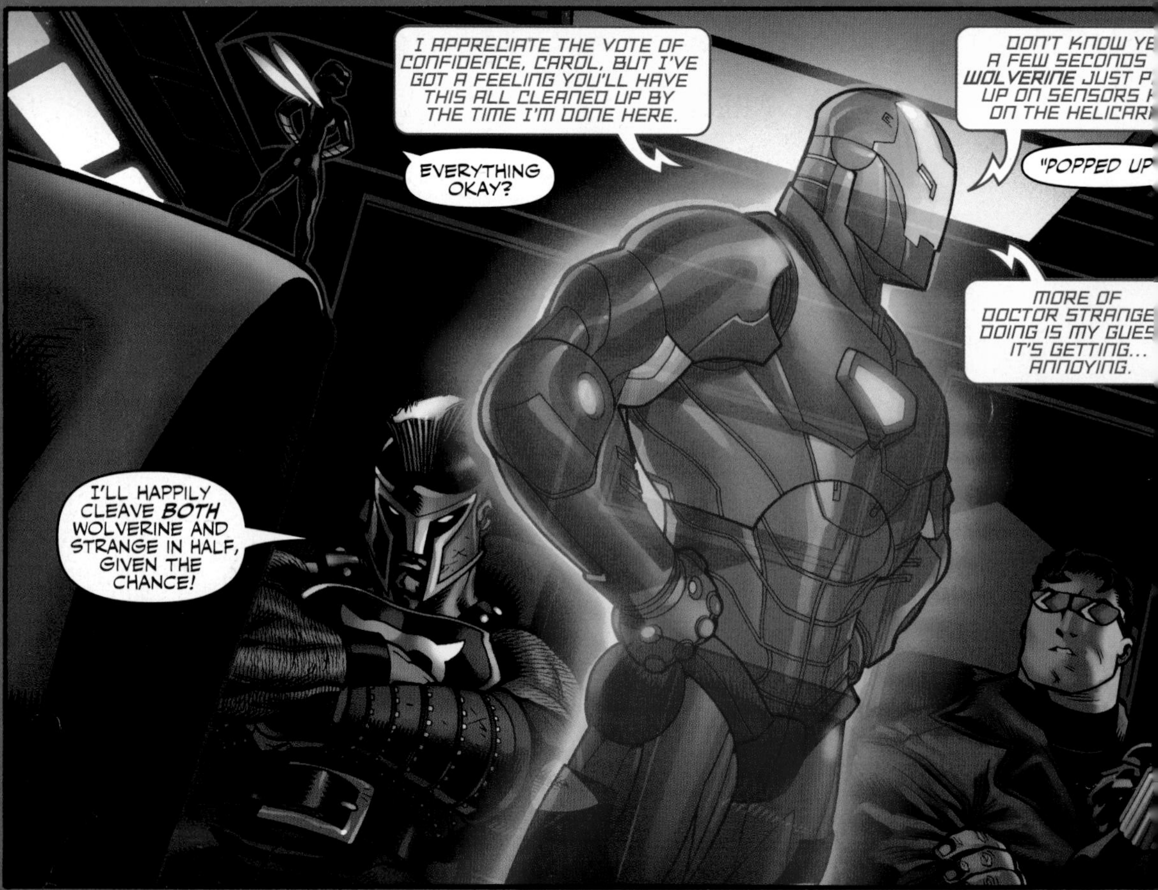

I APPRECIATE THE VOTE OF CONFIDENCE, CAROL, BUT I'VE GOT A FEELING YOU'LL HAVE THIS ALL CLEANED UP BY THE TIME I'M DONE HERE.
EVERYTHING OKAY?
DON'T KNOW YE
A FEW SECONDS
WOLVERINE JUST P
UP ON SENSORS
ON THE HELICAR
"POPPED UP
MORE OF DOCTOR STRANGE DOING IS MY GUES IT'S GETTING... ANNOYING.
I'LL HAPPILY CLEAVE BOTH WOLVERINE AND STRANGE IN HALF, GIVEN THE CHANCE!

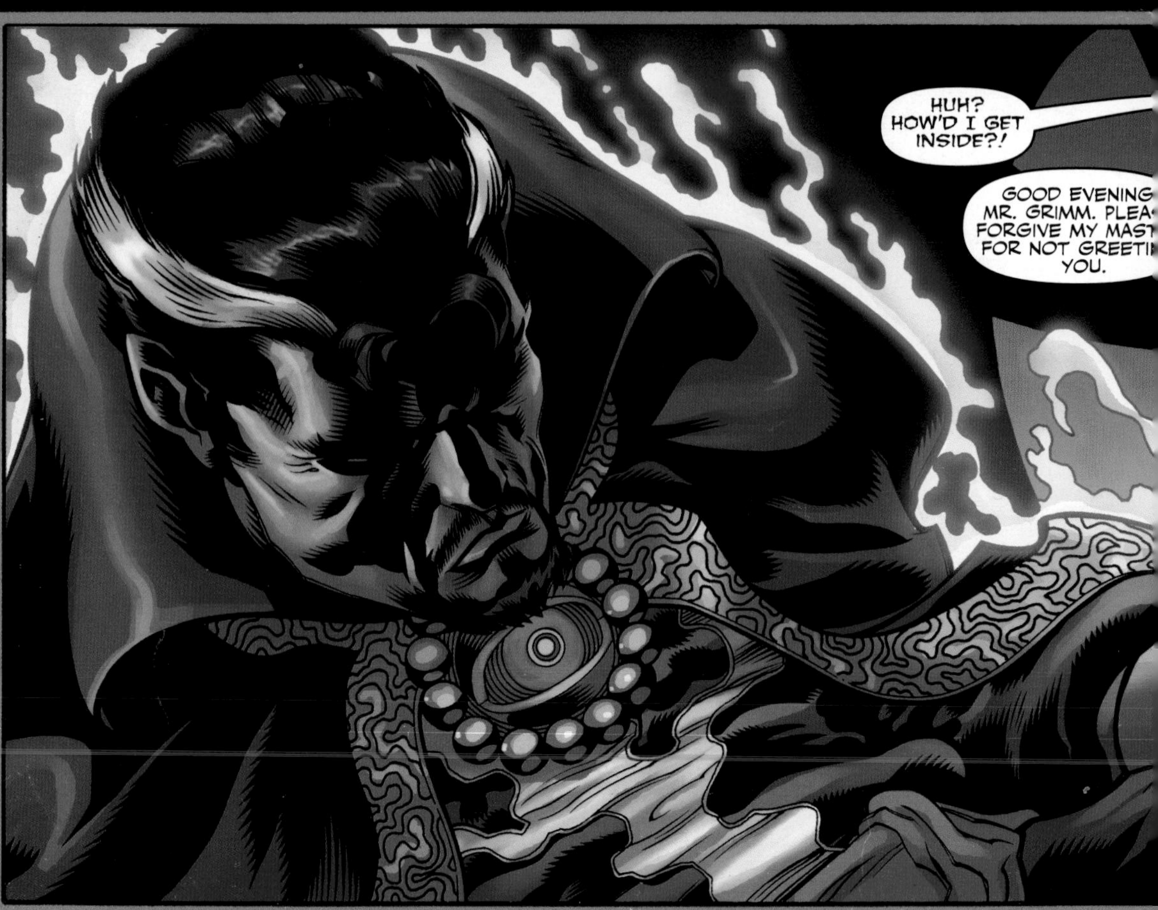

HUH? HOW'D I GET INSIDE?!
GOOD EVENING
MR. GRIMM. PLEA
FORGIVE MY MAST
FOR NOT GREETI
YOU.

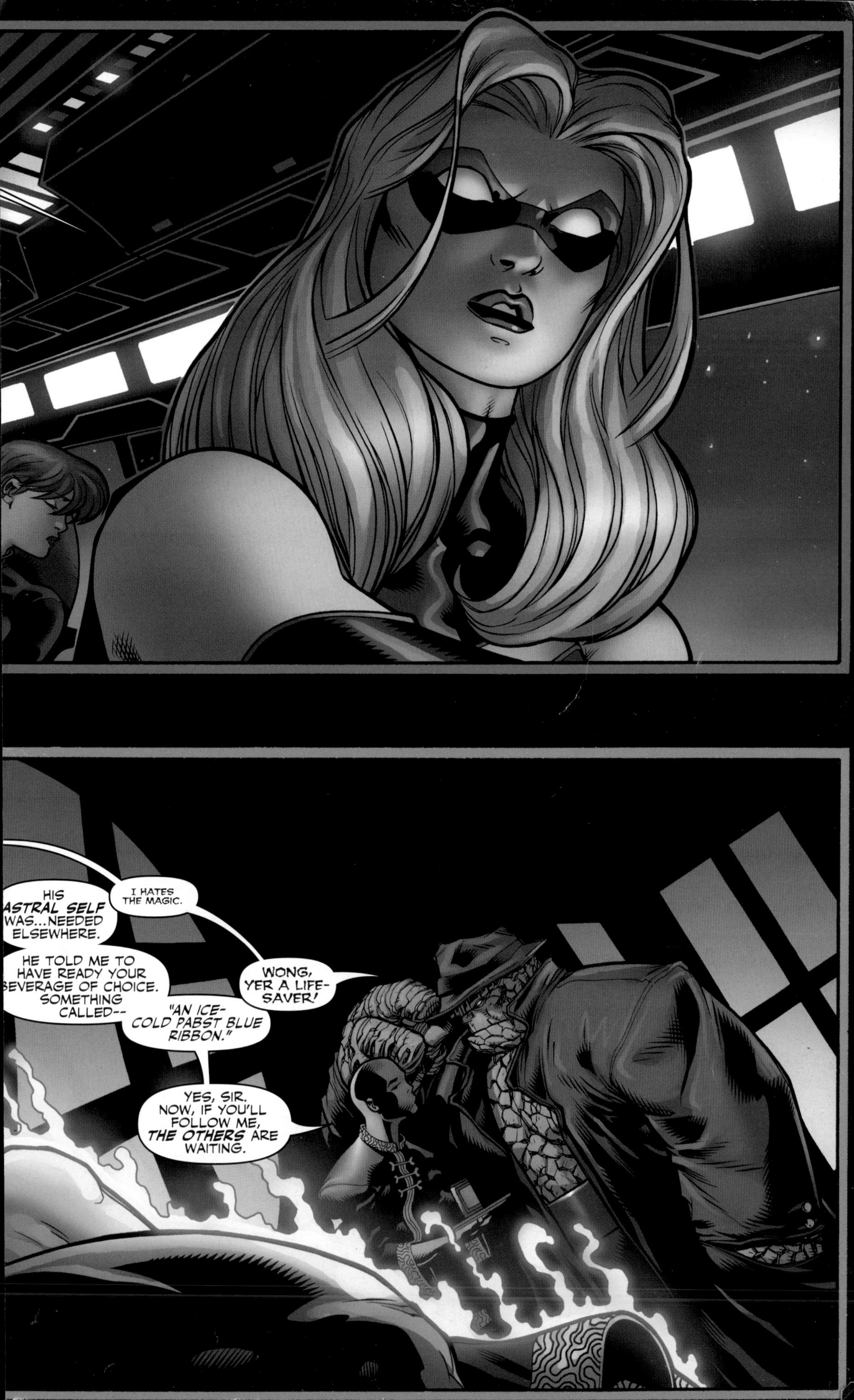
HIS ASTRAL SELF WAS...NEEDED ELSEWHERE.
I HATES THE MAGIC.
HE TOLD ME TO HAVE READY YOUR BEVERAGE OF CHOICE. SOMETHING CALLED--
"AN ICE-COLD PABST BLUE RIBBON."
WONG, YER A LIFE-SAVER!
YES, SIR. NOW, IF YOU'LL FOLLOW ME, THE OTHERS ARE WAITING.

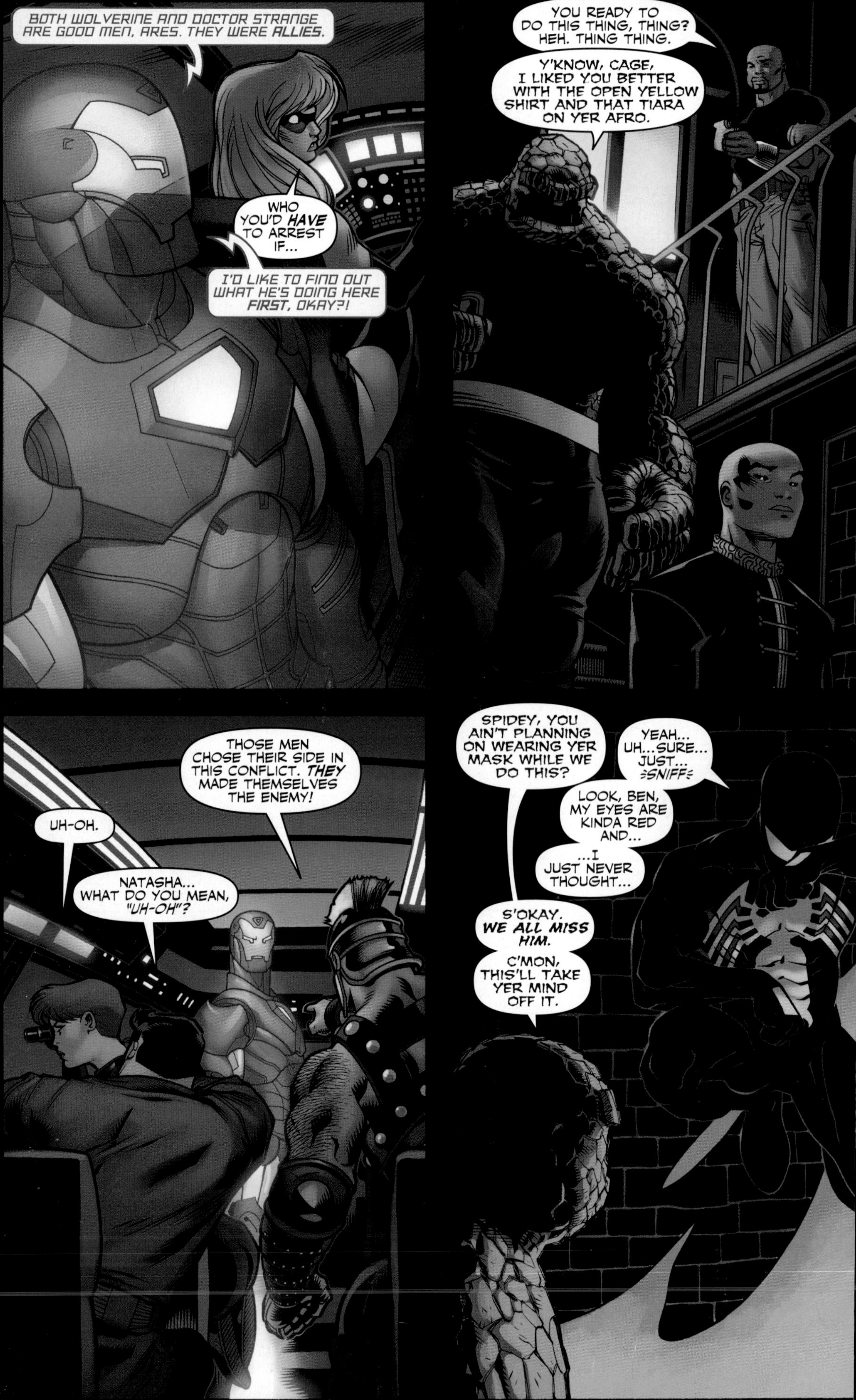
BOTH WOLVERINE AND DOCTOR STRANGE ARE GOOD MEN, ARES. THEY WERE ALLIES.
WHO YOU'D HAVE TO ARREST IF...
I'D LIKE TO FIND OUT WHAT HE'S DOING HERE FIRST, OKAY?!
YOU READY TO DO THIS THING, THING? HEH. THING THING.
Y'KNOW, CAGE, I LIKED YOU BETTER WITH THE OPEN YELLOW SHIRT AND THAT TIARA ON YER AFRO.
THOSE MEN CHOSE THEIR SIDE IN THIS CONFLICT. THEY MADE THEMSELVES THE ENEMY!
UH-OH.
NATASHA... WHAT DO YOU MEAN, "UH-OH"?
SPIDEY, YOU AIN'T PLANNING ON WEARING YER MASK WHILE WE DO THIS?
YEAH... UH...SURE... JUST... SNIFF
LOOK, BEN, MY EYES ARE KINDA RED AND...
...I JUST NEVER THOUGHT...
S'OKAY. WE ALL MISS HIM.
C'MON, THIS'LL TAKE YER MIND OFF IT.

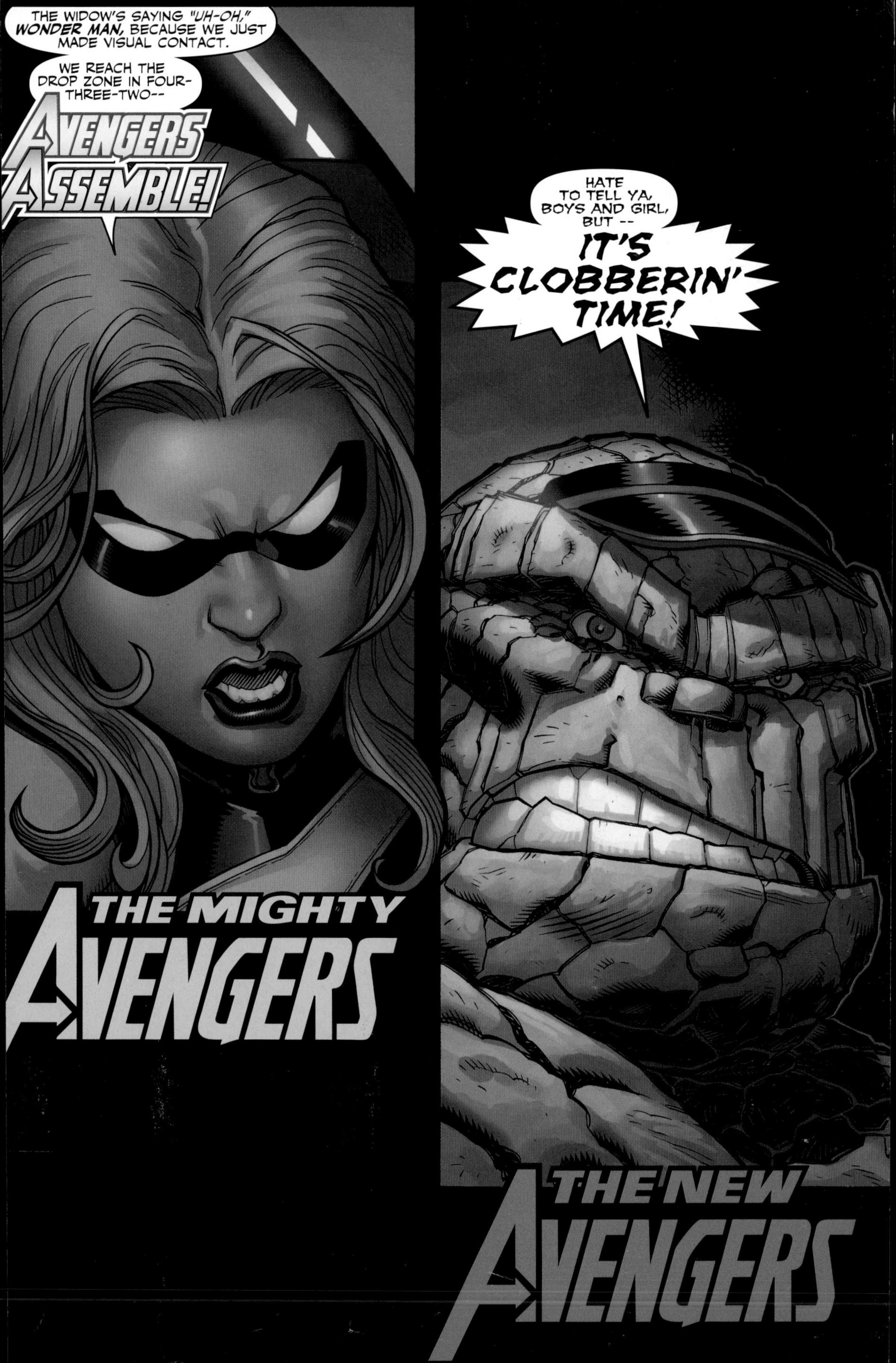
THE WIDOW'S SAYING "UH-OH," WONDER MAN, BECAUSE WE JUST MADE VISUAL CONTACT.
WE REACH THE DROP ZONE IN FOUR-THREE-TWO--
AVENGERS ASSEMBLE!
HATE TO TELL YA, BOYS AND GIRL, BUT --
IT'S CLOBBERIN' TIME!
THE MIGHTY AVENGERS
THE NEW AVENGERS

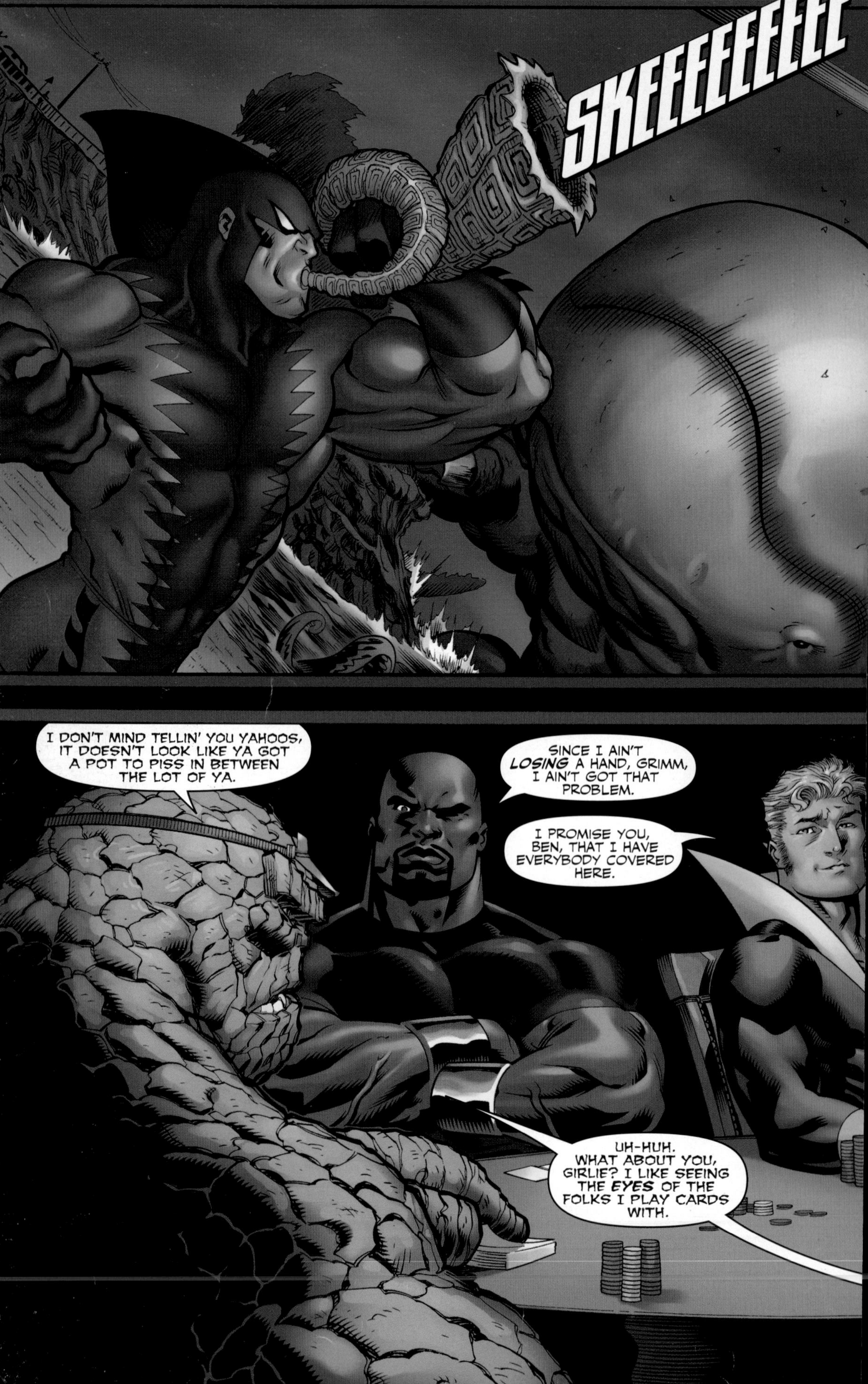
SKEEEEEEEEE
I DON'T MIND TELLIN' YOU YAHOOS, IT DOESN'T LOOK LIKE YA GOT A POT TO PISS IN BETWEEN THE LOT OF YA.
SINCE I AIN'T *LOSING* A HAND, GRIMM, I AIN'T GOT THAT PROBLEM.
I PROMISE YOU, BEN, THAT I HAVE EVERYBODY COVERED HERE.
UH-HUH. WHAT ABOUT YOU, GIRLIE? I LIKE SEEING THE *EYES* OF THE FOLKS I PLAY CARDS WITH.

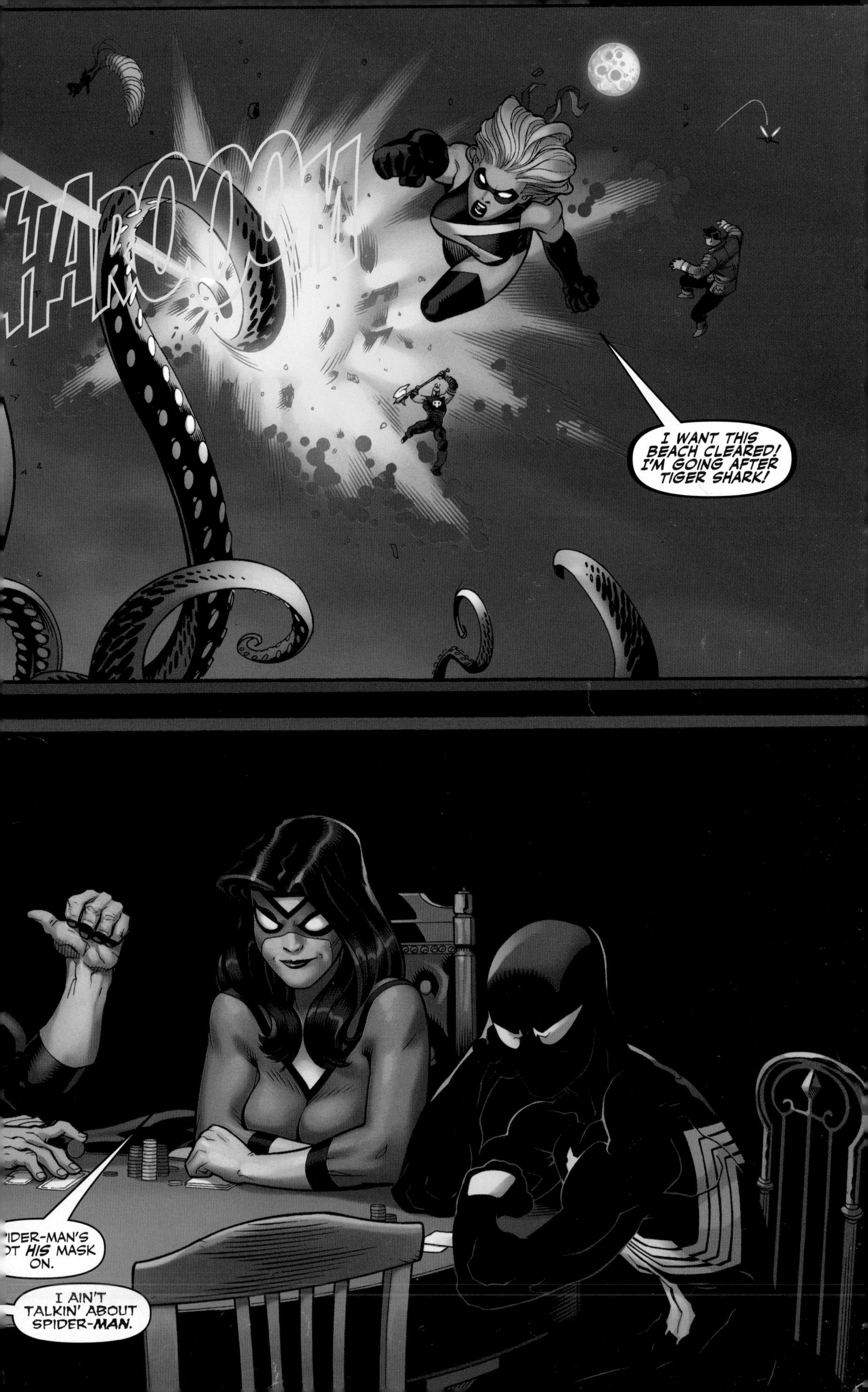
I WANT THIS BEACH CLEARED! I'M GOING AFTER TIGER SHARK!
PIDER-MAN'S OT *HIS* MASK ON.
I AIN'T TALKIN' ABOUT SPIDER-**MAN**.

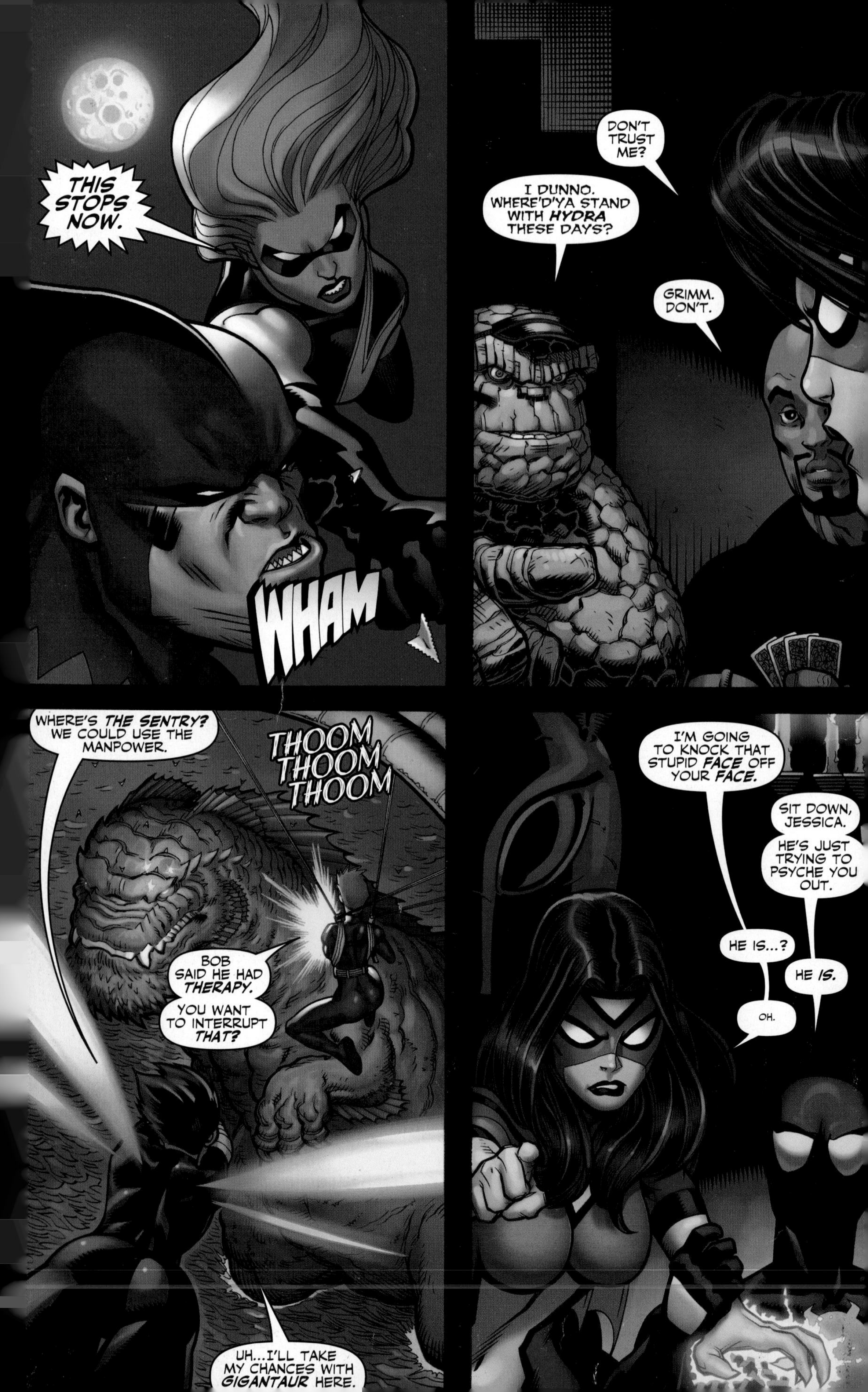
THIS STOPS NOW.
WHAM
DON'T TRUST ME?
I DUNNO. WHERE'D'YA STAND WITH HYDRA THESE DAYS?
GRIMM. DON'T.
WHERE'S THE SENTRY? WE COULD USE THE MANPOWER.
THOOM THOOM THOOM
BOB SAID HE HAD THERAPY.
YOU WANT TO INTERRUPT THAT?
UH...I'LL TAKE MY CHANCES WITH GIGANTAUR HERE.
I'M GOING TO KNOCK THAT STUPID FACE OFF YOUR FACE.
SIT DOWN, JESSICA.
HE'S JUST TRYING TO PSYCHE YOU OUT.
HE IS...?
HE IS.
OH.

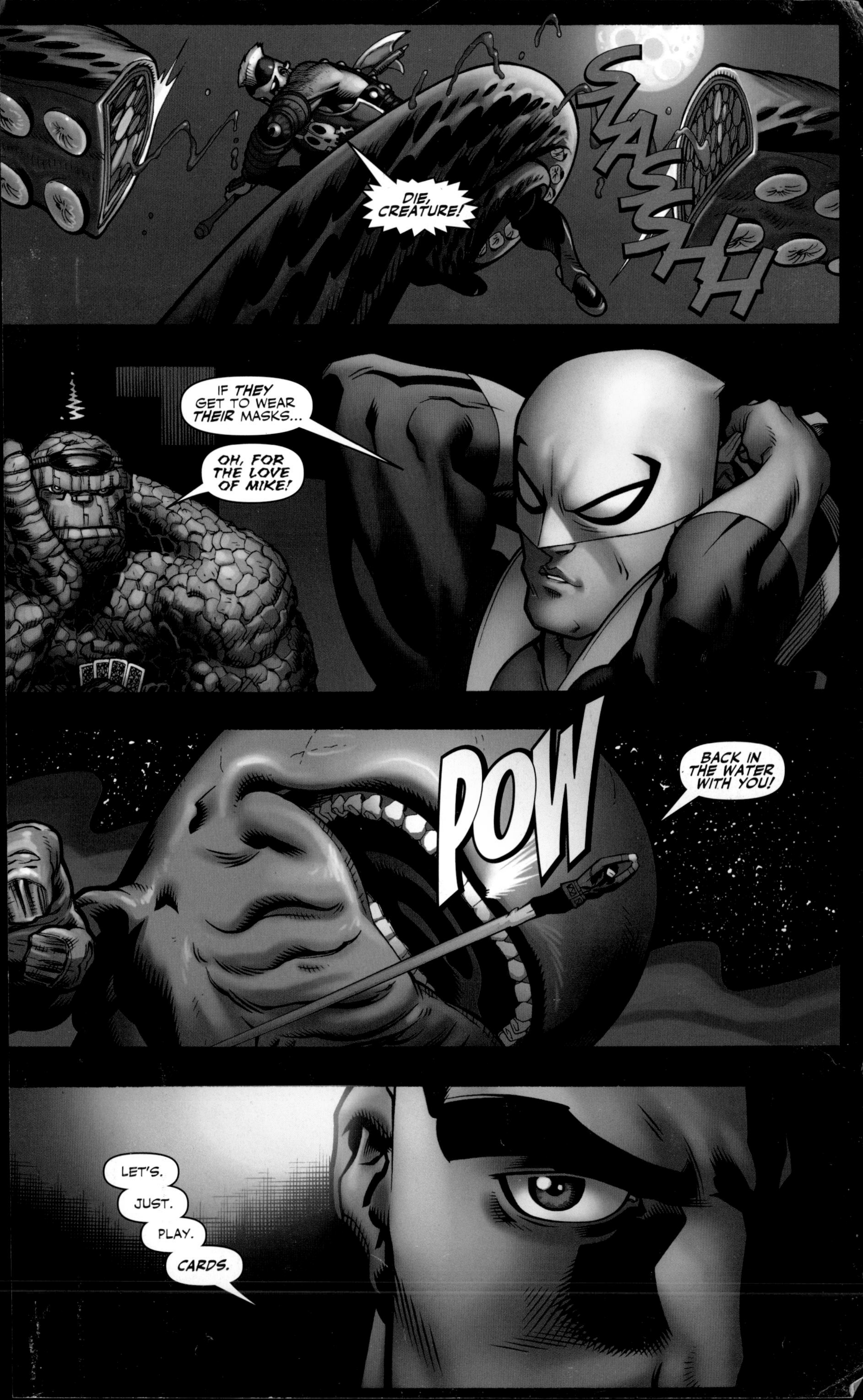

DIE, CREATURE!
SLASSHH
IF THEY GET TO WEAR THEIR MASKS...
OH, FOR THE LOVE OF MIKE!
POW
BACK IN THE WATER WITH YOU!
LET'S.
JUST.
PLAY.
CARDS.

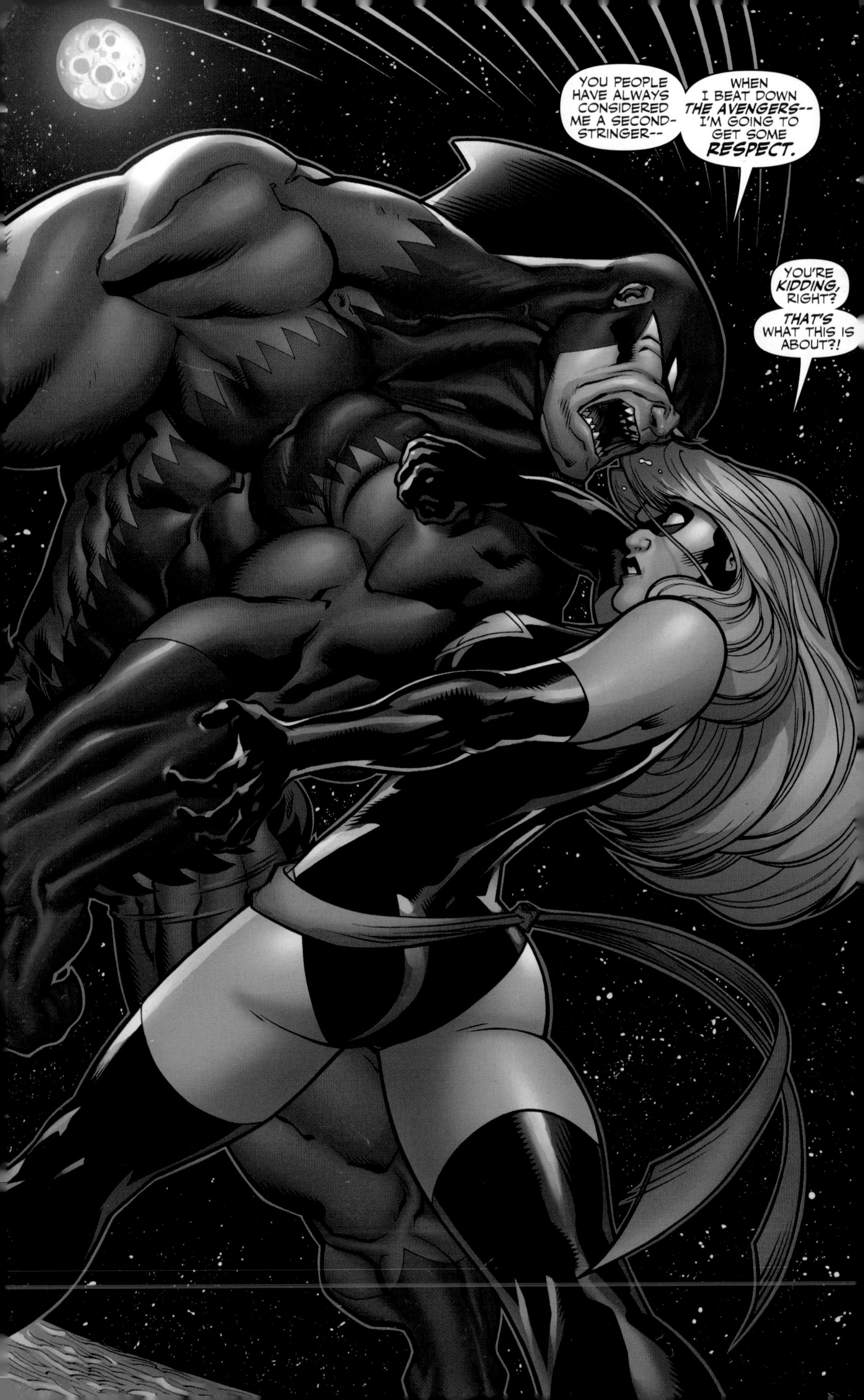
YOU PEOPLE HAVE ALWAYS CONSIDERED ME A SECOND-STRINGER--
WHEN I BEAT DOWN THE AVENGERS-- I'M GOING TO GET SOME RESPECT.
YOU'RE KIDDING, RIGHT? THAT'S WHAT THIS IS ABOUT?!

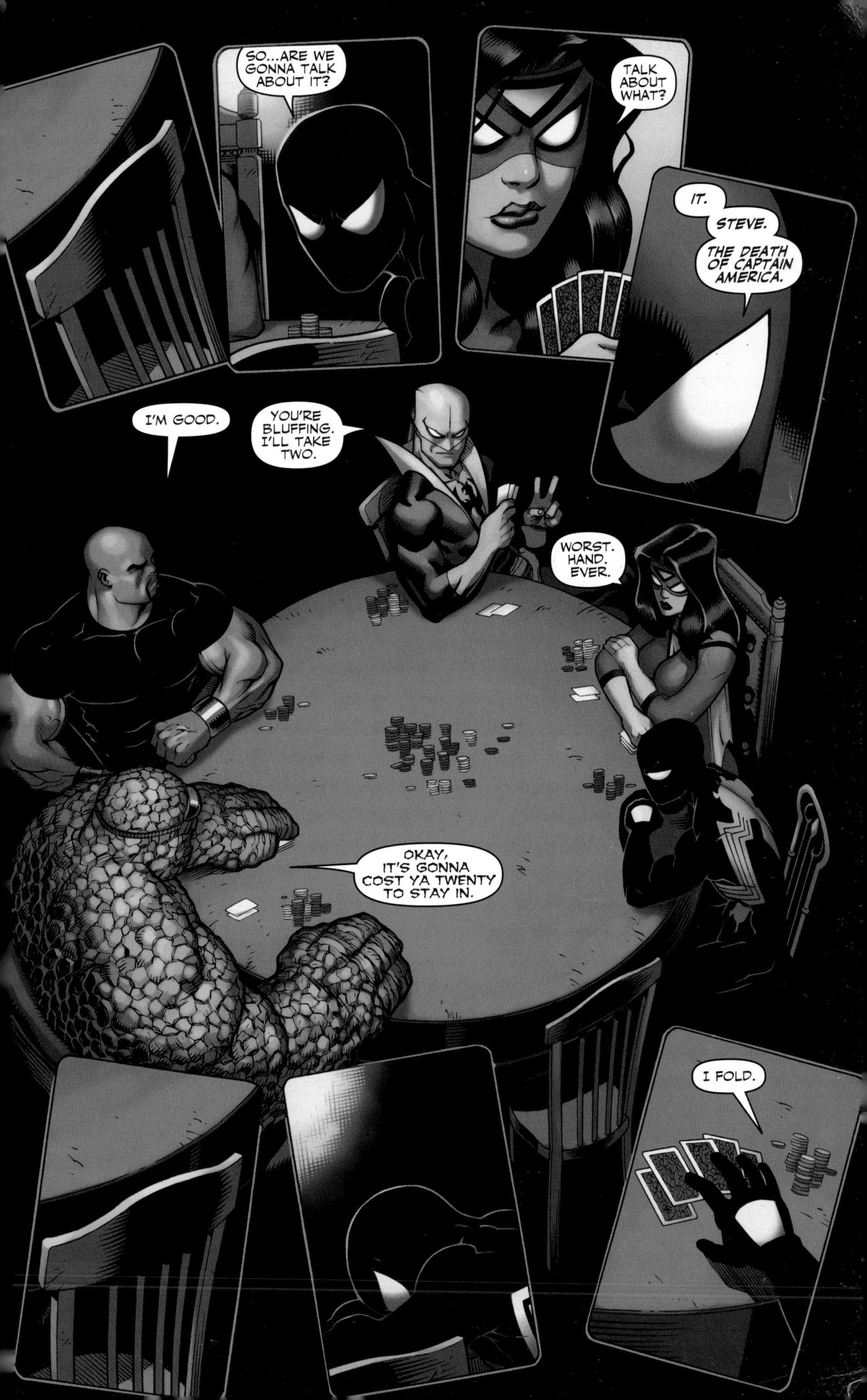
SO...ARE WE GONNA TALK ABOUT IT?
TALK ABOUT WHAT?
IT.
STEVE.
THE DEATH OF CAPTAIN AMERICA.
I'M GOOD.
YOU'RE BLUFFING. I'LL TAKE TWO.
WORST. HAND. EVER.
OKAY, IT'S GONNA COST YA TWENTY TO STAY IN.
I FOLD.

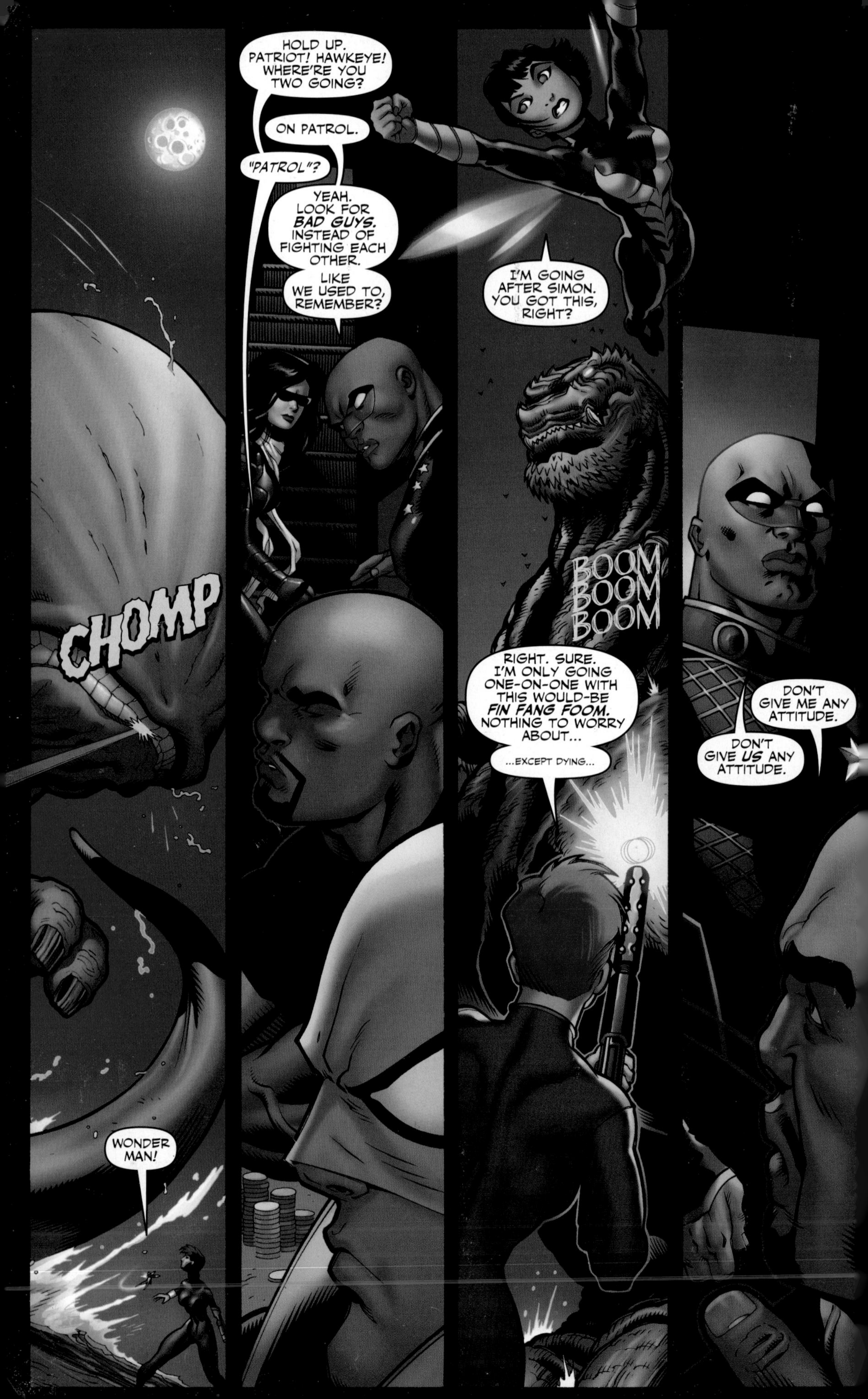
CHOMP
WONDER MAN!
HOLD UP. PATRIOT! HAWKEYE! WHERE'RE YOU TWO GOING?
ON PATROL.
"PATROL"?
YEAH. LOOK FOR BAD GUYS. INSTEAD OF FIGHTING EACH OTHER.
LIKE WE USED TO, REMEMBER?
I'M GOING AFTER SIMON. YOU GOT THIS, RIGHT?
BOOM BOOM BOOM
RIGHT. SURE. I'M ONLY GOING ONE-ON-ONE WITH THIS WOULD-BE FIN FANG FOOM. NOTHING TO WORRY ABOUT...
...EXCEPT DYING...
DON'T GIVE ME ANY ATTITUDE.
DON'T GIVE US ANY ATTITUDE.

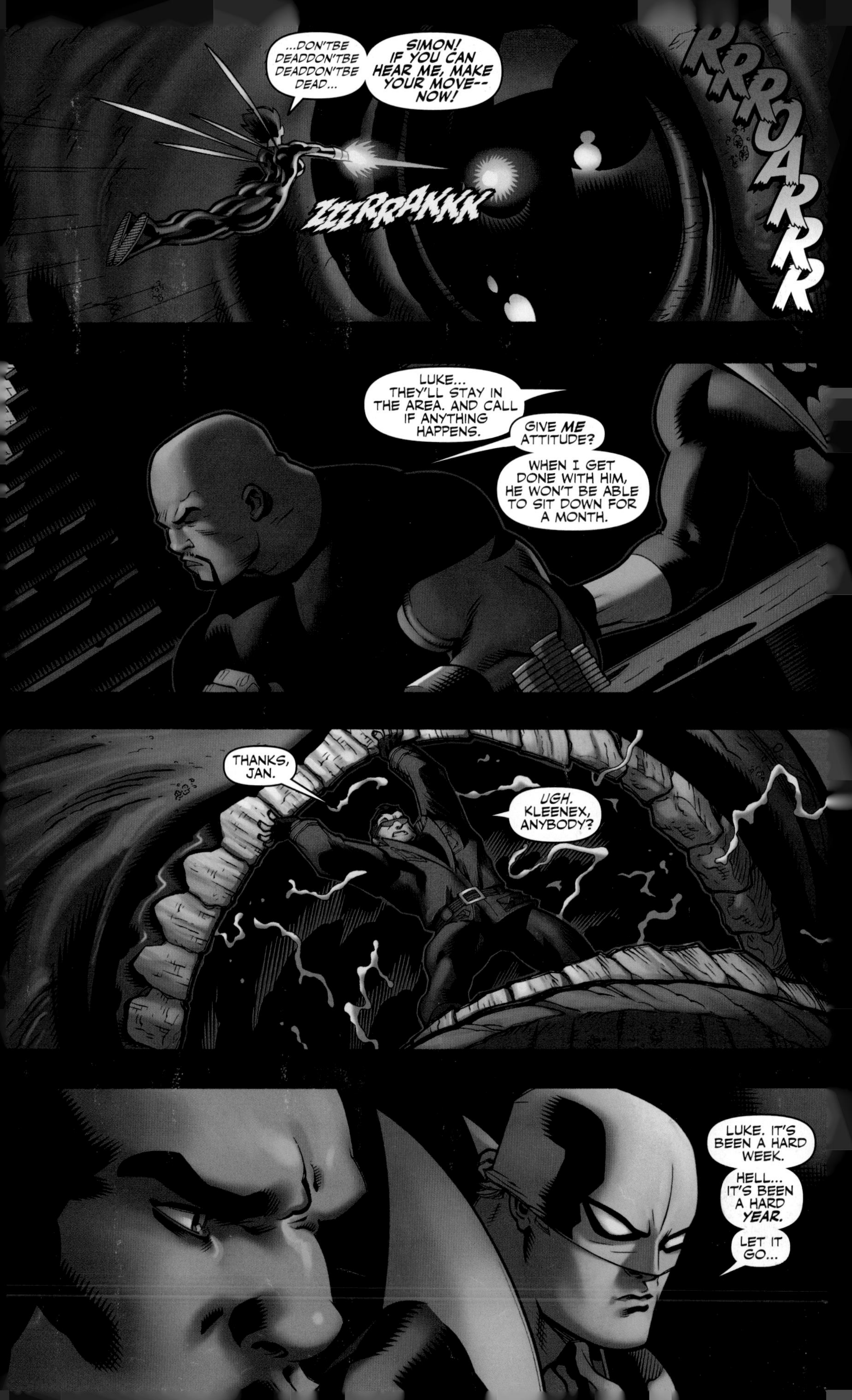
...DON'TBE DEADDON'TBE DEADDON'TBE DEAD...
SIMON! IF YOU CAN HEAR ME, MAKE YOUR MOVE-- NOW!
RRRROARRRR
ZZZRRAKKK
LUKE... THEY'LL STAY IN THE AREA. AND CALL IF ANYTHING HAPPENS.
GIVE ME ATTITUDE?
WHEN I GET DONE WITH HIM, HE WON'T BE ABLE TO SIT DOWN FOR A MONTH.
THANKS, JAN.
UGH. KLEENEX, ANYBODY?
LUKE. IT'S BEEN A HARD WEEK.
HELL... IT'S BEEN A HARD YEAR.
LET IT GO...

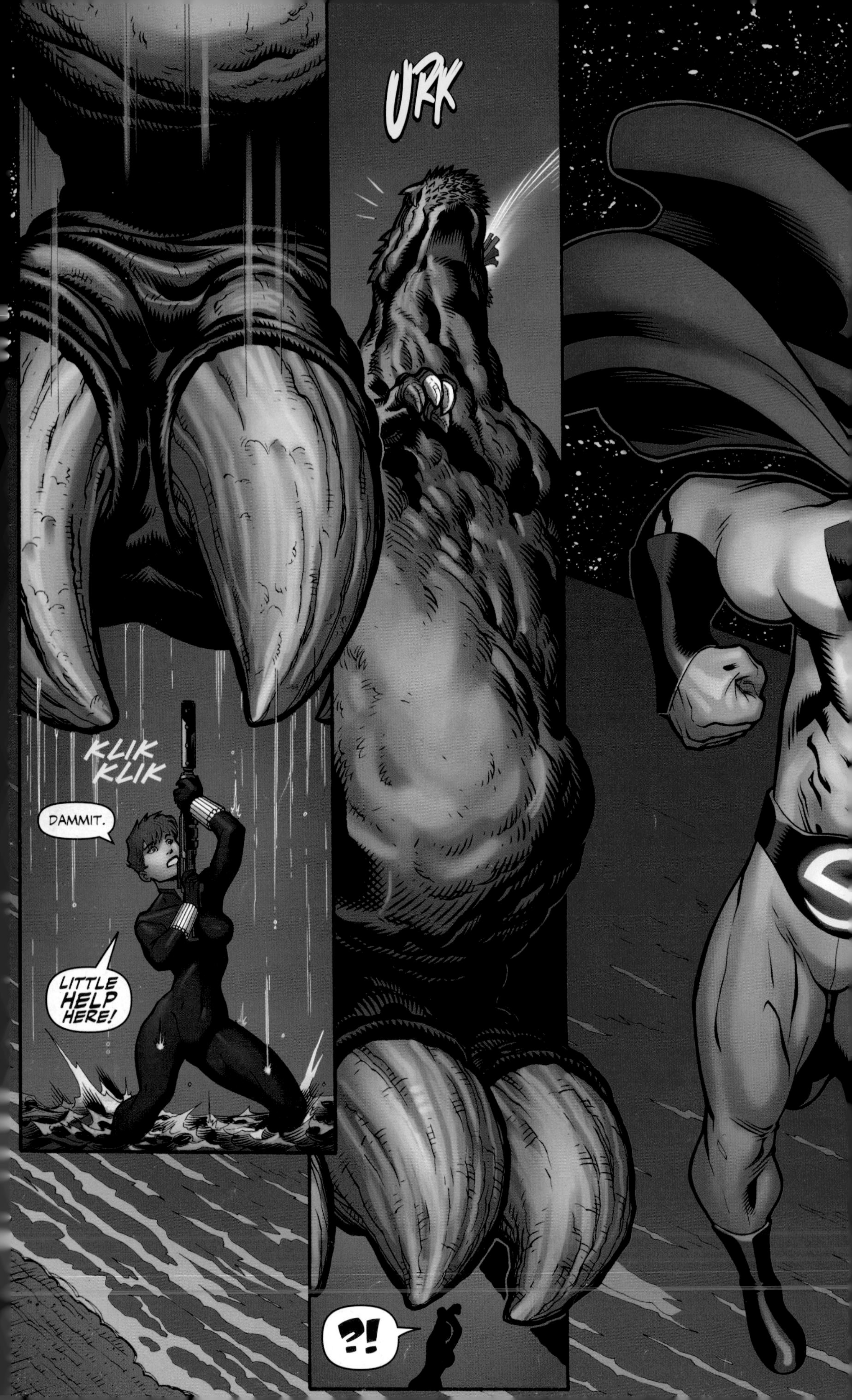
URK
KLIK
KLIK
DAMMIT.
LITTLE HELP HERE!
?!

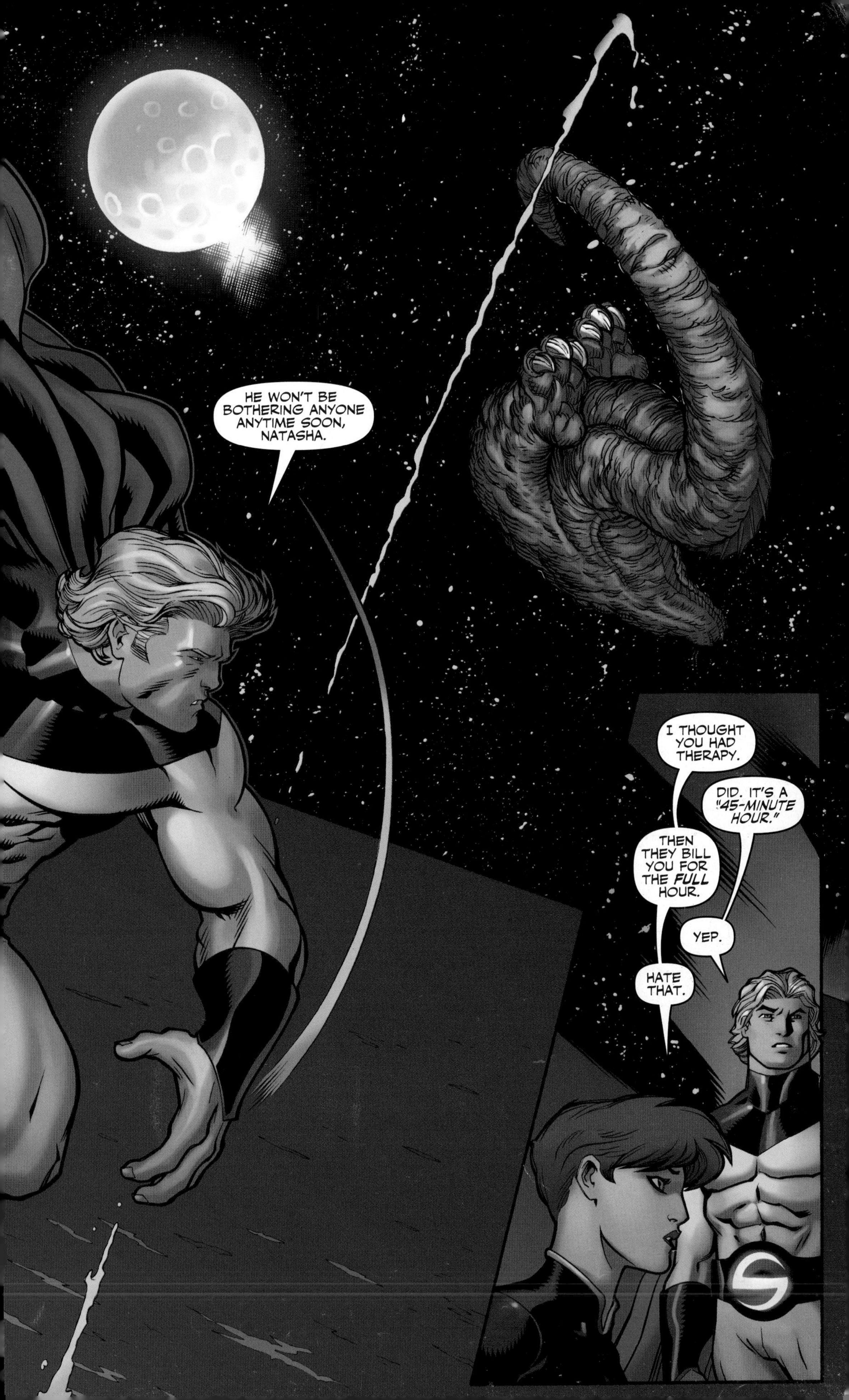
HE WON'T BE BOTHERING ANYONE ANYTIME SOON, NATASHA.
I THOUGHT YOU HAD THERAPY.
DID. IT'S A "45-MINUTE HOUR."
THEN THEY BILL YOU FOR THE *FULL* HOUR.
YEP.
HATE THAT.

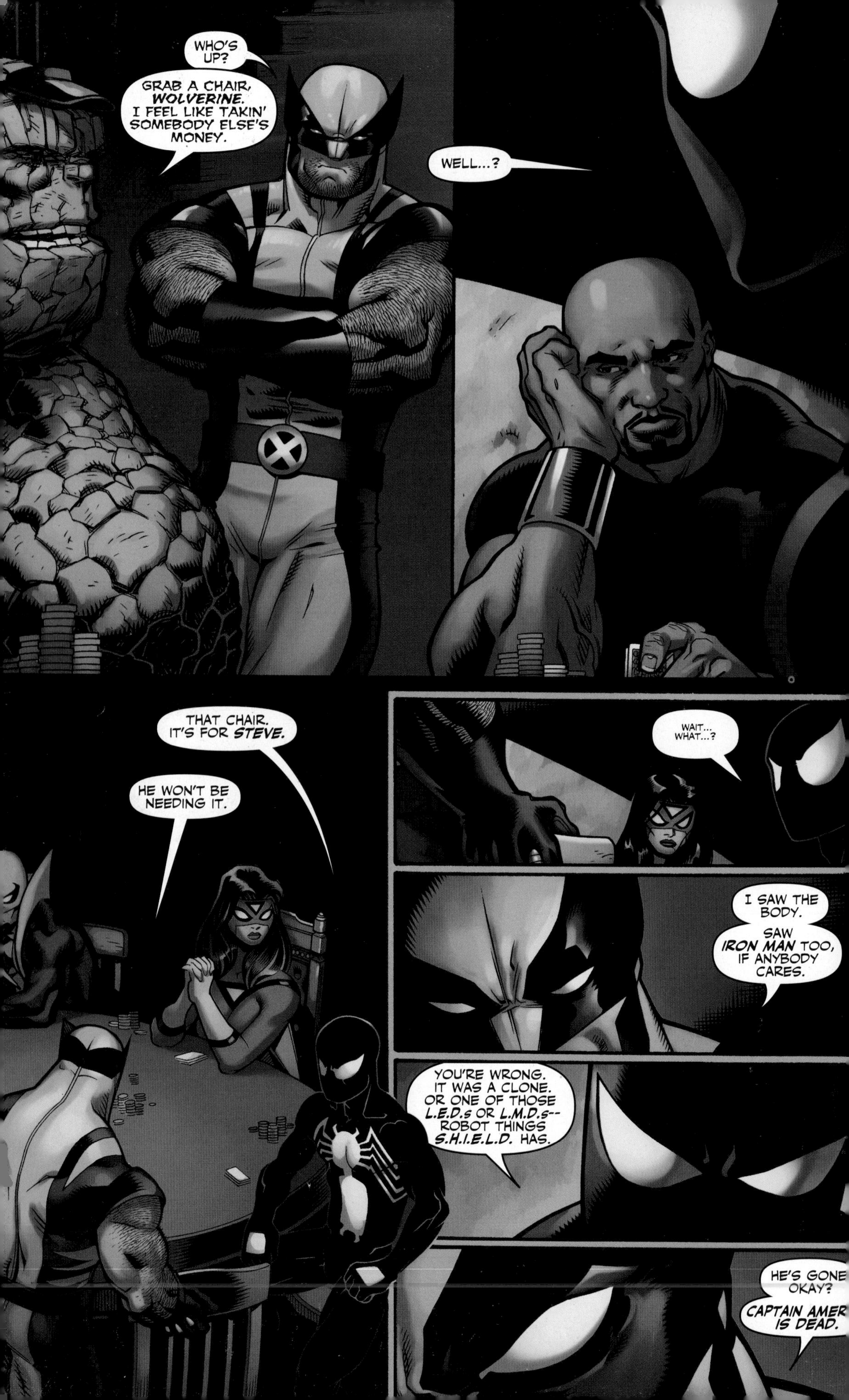
WHO'S UP?
GRAB A CHAIR, WOLVERINE. I FEEL LIKE TAKIN' SOMEBODY ELSE'S MONEY.
WELL...?
THAT CHAIR. IT'S FOR STEVE.
HE WON'T BE NEEDING IT.
WAIT... WHAT...?
I SAW THE BODY.
SAW IRON MAN TOO, IF ANYBODY CARES.
YOU'RE WRONG. IT WAS A CLONE. OR ONE OF THOSE L.E.D.s OR L.M.D.s-- ROBOT THINGS S.H.I.E.L.D. HAS.
HE'S GONE OKAY?
CAPTAIN AMER IS DEAD.

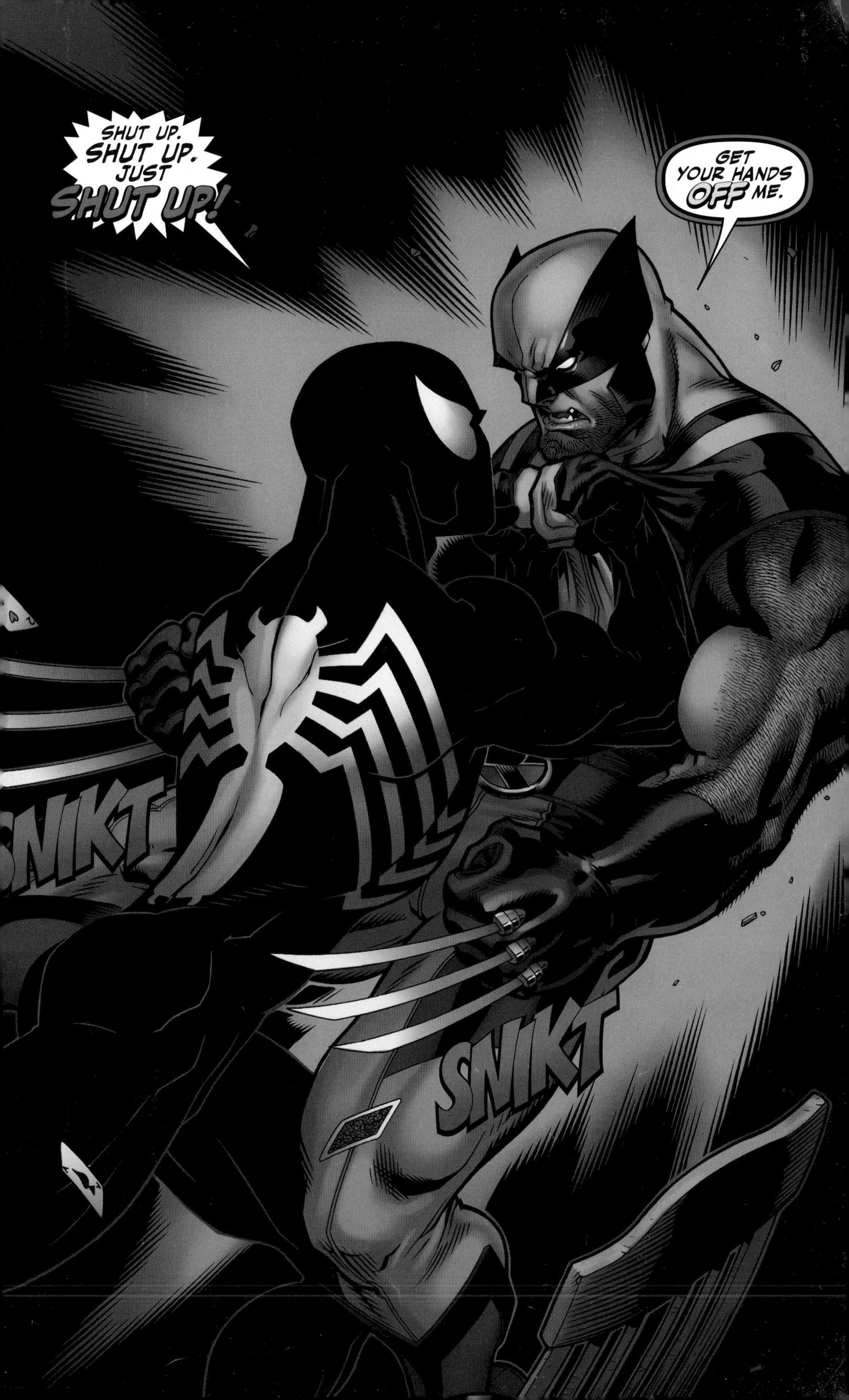
SHUT UP. SHUT UP. JUST SHUT UP!
GET YOUR HANDS OFF ME.
SNIKT
SNIKT

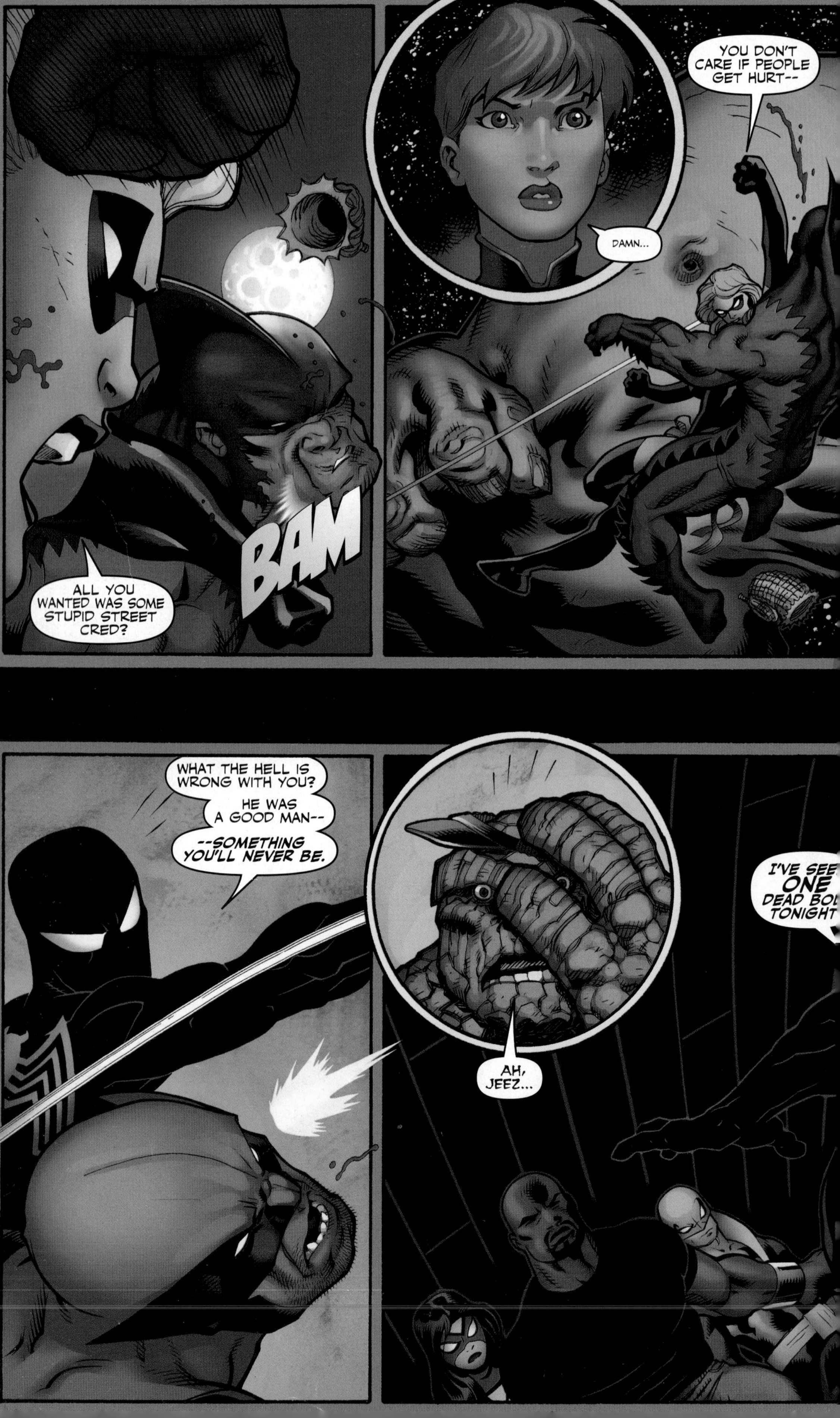
ALL YOU WANTED WAS SOME STUPID STREET CRED?
BAM
YOU DON'T CARE IF PEOPLE GET HURT--
DAMN...
WHAT THE HELL IS WRONG WITH YOU?
HE WAS A GOOD MAN--
--SOMETHING YOU'LL NEVER BE.
AH, JEEZ...
I'VE SEE ONE DEAD BO TONIGHT

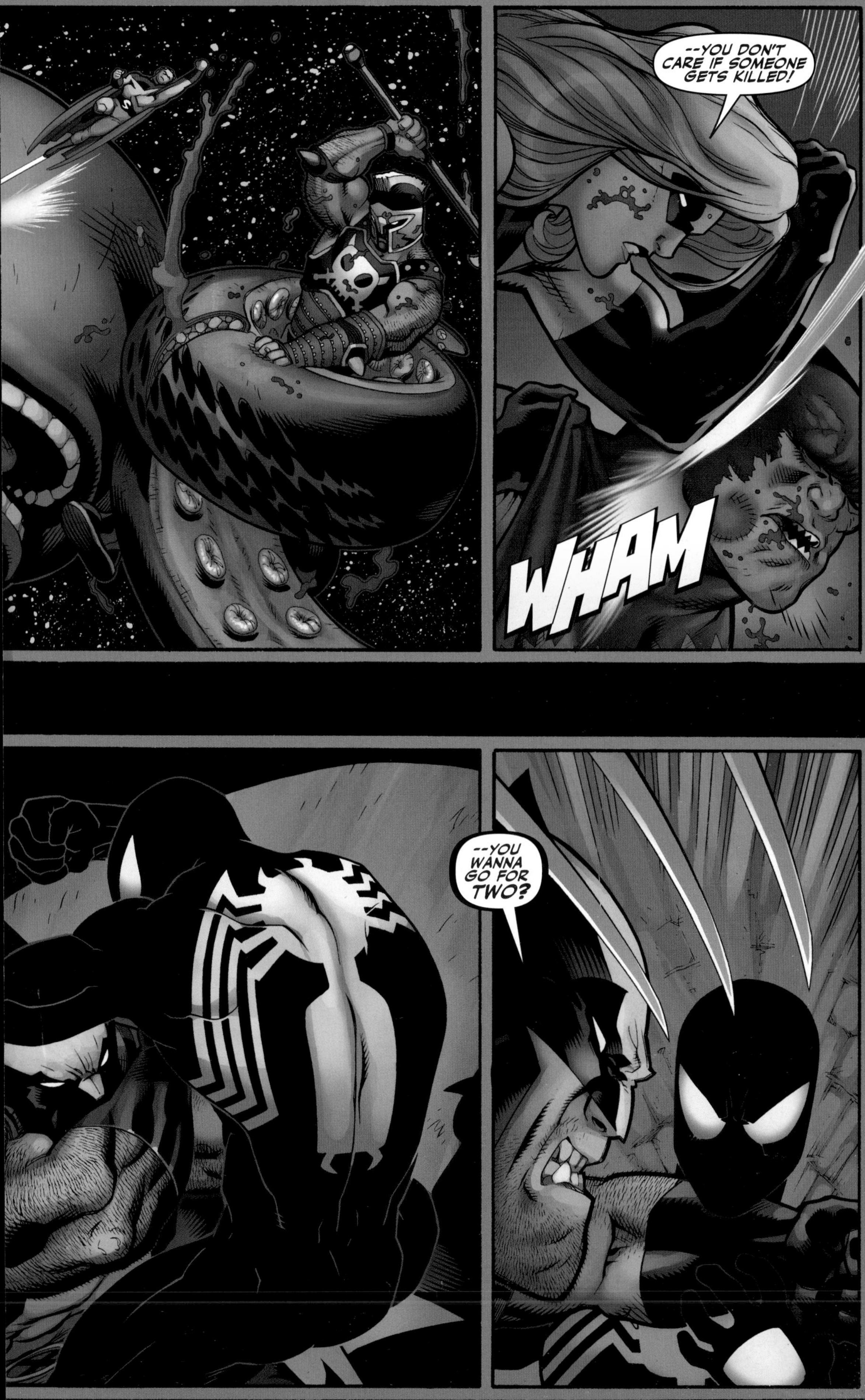
--YOU DON'T CARE IF SOMEONE GETS KILLED!
WHAM
--YOU WANNA GO FOR TWO?

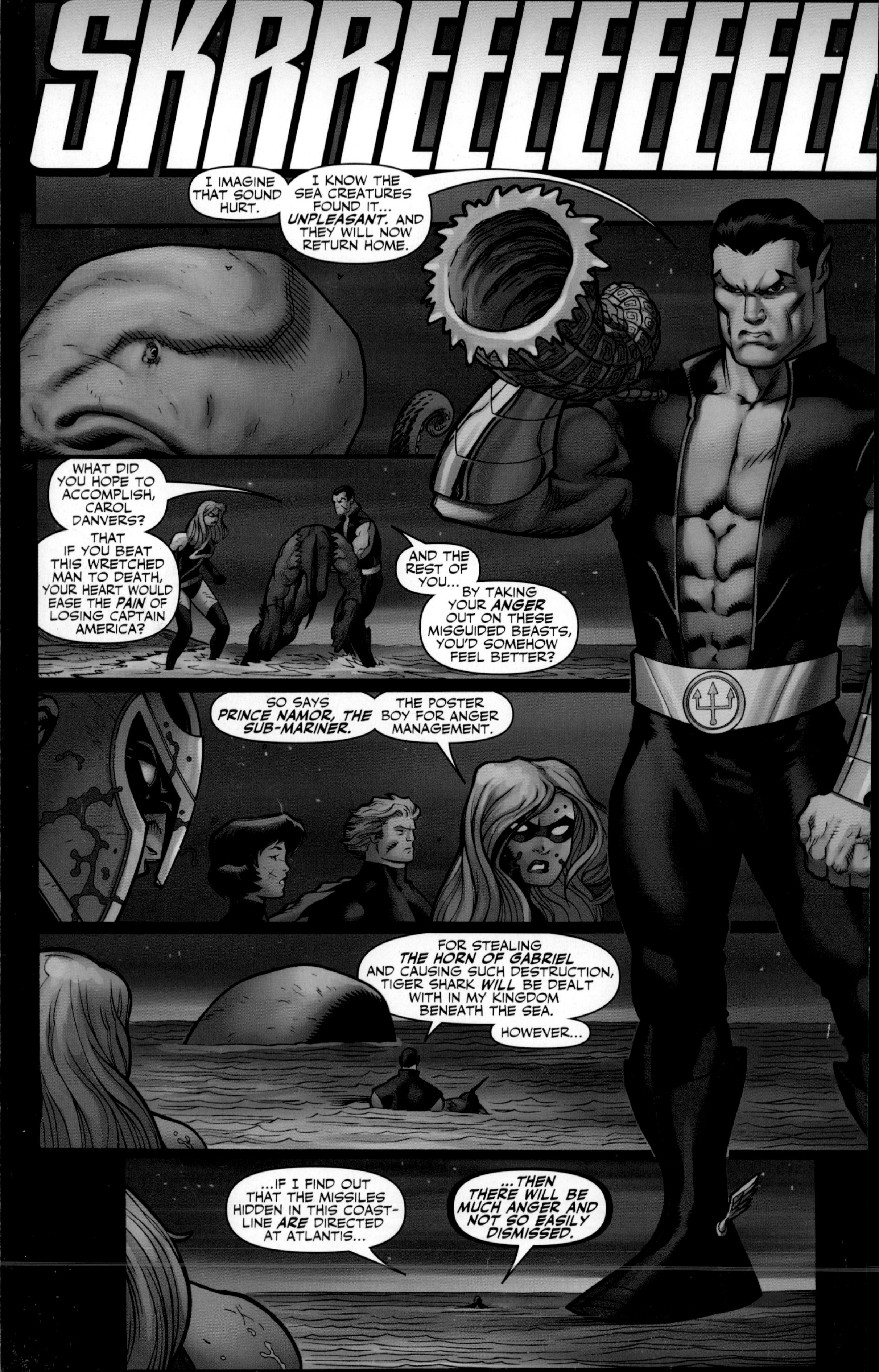
SKRREEEEEEEEL
I IMAGINE THAT SOUND HURT.
I KNOW THE SEA CREATURES FOUND IT... UNPLEASANT. AND THEY WILL NOW RETURN HOME.
WHAT DID YOU HOPE TO ACCOMPLISH, CAROL DANVERS?
THAT IF YOU BEAT THIS WRETCHED MAN TO DEATH, YOUR HEART WOULD EASE THE PAIN OF LOSING CAPTAIN AMERICA?
AND THE REST OF YOU...
BY TAKING YOUR ANGER OUT ON THESE MISGUIDED BEASTS, YOU'D SOMEHOW FEEL BETTER?
SO SAYS PRINCE NAMOR, THE SUB-MARINER.
THE POSTER BOY FOR ANGER MANAGEMENT.
FOR STEALING THE HORN OF GABRIEL AND CAUSING SUCH DESTRUCTION, TIGER SHARK WILL BE DEALT WITH IN MY KINGDOM BENEATH THE SEA.
HOWEVER...
...IF I FIND OUT THAT THE MISSILES HIDDEN IN THIS COAST-LINE ARE DIRECTED AT ATLANTIS...
...THEN THERE WILL BE MUCH ANGER AND NOT SO EASILY DISMISSED.

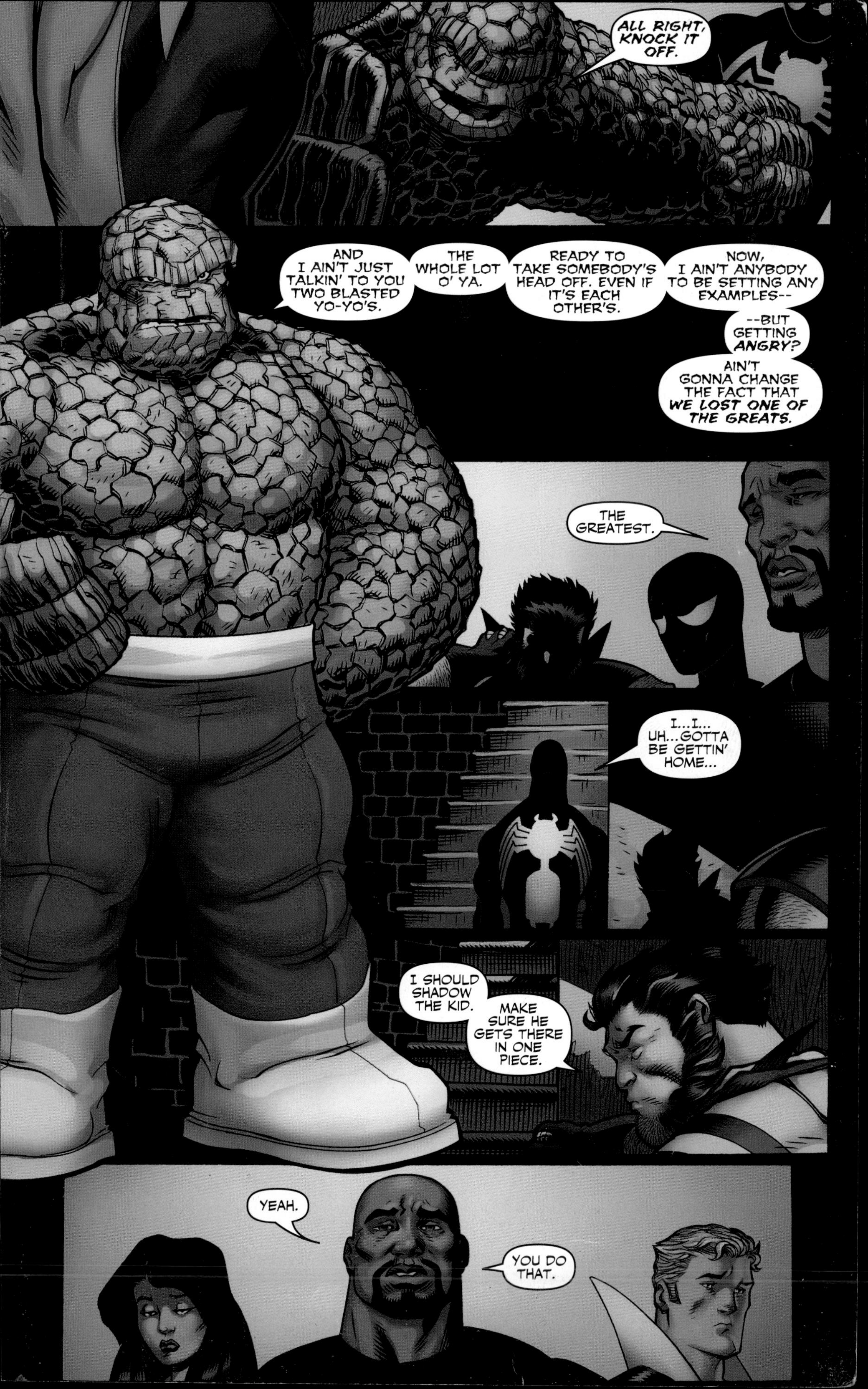
ALL RIGHT, KNOCK IT OFF.
AND I AIN'T JUST TALKIN' TO YOU TWO BLASTED YO-YO'S.
THE WHOLE LOT O' YA.
READY TO TAKE SOMEBODY'S HEAD OFF. EVEN IF IT'S EACH OTHER'S.
NOW, I AIN'T ANYBODY TO BE SETTING ANY EXAMPLES--
--BUT GETTING ANGRY?
AIN'T GONNA CHANGE THE FACT THAT WE LOST ONE OF THE GREATS.
THE GREATEST.
I...I... UH...GOTTA BE GETTIN' HOME...
I SHOULD SHADOW THE KID.
MAKE SURE HE GETS THERE IN ONE PIECE.
YEAH.
YOU DO THAT.

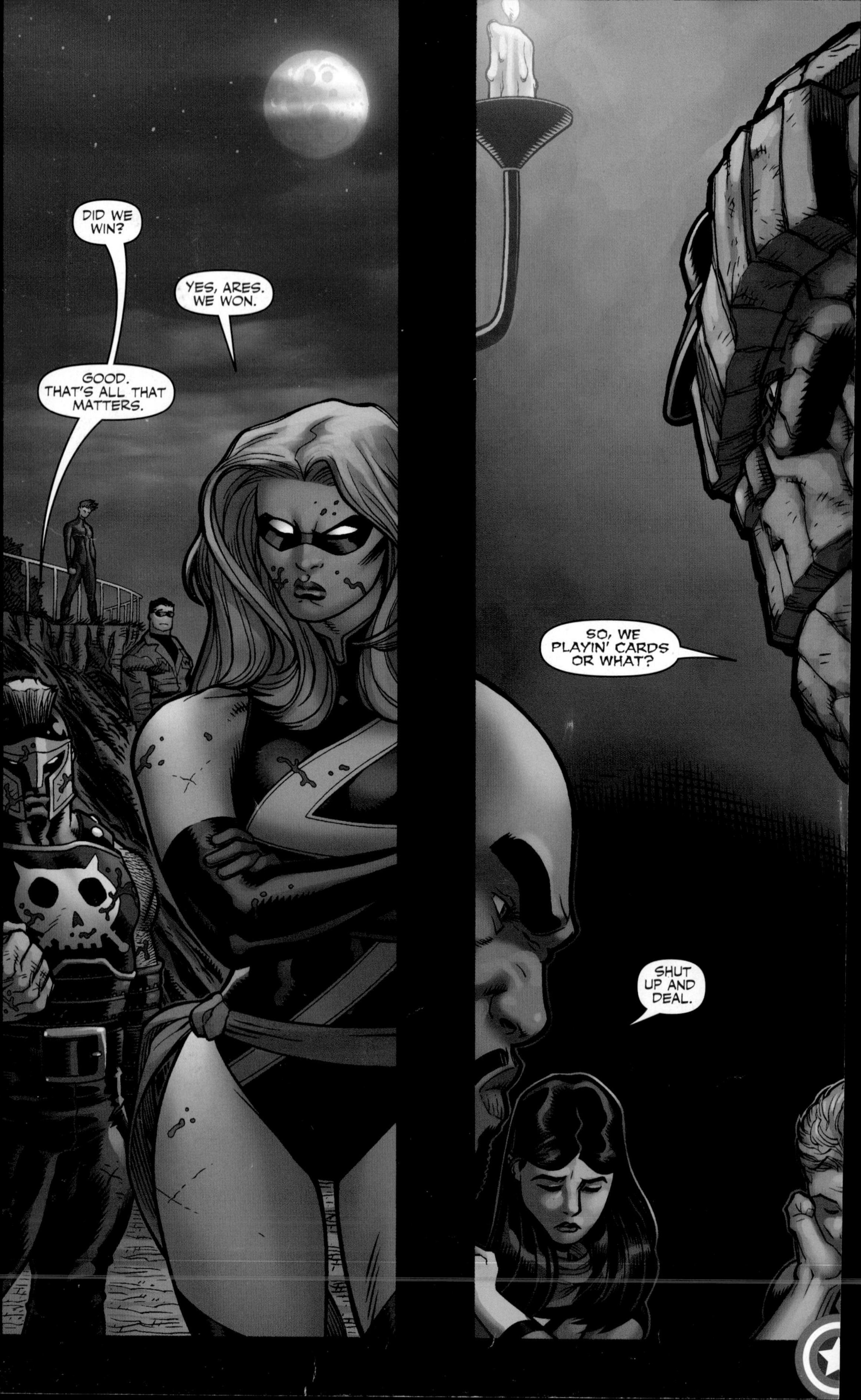
DID WE WIN?
YES, ARES. WE WON.
GOOD. THAT'S ALL THAT MATTERS.
SO, WE PLAYIN' CARDS OR WHAT?
SHUT UP AND DEAL.

FALLEN 3 SON

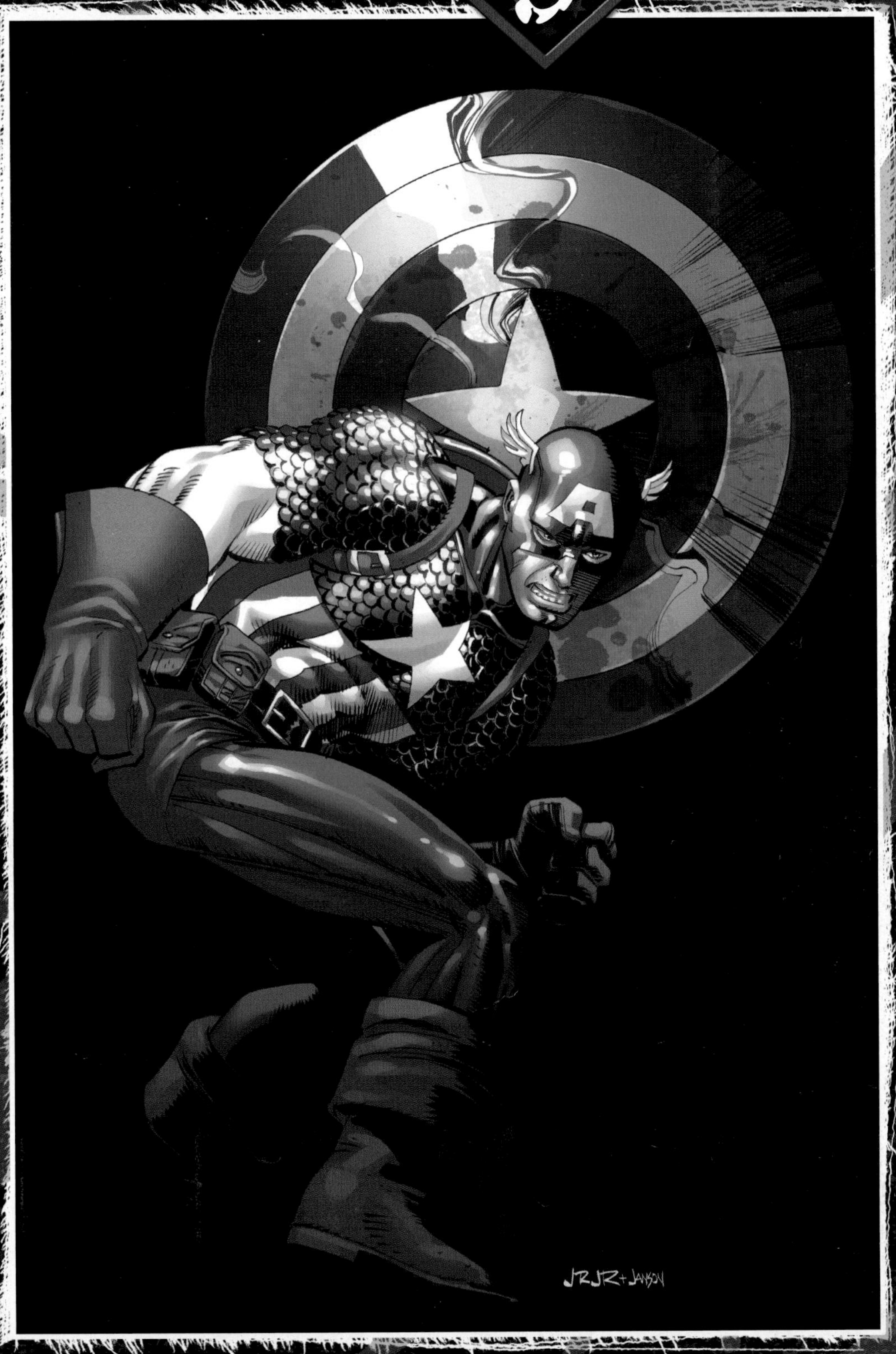
JRJR + JANSON

Bargaining

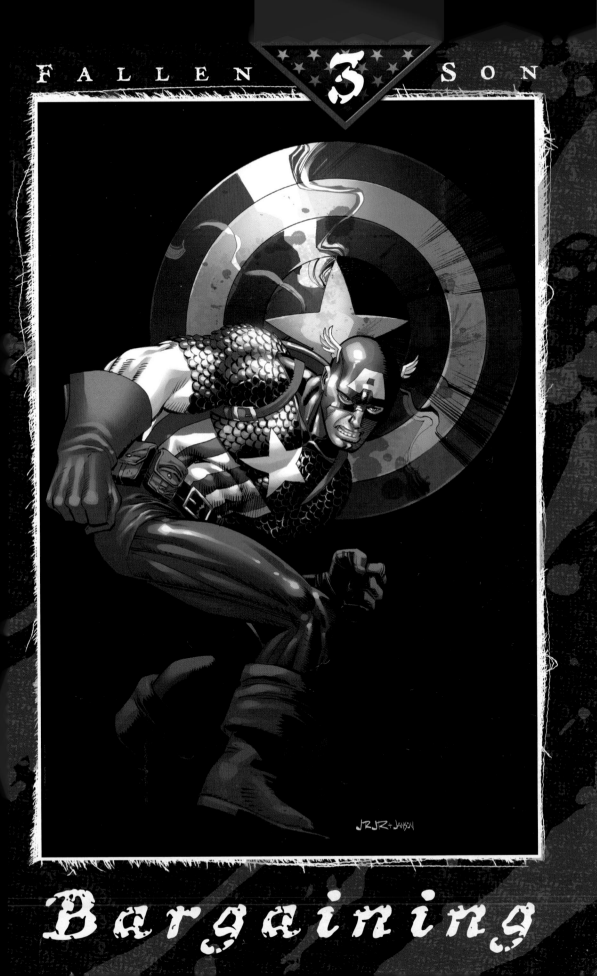

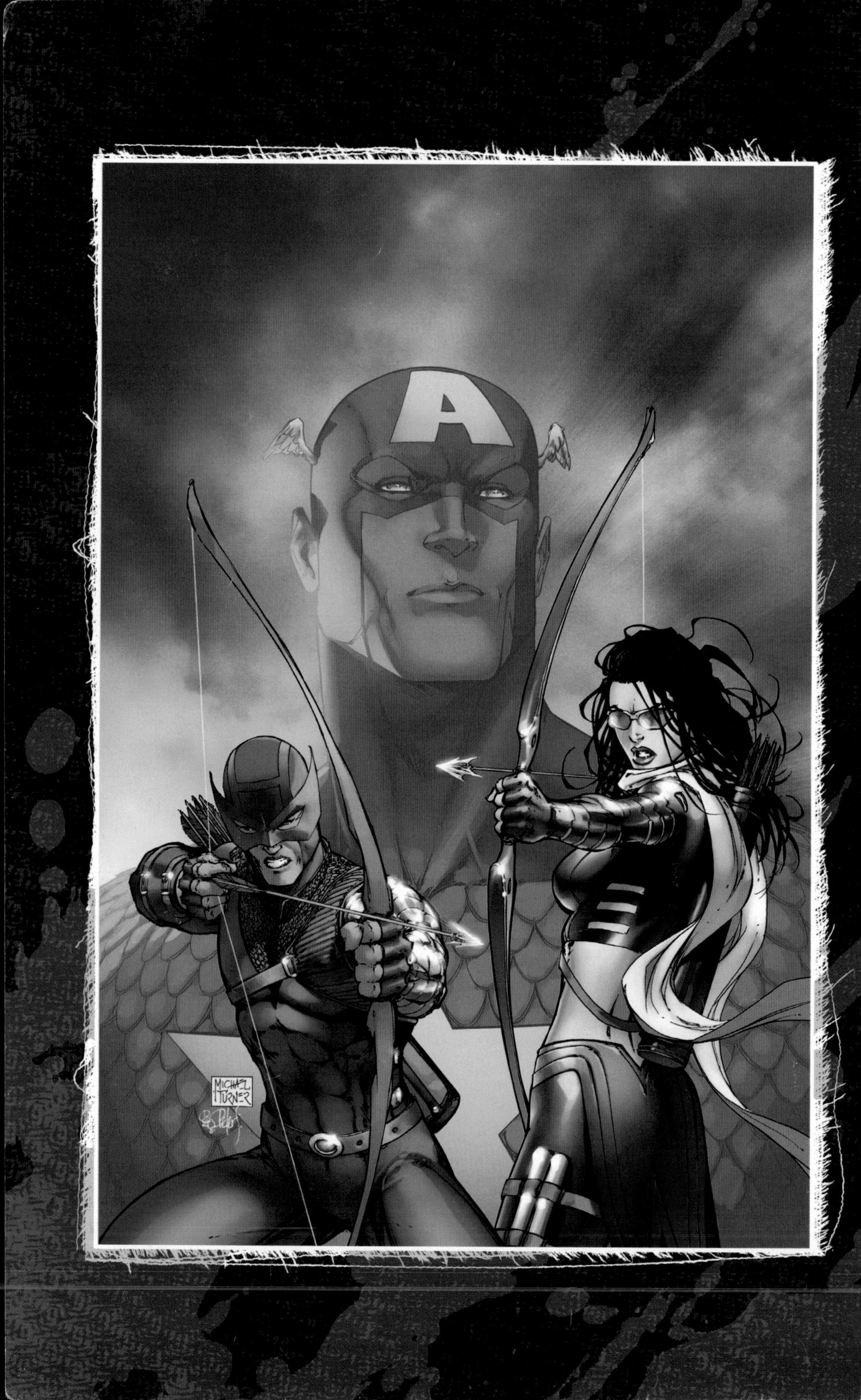
MICHAEL TURNER

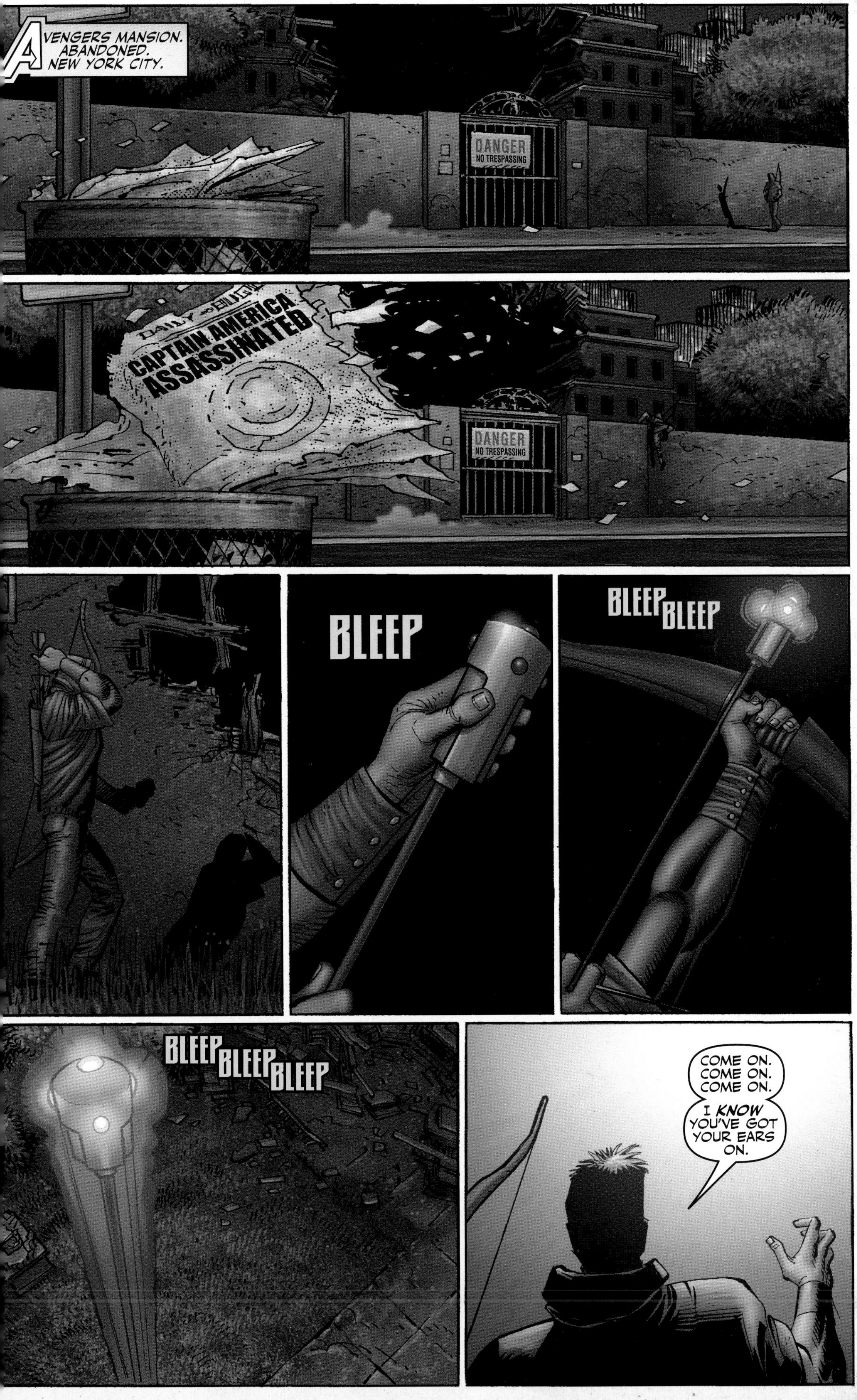
AVENGERS MANSION. ABANDONED. NEW YORK CITY.
DANGER
NO TRESPASSING
CAPTAIN AMERICA ASSASSINATED
DANGER
NO TRESPASSING
BLEEP
BLEEP BLEEP
BLEEP BLEEP BLEEP
COME ON. COME ON. COME ON.
I KNOW YOU'VE GOT YOUR EARS ON.

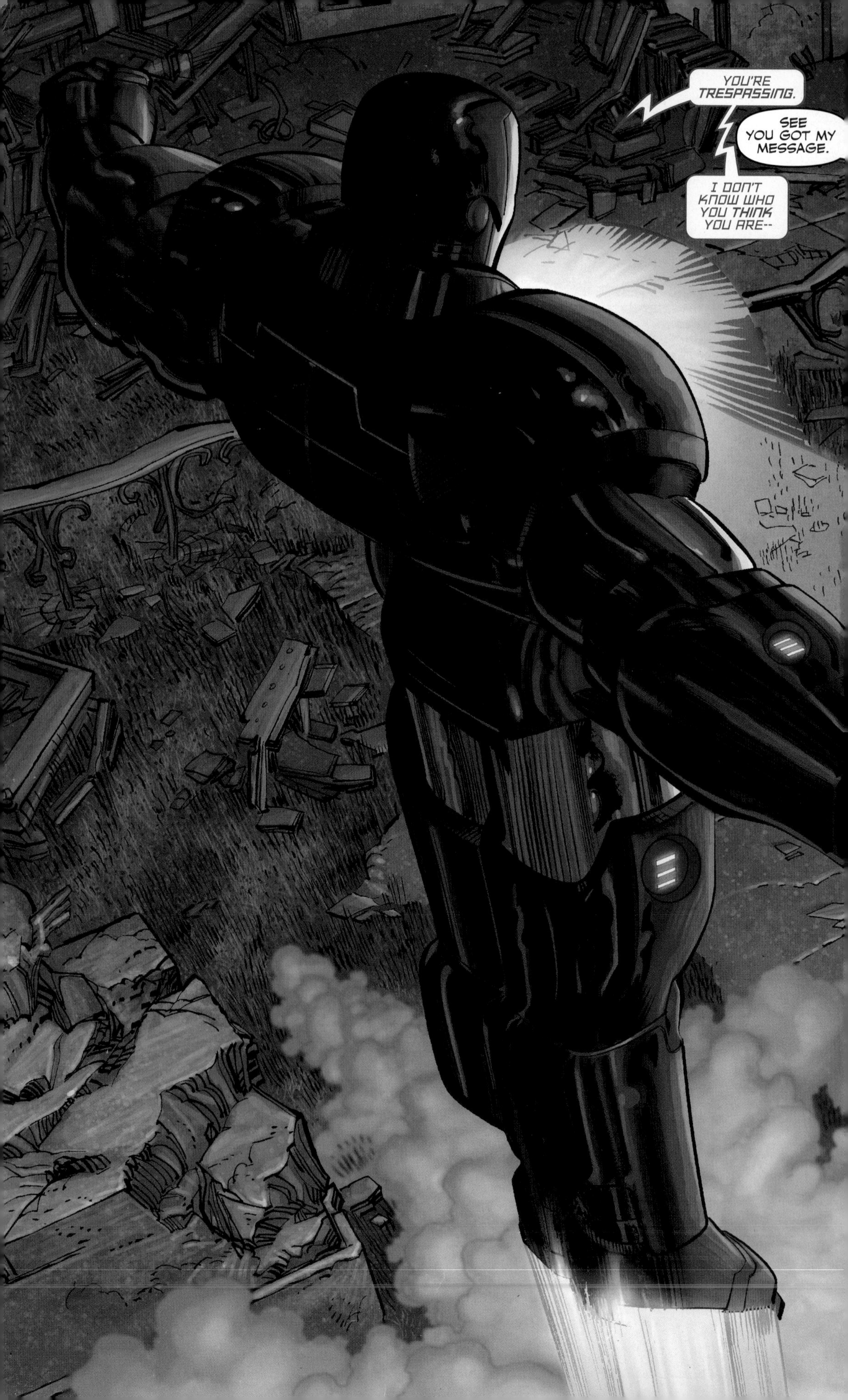
YOU'RE TRESPASSING.
SEE YOU GOT MY MESSAGE.
I DON'T KNOW WHO YOU THINK YOU ARE--

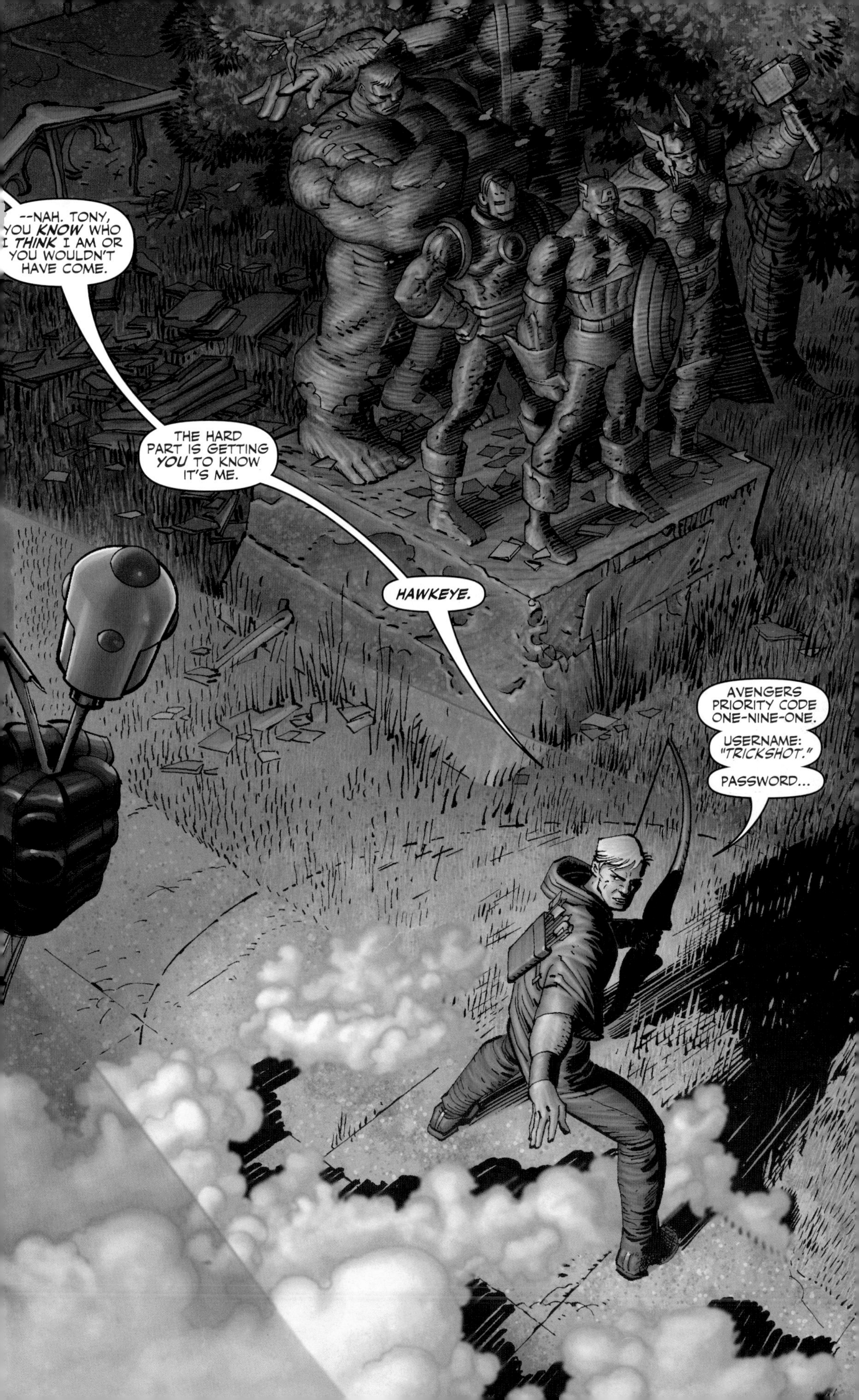
--NAH. TONY, YOU KNOW WHO I THINK I AM OR YOU WOULDN'T HAVE COME.
THE HARD PART IS GETTING YOU TO KNOW IT'S ME.
HAWKEYE.
AVENGERS PRIORITY CODE ONE-NINE-ONE.
USERNAME: "TRICKSHOT."
PASSWORD...

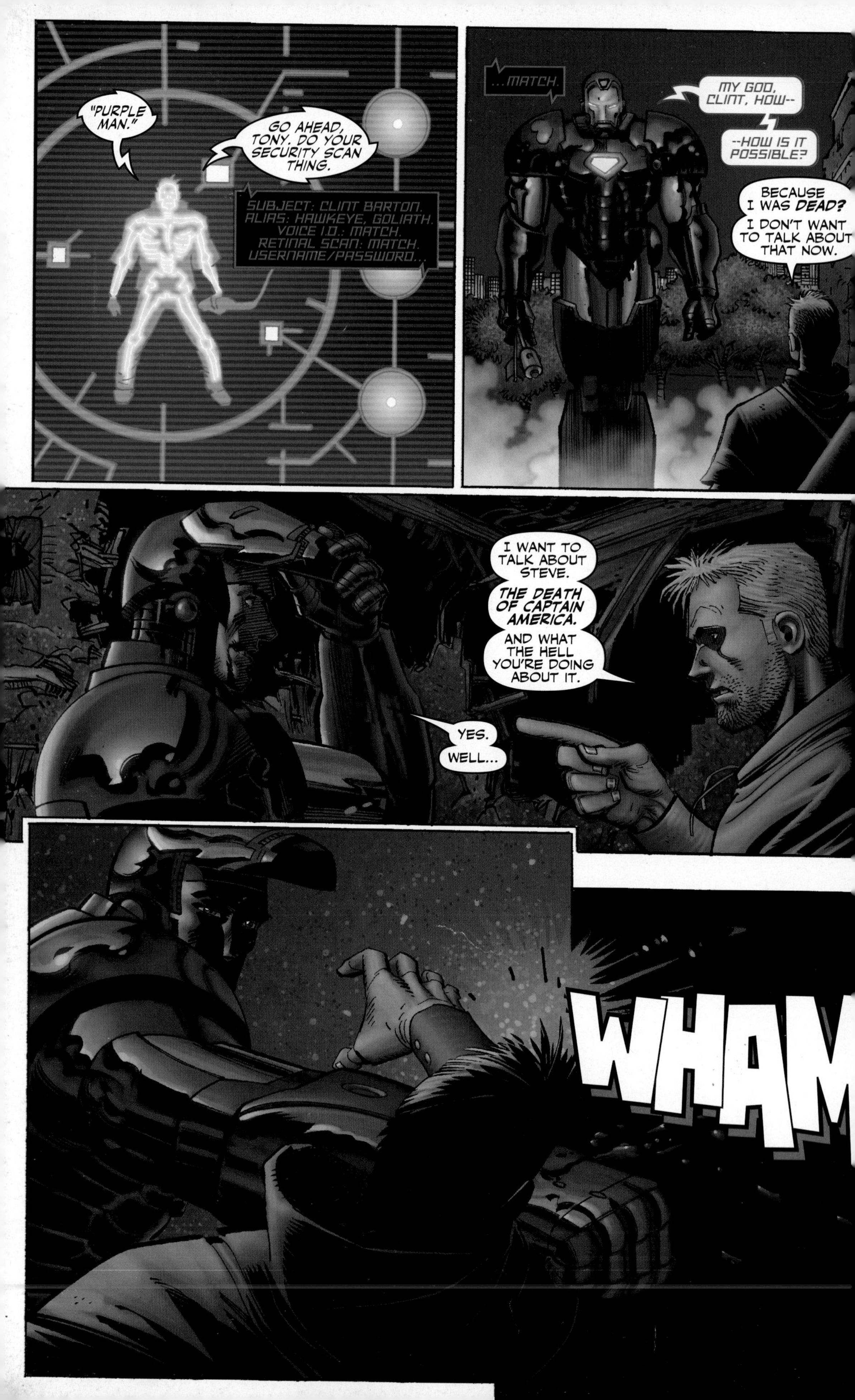
"PURPLE MAN."
GO AHEAD, TONY. DO YOUR SECURITY SCAN THING.
SUBJECT: CLINT BARTON. ALIAS: HAWKEYE, GOLIATH. VOICE I.D.: MATCH. RETINAL SCAN: MATCH. USERNAME/PASSWORD...
...MATCH.
MY GOD, CLINT, HOW--
--HOW IS IT POSSIBLE?
BECAUSE I WAS *DEAD?*
I DON'T WANT TO TALK ABOUT THAT NOW.
I WANT TO TALK ABOUT STEVE.
THE DEATH OF CAPTAIN AMERICA.
AND WHAT THE HELL YOU'RE DOING ABOUT IT.
YES.
WELL...
WHAM

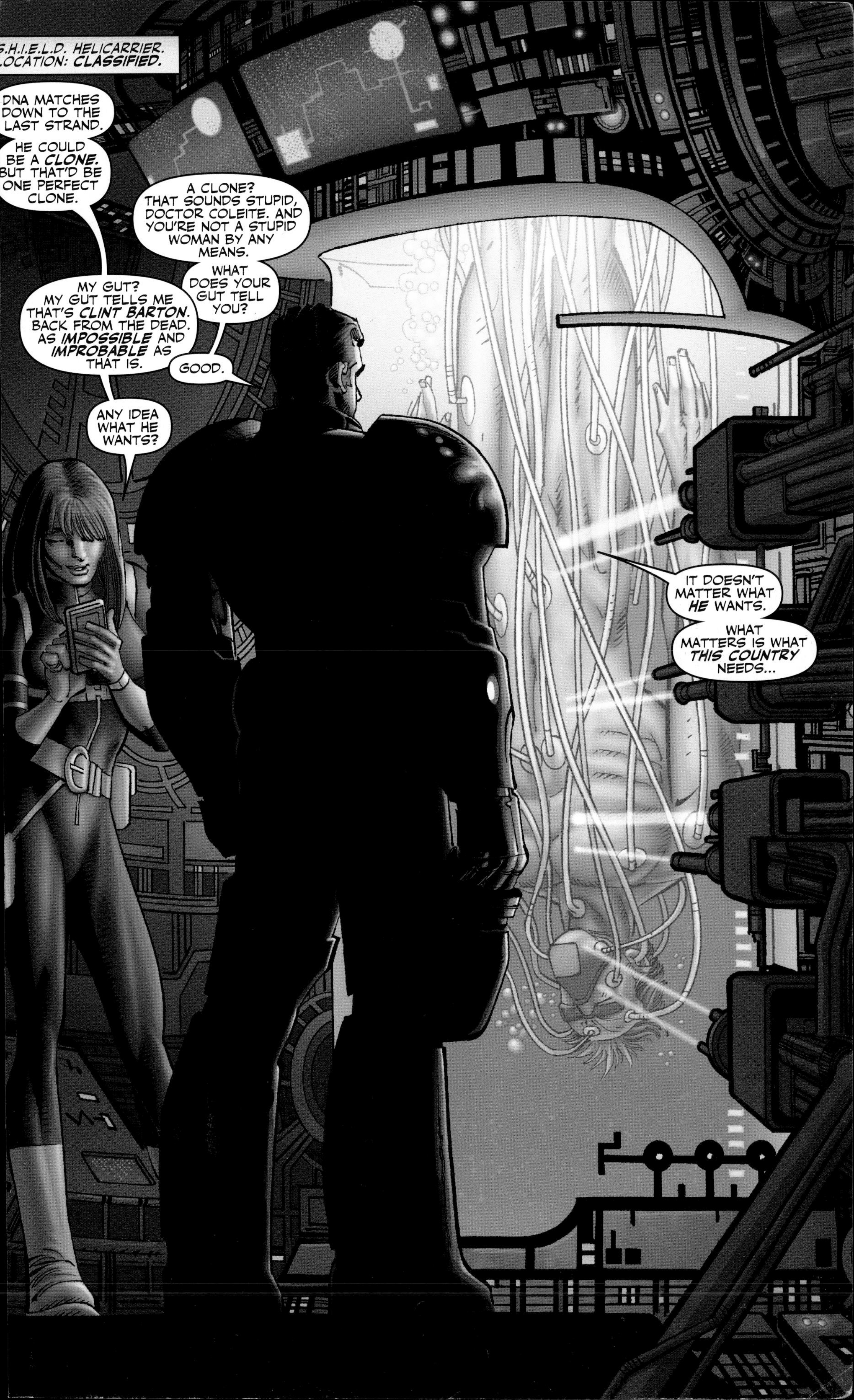
S.H.I.E.L.D. HELICARRIER.
LOCATION: CLASSIFIED.
DNA MATCHES DOWN TO THE LAST STRAND.
HE COULD BE A CLONE. BUT THAT'D BE ONE PERFECT CLONE.
A CLONE? THAT SOUNDS STUPID, DOCTOR COLEITE. AND YOU'RE NOT A STUPID WOMAN BY ANY MEANS.
WHAT DOES YOUR GUT TELL YOU?
MY GUT? MY GUT TELLS ME THAT'S CLINT BARTON. BACK FROM THE DEAD. AS IMPOSSIBLE AND IMPROBABLE AS THAT IS.
GOOD.
ANY IDEA WHAT HE WANTS?
IT DOESN'T MATTER WHAT HE WANTS.
WHAT MATTERS IS WHAT THIS COUNTRY NEEDS...

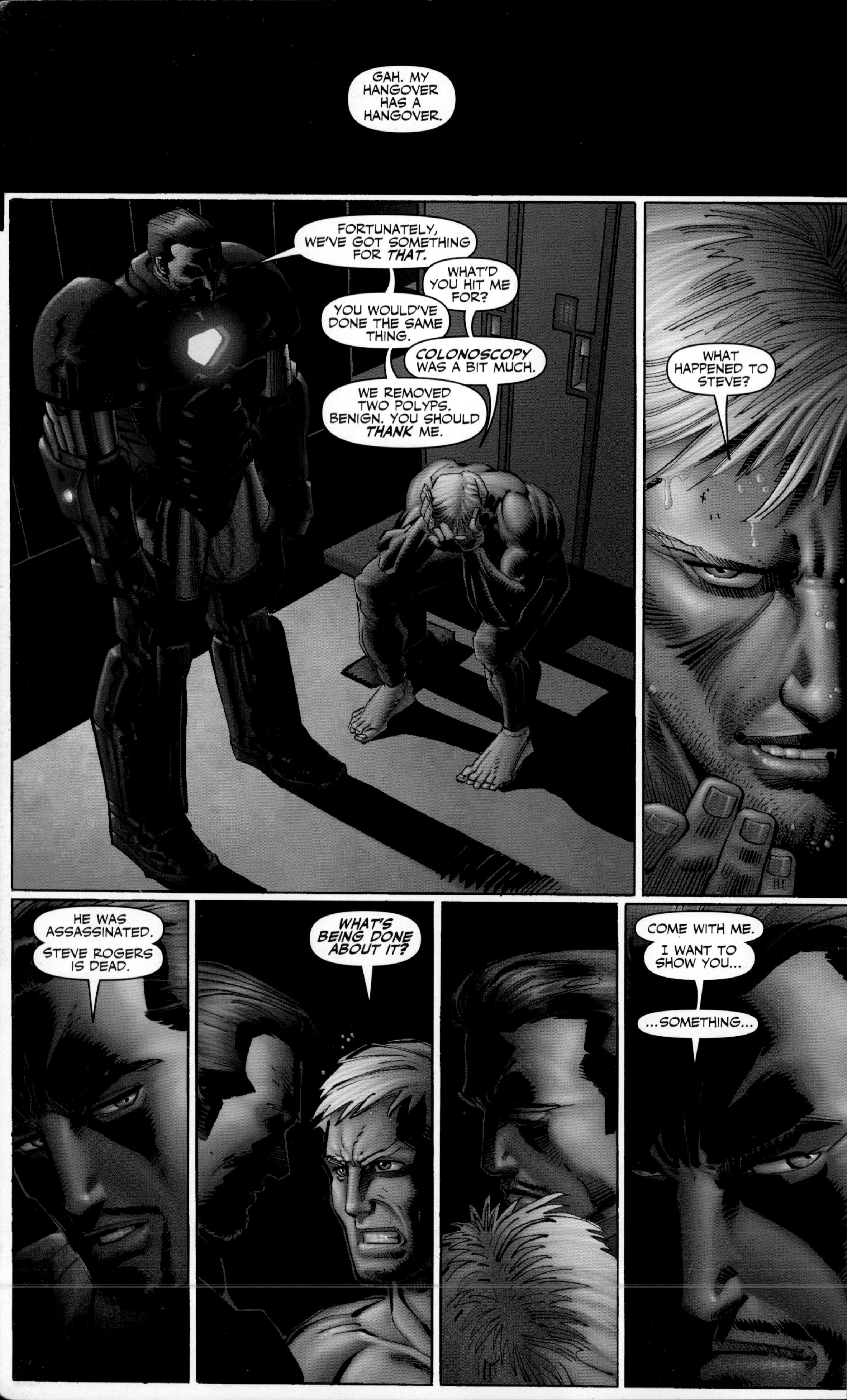
GAH. MY HANGOVER HAS A HANGOVER.
FORTUNATELY, WE'VE GOT SOMETHING FOR THAT.
WHAT'D YOU HIT ME FOR?
YOU WOULD'VE DONE THE SAME THING.
COLONOSCOPY WAS A BIT MUCH.
WE REMOVED TWO POLYPS. BENIGN. YOU SHOULD THANK ME.
WHAT HAPPENED TO STEVE?
HE WAS ASSASSINATED.
STEVE ROGERS IS DEAD.
WHAT'S BEING DONE ABOUT IT?
COME WITH ME.
I WANT TO SHOW YOU...
...SOMETHING...

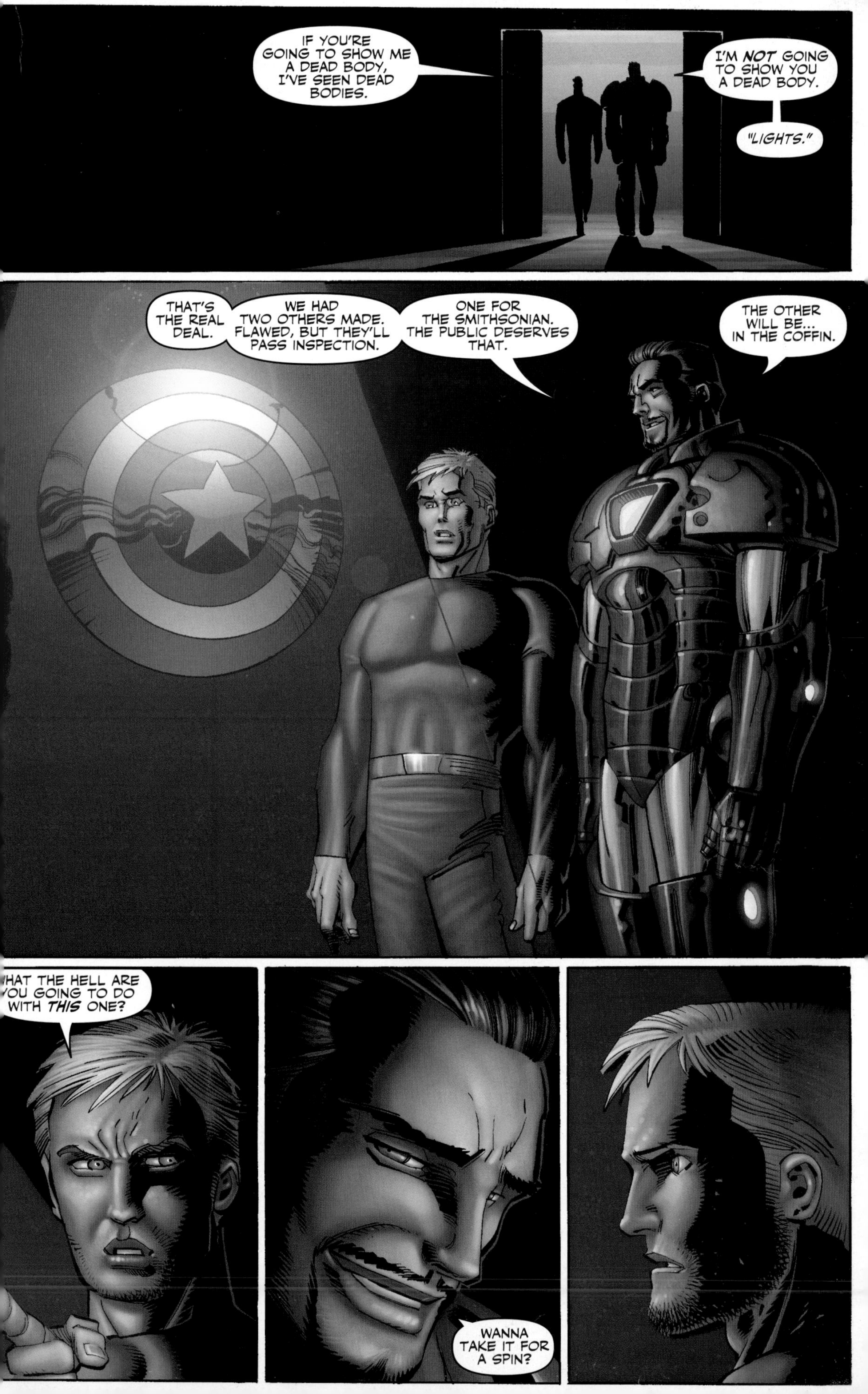
IF YOU'RE GOING TO SHOW ME A DEAD BODY, I'VE SEEN DEAD BODIES.
I'M *NOT* GOING TO SHOW YOU A DEAD BODY.
"LIGHTS."
THAT'S THE REAL DEAL.
WE HAD TWO OTHERS MADE. FLAWED, BUT THEY'LL PASS INSPECTION.
ONE FOR THE SMITHSONIAN. THE PUBLIC DESERVES THAT.
THE OTHER WILL BE... IN THE COFFIN.
HAT THE HELL ARE OU GOING TO DO WITH *THIS* ONE?
WANNA TAKE IT FOR A SPIN?

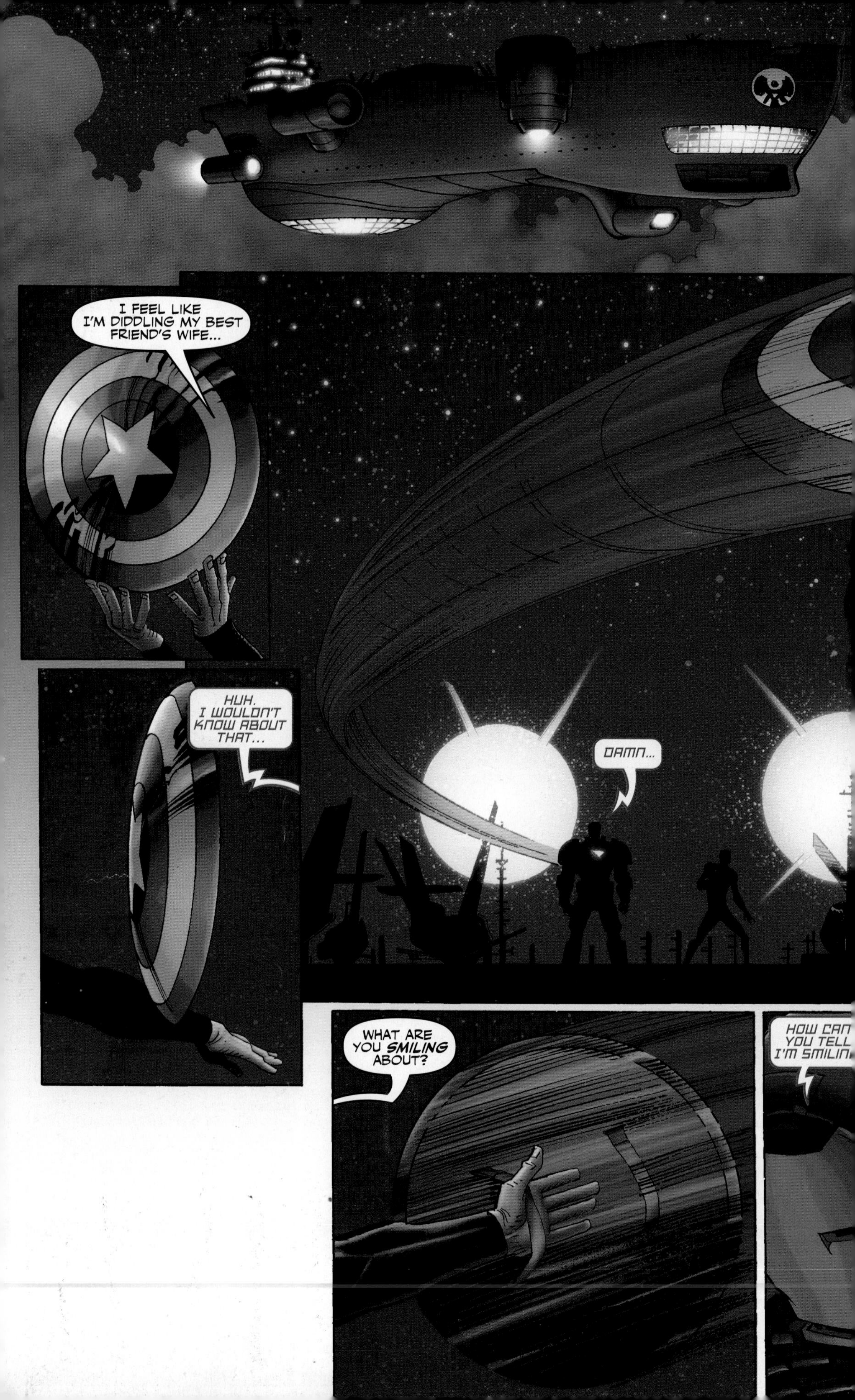
I FEEL LIKE I'M DIDDLING MY BEST FRIEND'S WIFE...
HUH. I WOULDN'T KNOW ABOUT THAT...
DAMN...
WHAT ARE YOU SMILING ABOUT?
HOW CAN YOU TELL I'M SMILIN

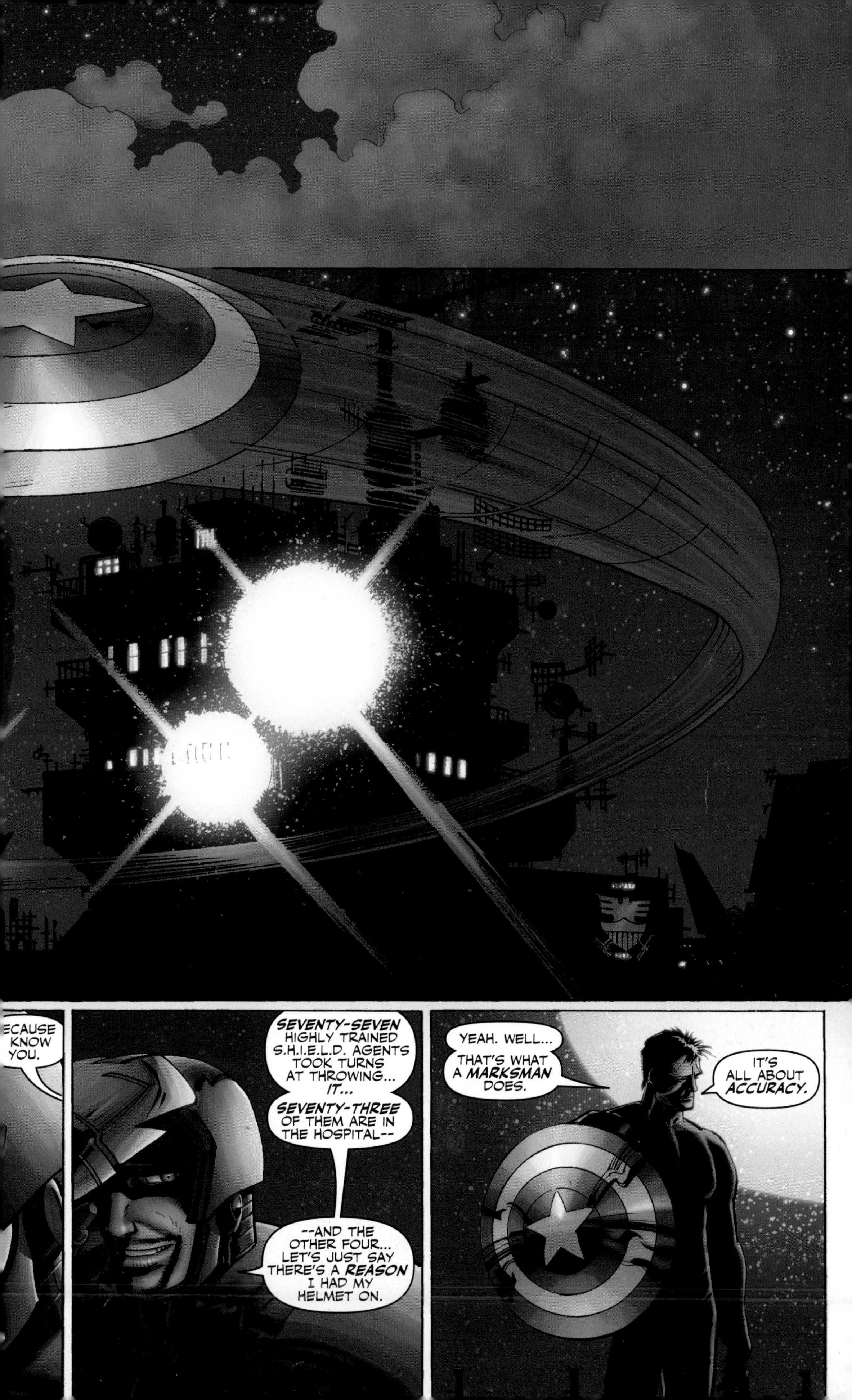
ECAUSE KNOW YOU.
SEVENTY-SEVEN HIGHLY TRAINED S.H.I.E.L.D. AGENTS TOOK TURNS AT THROWING... IT...
SEVENTY-THREE OF THEM ARE IN THE HOSPITAL--
--AND THE OTHER FOUR... LET'S JUST SAY THERE'S A REASON I HAD MY HELMET ON.
YEAH. WELL...
THAT'S WHAT A MARKSMAN DOES.
IT'S ALL ABOUT ACCURACY.

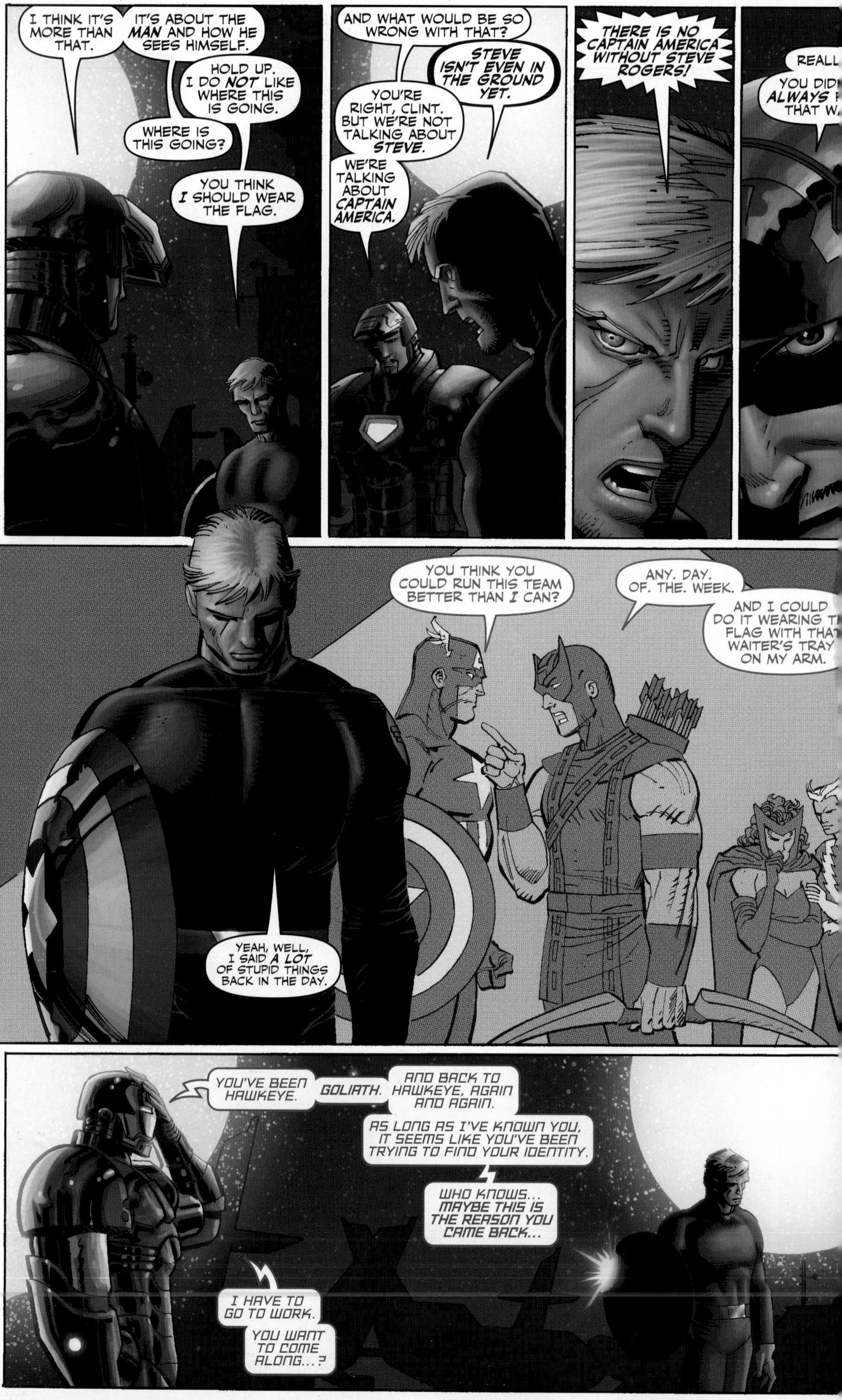

I THINK IT'S MORE THAN THAT.
IT'S ABOUT THE MAN AND HOW HE SEES HIMSELF.
HOLD UP. I DO NOT LIKE WHERE THIS IS GOING.
WHERE IS THIS GOING?
YOU THINK I SHOULD WEAR THE FLAG.
AND WHAT WOULD BE SO WRONG WITH THAT?
STEVE ISN'T EVEN IN THE GROUND YET.
YOU'RE RIGHT, CLINT. BUT WE'RE NOT TALKING ABOUT STEVE.
WE'RE TALKING ABOUT CAPTAIN AMERICA.
THERE IS NO CAPTAIN AMERICA WITHOUT STEVE ROGERS!
REALL
YOU DID ALWAYS THAT W
YOU THINK YOU COULD RUN THIS TEAM BETTER THAN I CAN?
ANY. DAY. OF. THE. WEEK.
AND I COULD DO IT WEARING T FLAG WITH THAT WAITER'S TRAY ON MY ARM.
YEAH, WELL, I SAID A LOT OF STUPID THINGS BACK IN THE DAY.
YOU'VE BEEN HAWKEYE.
GOLIATH.
AND BACK TO HAWKEYE, AGAIN AND AGAIN.
AS LONG AS I'VE KNOWN YOU, IT SEEMS LIKE YOU'VE BEEN TRYING TO FIND YOUR IDENTITY.
WHO KNOWS... MAYBE THIS IS THE REASON YOU CAME BACK...
I HAVE TO GO TO WORK.
YOU WANT TO COME ALONG...?

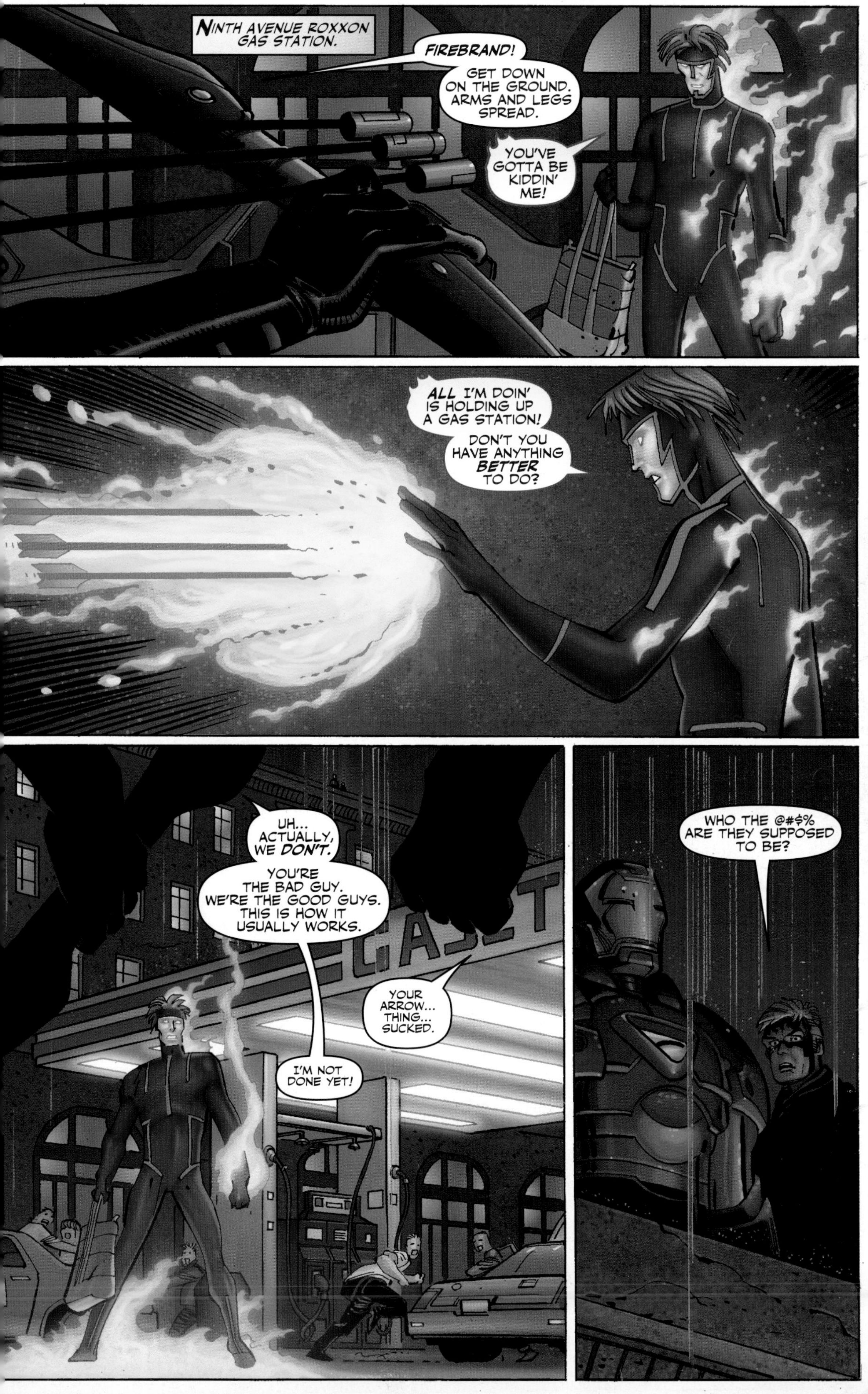
NINTH AVENUE ROXXON GAS STATION.
FIREBRAND!
GET DOWN ON THE GROUND. ARMS AND LEGS SPREAD.
YOU'VE GOTTA BE KIDDIN' ME!
ALL I'M DOIN' IS HOLDING UP A GAS STATION!
DON'T YOU HAVE ANYTHING BETTER TO DO?
UH... ACTUALLY, WE DON'T.
YOU'RE THE BAD GUY. WE'RE THE GOOD GUYS. THIS IS HOW IT USUALLY WORKS.
YOUR ARROW... THING... SUCKED.
I'M NOT DONE YET!
WHO THE @#$% ARE THEY SUPPOSED TO BE?

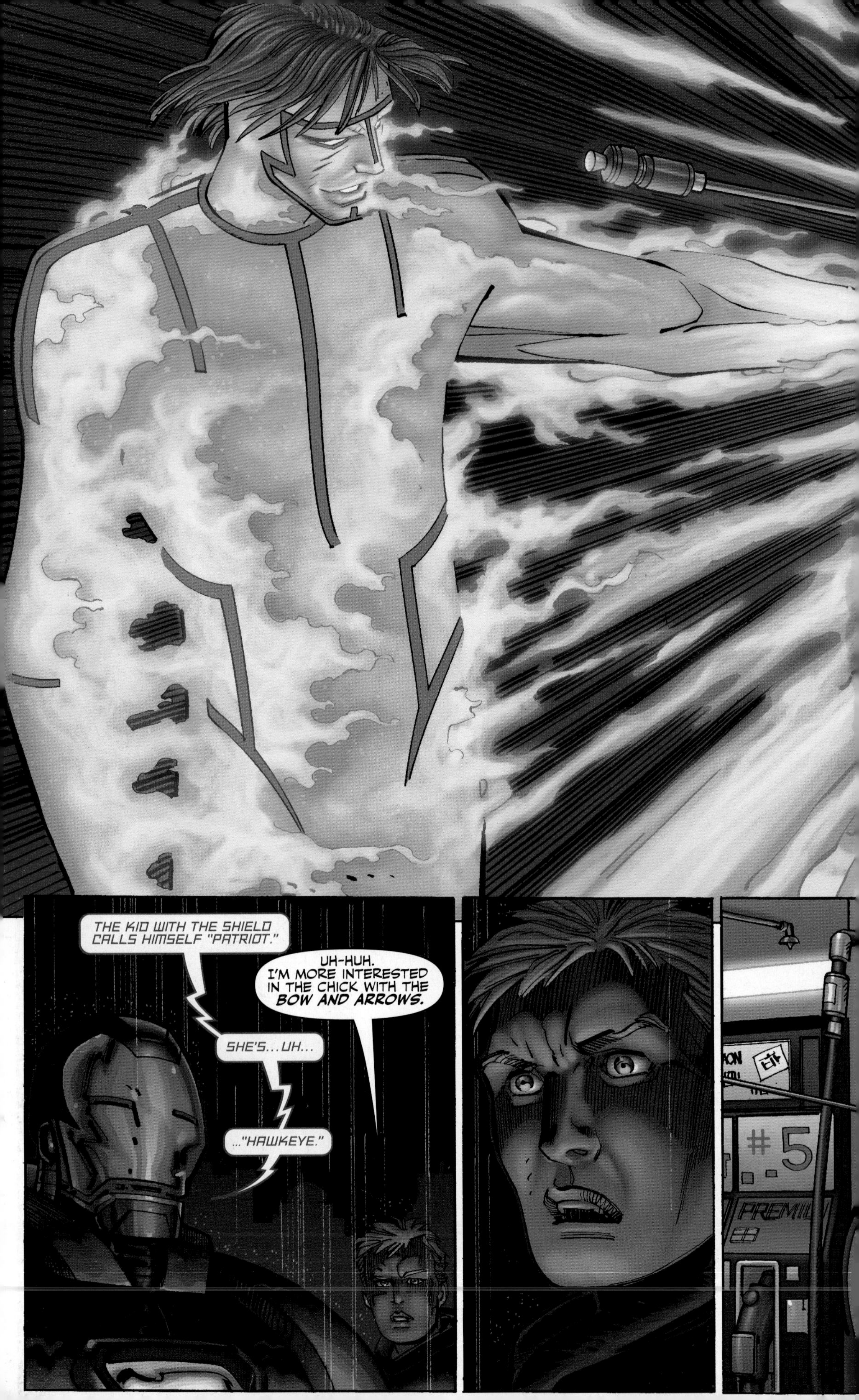
THE KID WITH THE SHIELD CALLS HIMSELF "PATRIOT."
UH-HUH. I'M MORE INTERESTED IN THE CHICK WITH THE BOW AND ARROWS.
SHE'S...UH...
..."HAWKEYE."
#5
PREMIU

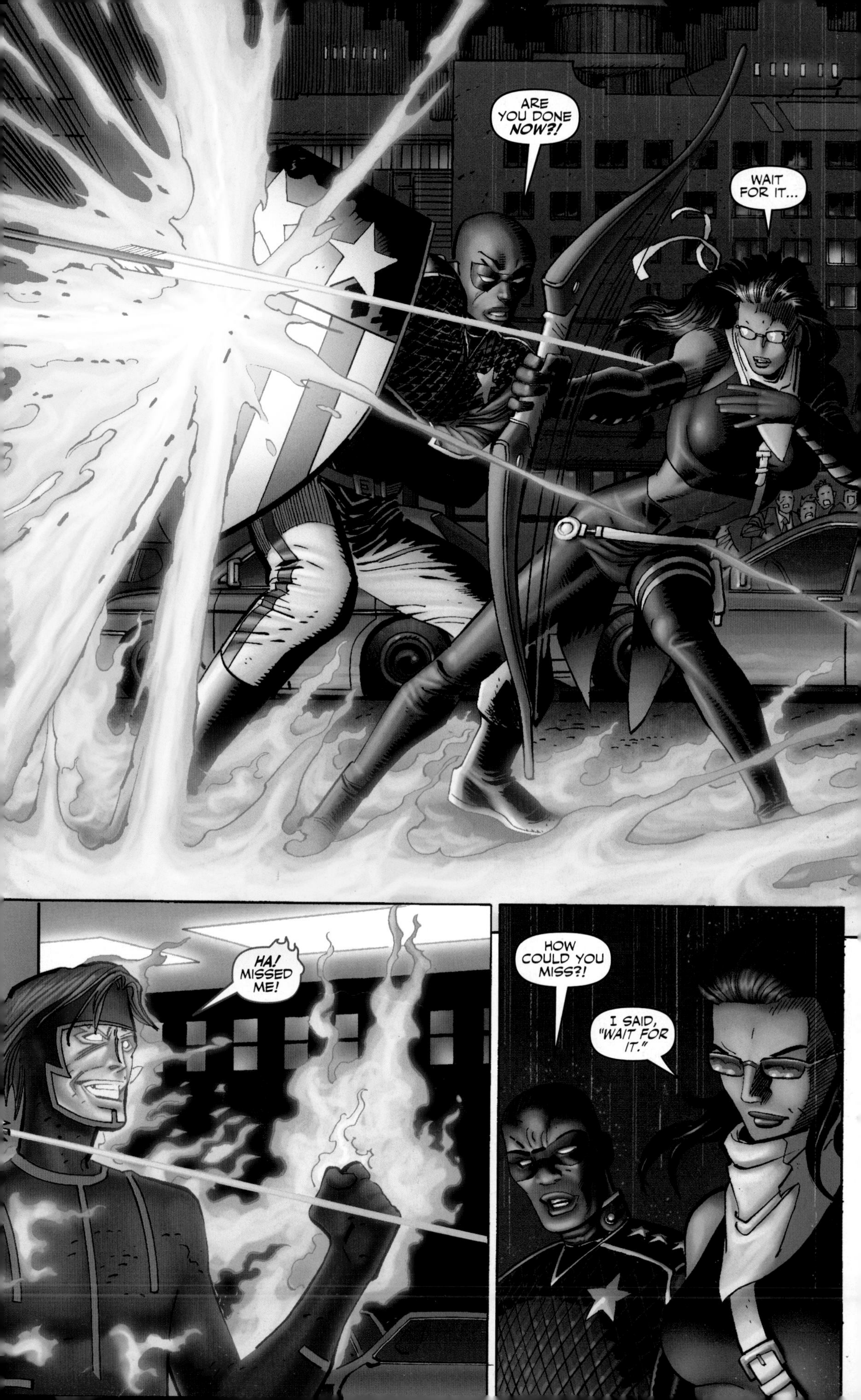
ARE YOU DONE NOW?!
WAIT FOR IT...
HA! MISSED ME!
HOW COULD YOU MISS?!
I SAID, "WAIT FOR IT."

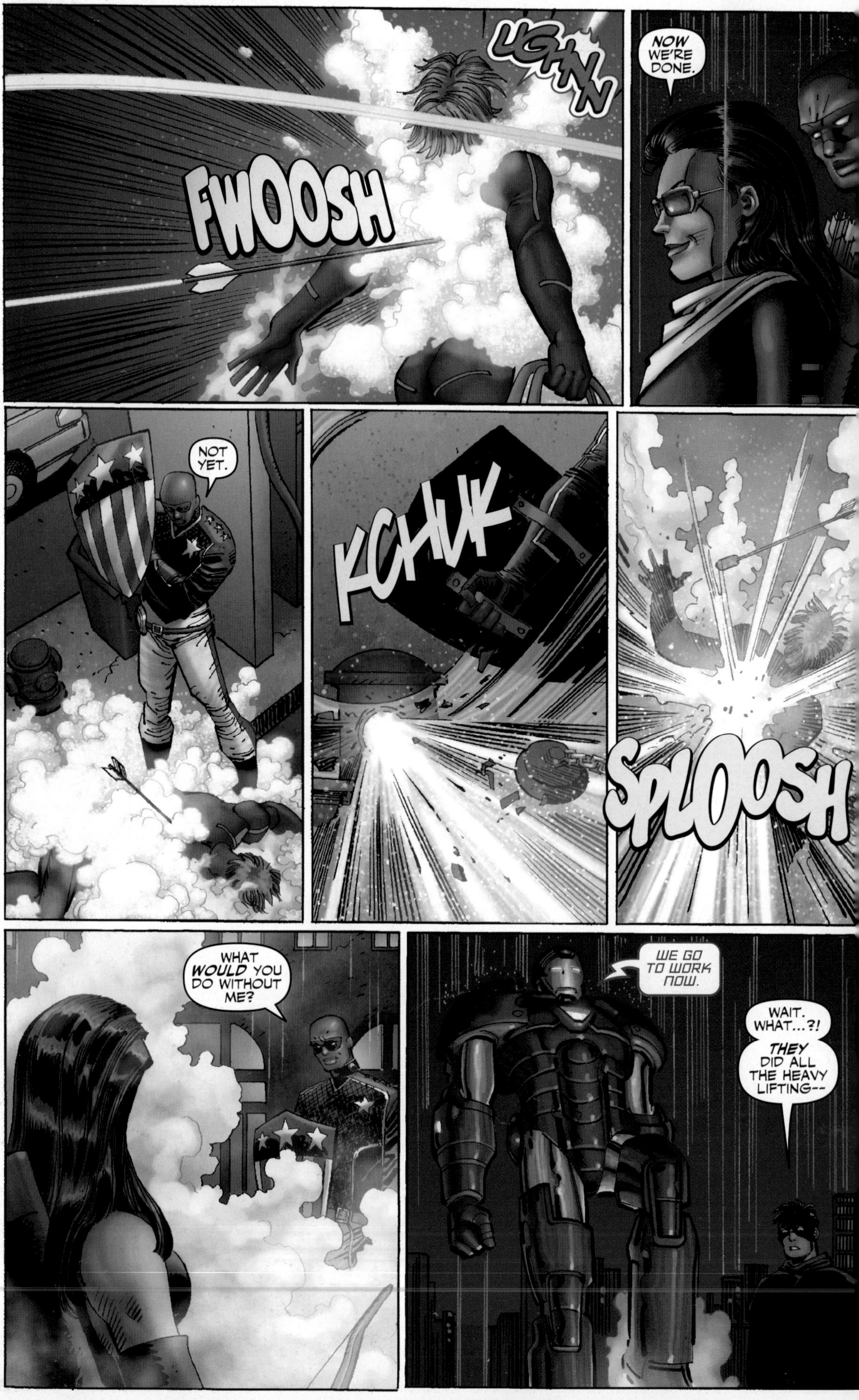
UGHNN
FWOOSH
NOW WE'RE DONE.
NOT YET.
KCHUK
SPLOOSH
WHAT WOULD YOU DO WITHOUT ME?
WE GO TO WORK NOW.
WAIT. WHAT...?! THEY DID ALL THE HEAVY LIFTING--

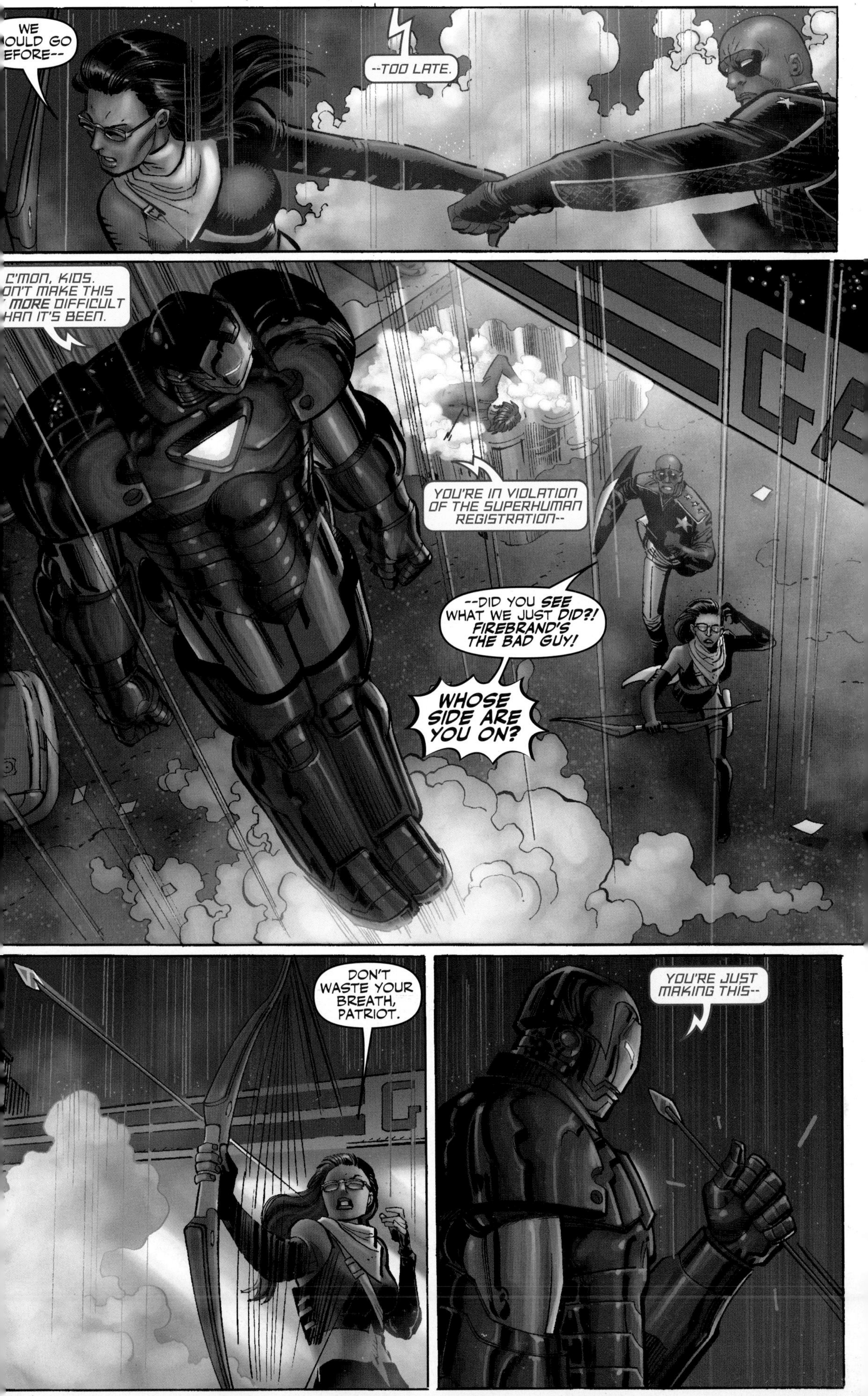

WE OULD GO EFORE--
--TOO LATE.
C'MON, KIDS. ON'T MAKE THIS MORE DIFFICULT HAN IT'S BEEN.
YOU'RE IN VIOLATION OF THE SUPERHUMAN REGISTRATION--
--DID YOU SEE WHAT WE JUST DID?! FIREBRAND'S THE BAD GUY!
WHOSE SIDE ARE YOU ON?
DON'T WASTE YOUR BREATH, PATRIOT.
YOU'RE JUST MAKING THIS--

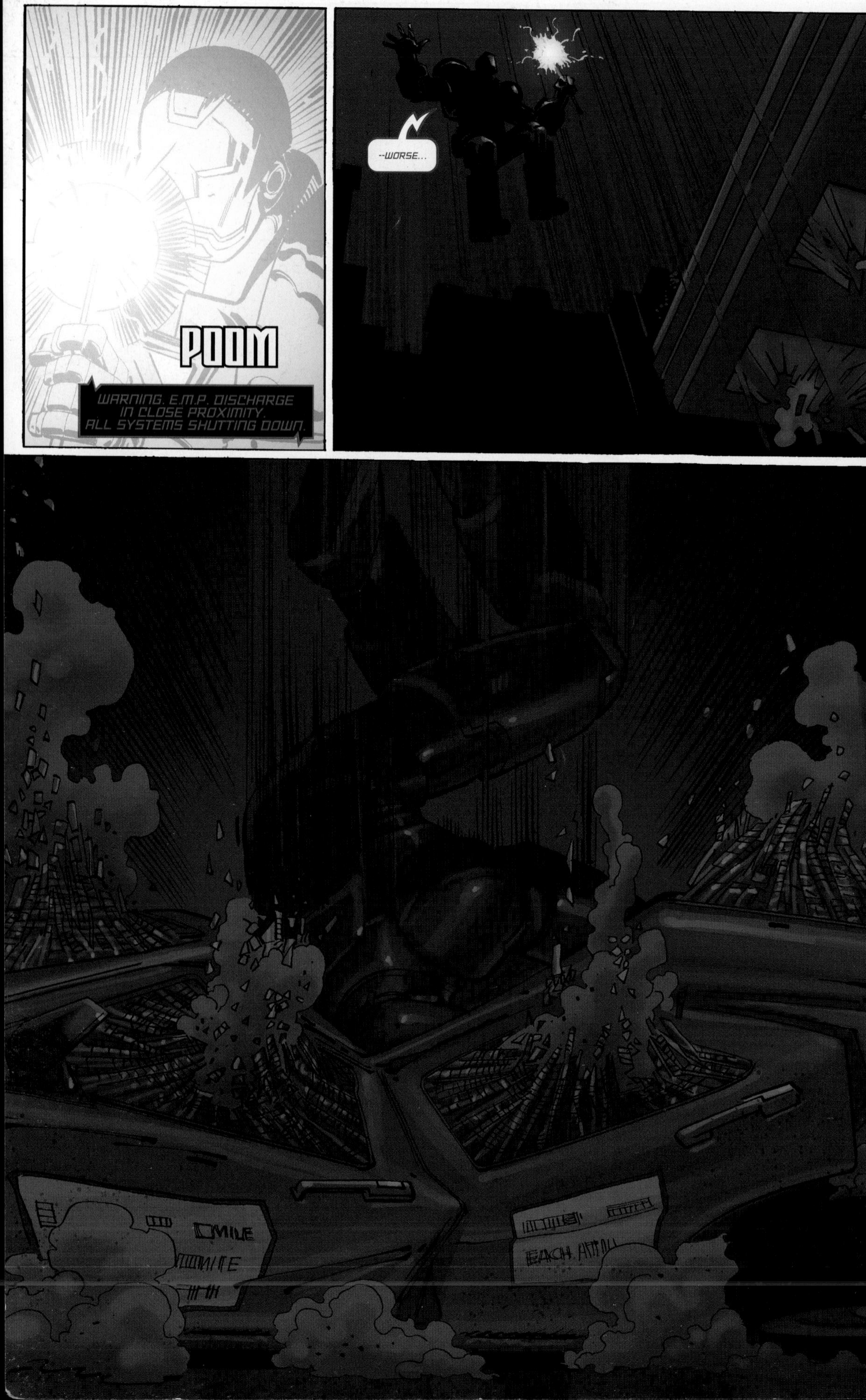
POOM
WARNING. E.M.P. DISCHARGE IN CLOSE PROXIMITY. ALL SYSTEMS SHUTTING DOWN.
--WORSE...

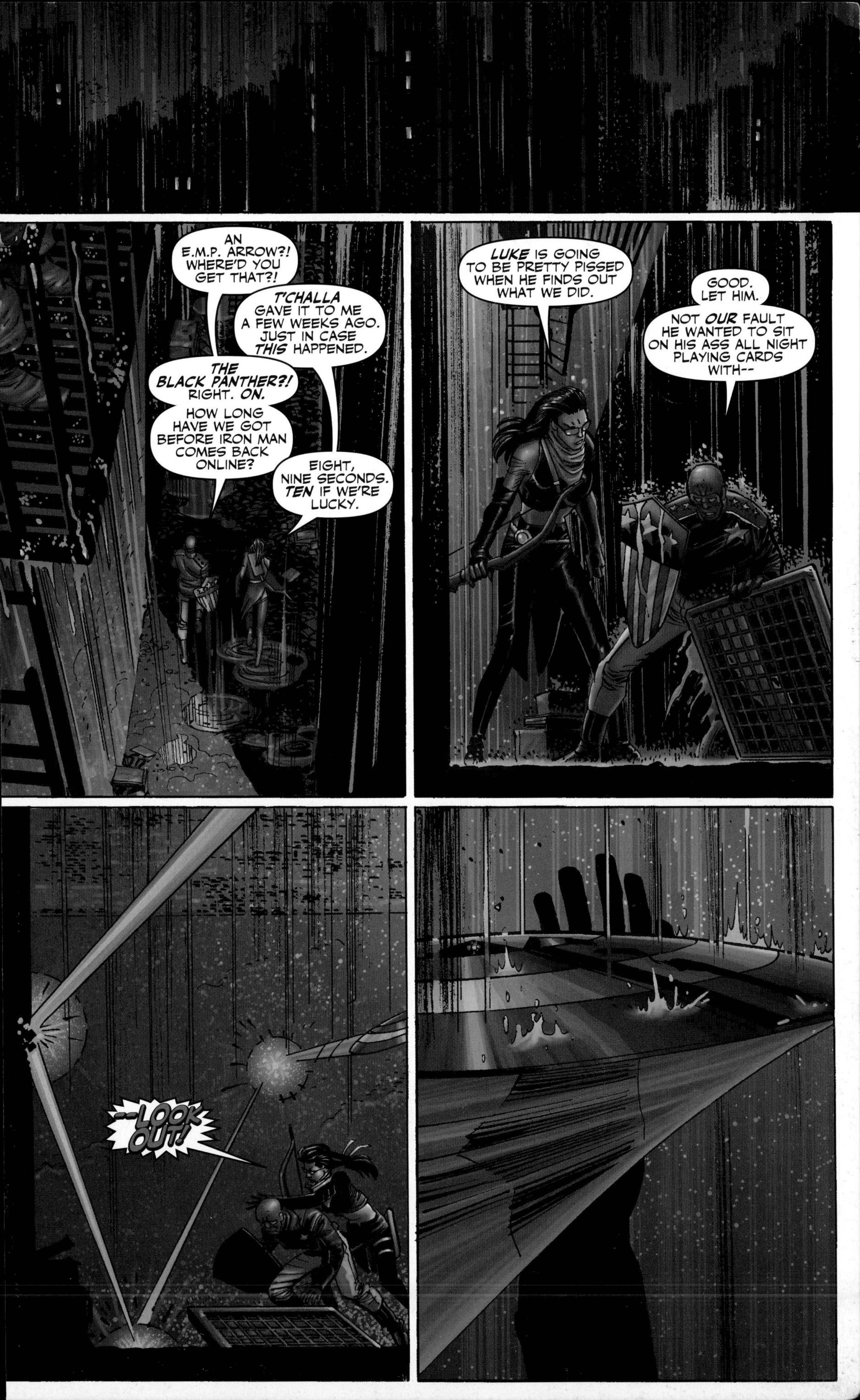

AN E.M.P. ARROW?! WHERE'D YOU GET THAT?!
T'CHALLA GAVE IT TO ME A FEW WEEKS AGO. JUST IN CASE THIS HAPPENED.
THE BLACK PANTHER?! RIGHT. ON.
HOW LONG HAVE WE GOT BEFORE IRON MAN COMES BACK ONLINE?
EIGHT, NINE SECONDS. TEN IF WE'RE LUCKY.
LUKE IS GOING TO BE PRETTY PISSED WHEN HE FINDS OUT WHAT WE DID.
GOOD. LET HIM.
NOT OUR FAULT HE WANTED TO SIT ON HIS ASS ALL NIGHT PLAYING CARDS WITH--
--LOOK OUT!

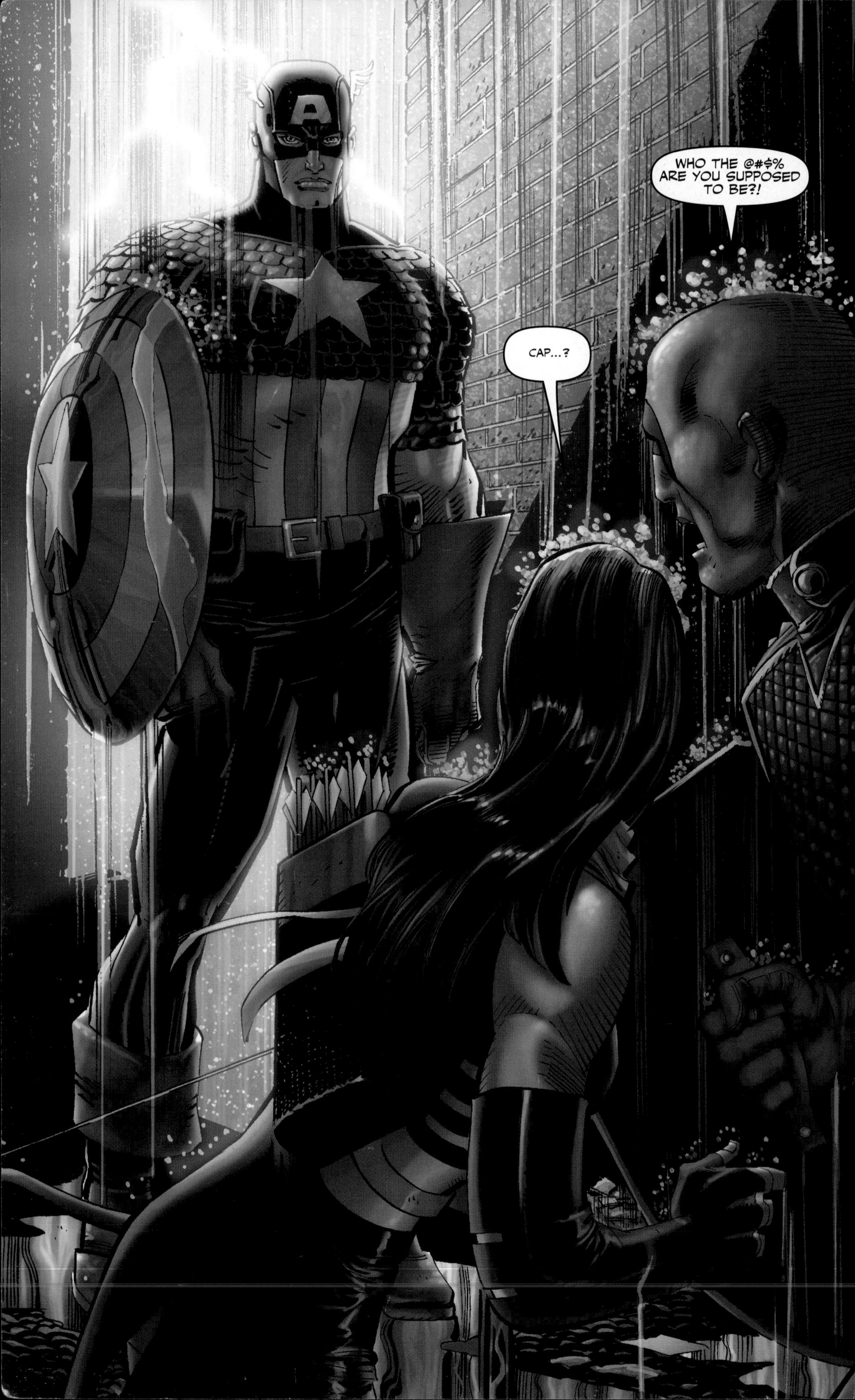
CAP...?
WHO THE @#$% ARE YOU SUPPOSED TO BE?!

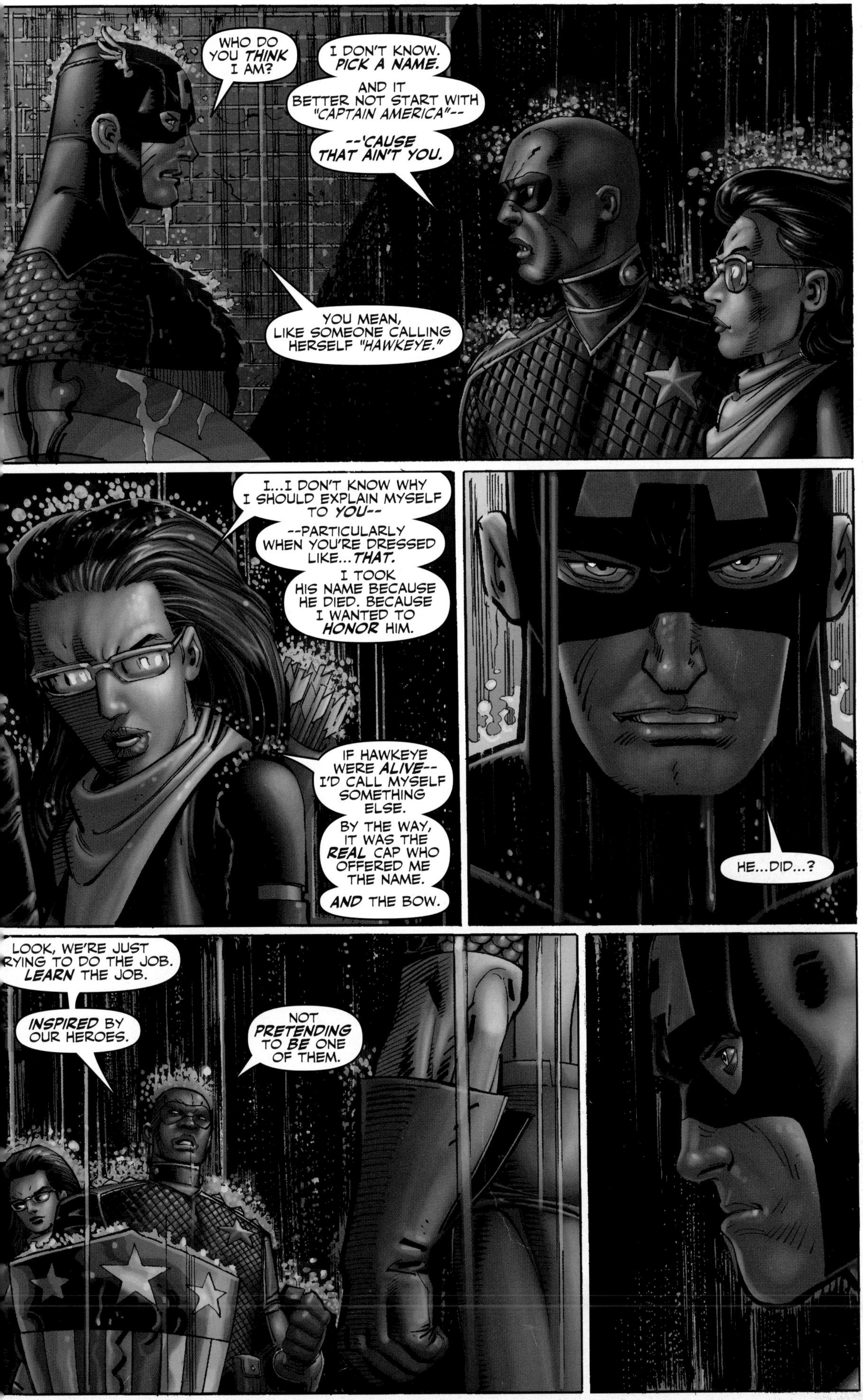
WHO DO YOU *THINK* I AM?
I DON'T KNOW. *PICK A NAME.*
AND IT BETTER NOT START WITH *"CAPTAIN AMERICA"*--
--'CAUSE THAT AIN'T YOU.
YOU MEAN, LIKE SOMEONE CALLING HERSELF *"HAWKEYE."*
I...I DON'T KNOW WHY I SHOULD EXPLAIN MYSELF TO *YOU*--
--PARTICULARLY WHEN YOU'RE DRESSED LIKE...*THAT.*
I TOOK HIS NAME BECAUSE HE DIED. BECAUSE I WANTED TO *HONOR* HIM.
IF HAWKEYE WERE *ALIVE*-- I'D CALL MYSELF SOMETHING ELSE.
BY THE WAY, IT WAS THE *REAL* CAP WHO OFFERED ME THE NAME.
AND THE BOW.
HE...DID...?
LOOK, WE'RE JUST RYING TO DO THE JOB. *LEARN* THE JOB.
INSPIRED BY OUR HEROES.
NOT *PRETENDING* TO *BE* ONE OF THEM.

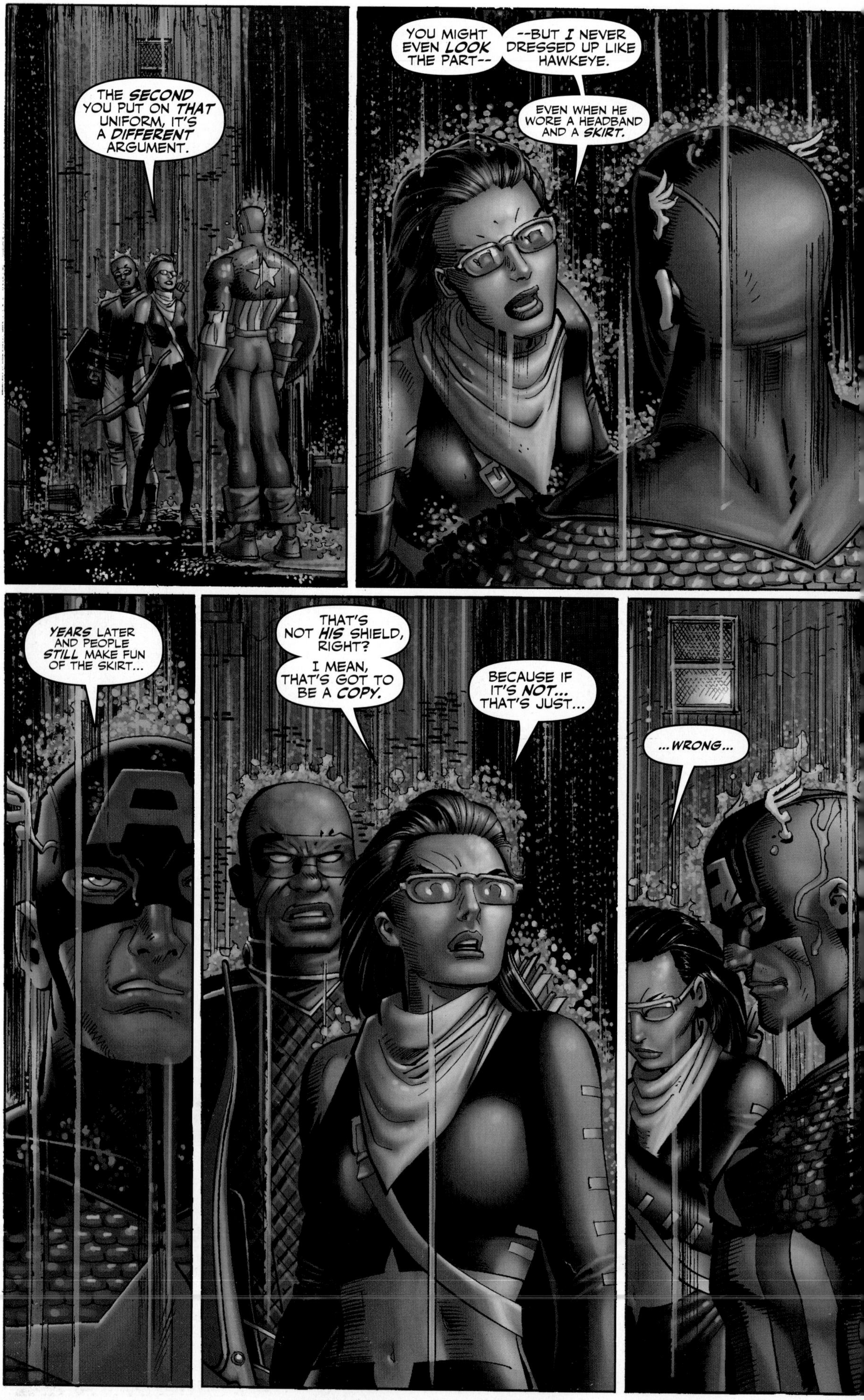
THE SECOND YOU PUT ON THAT UNIFORM, IT'S A DIFFERENT ARGUMENT.
YOU MIGHT EVEN LOOK THE PART--
--BUT I NEVER DRESSED UP LIKE HAWKEYE.
EVEN WHEN HE WORE A HEADBAND AND A SKIRT.
YEARS LATER AND PEOPLE STILL MAKE FUN OF THE SKIRT...
THAT'S NOT HIS SHIELD, RIGHT?
I MEAN, THAT'S GOT TO BE A COPY.
BECAUSE IF IT'S NOT... THAT'S JUST...
...WRONG...

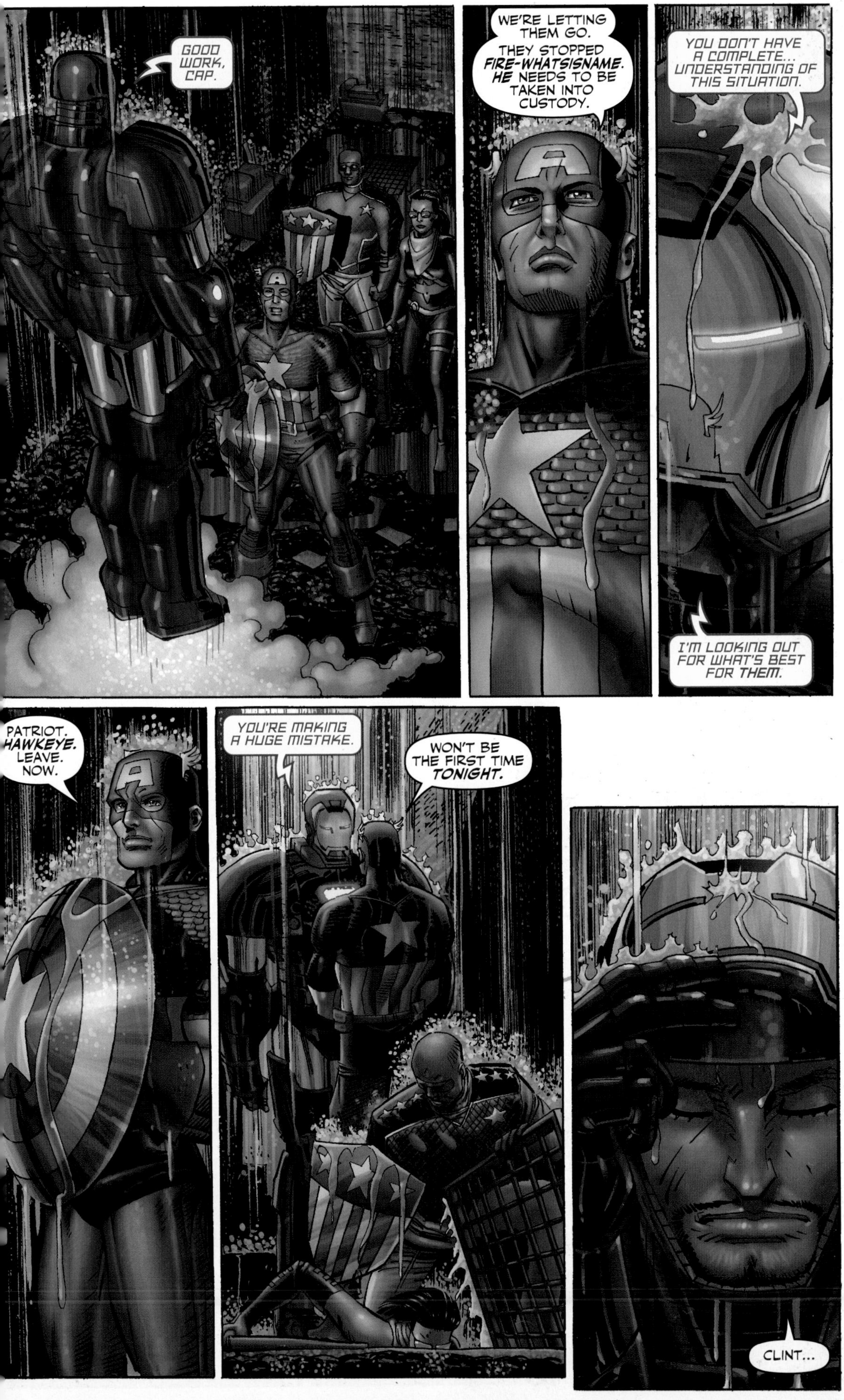

GOOD WORK, CAP.
WE'RE LETTING THEM GO.
THEY STOPPED FIRE-WHATSISNAME. HE NEEDS TO BE TAKEN INTO CUSTODY.
YOU DON'T HAVE A COMPLETE... UNDERSTANDING OF THIS SITUATION.
I'M LOOKING OUT FOR WHAT'S BEST FOR THEM.
PATRIOT. HAWKEYE. LEAVE. NOW.
YOU'RE MAKING A HUGE MISTAKE.
WON'T BE THE FIRST TIME TONIGHT.
CLINT...

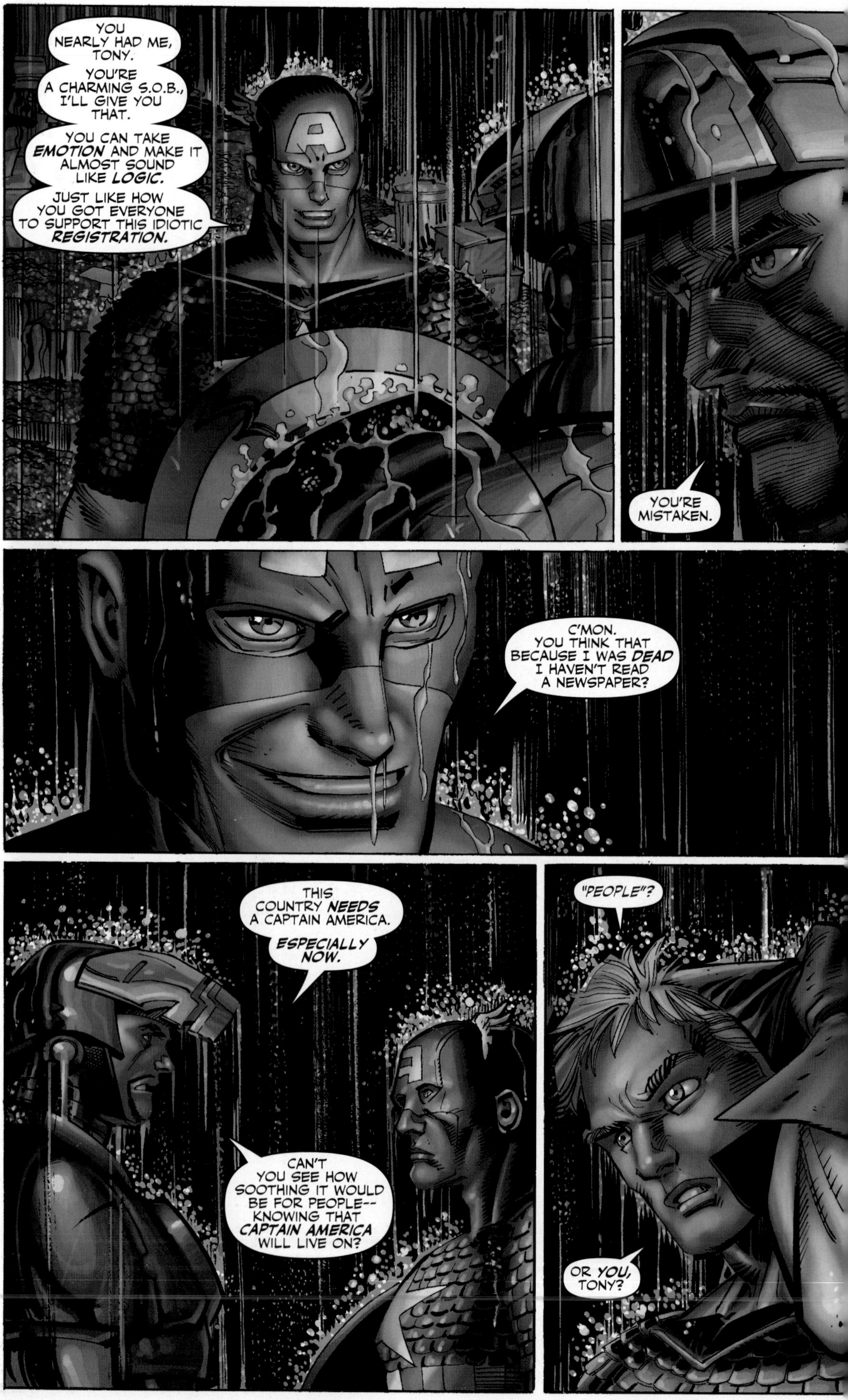
YOU NEARLY HAD ME, TONY.
YOU'RE A CHARMING S.O.B., I'LL GIVE YOU THAT.
YOU CAN TAKE EMOTION AND MAKE IT ALMOST SOUND LIKE LOGIC.
JUST LIKE HOW YOU GOT EVERYONE TO SUPPORT THIS IDIOTIC REGISTRATION.
YOU'RE MISTAKEN.
C'MON. YOU THINK THAT BECAUSE I WAS DEAD I HAVEN'T READ A NEWSPAPER?
THIS COUNTRY NEEDS A CAPTAIN AMERICA.
ESPECIALLY NOW.
CAN'T YOU SEE HOW SOOTHING IT WOULD BE FOR PEOPLE-- KNOWING THAT CAPTAIN AMERICA WILL LIVE ON?
"PEOPLE"?
OR YOU, TONY?

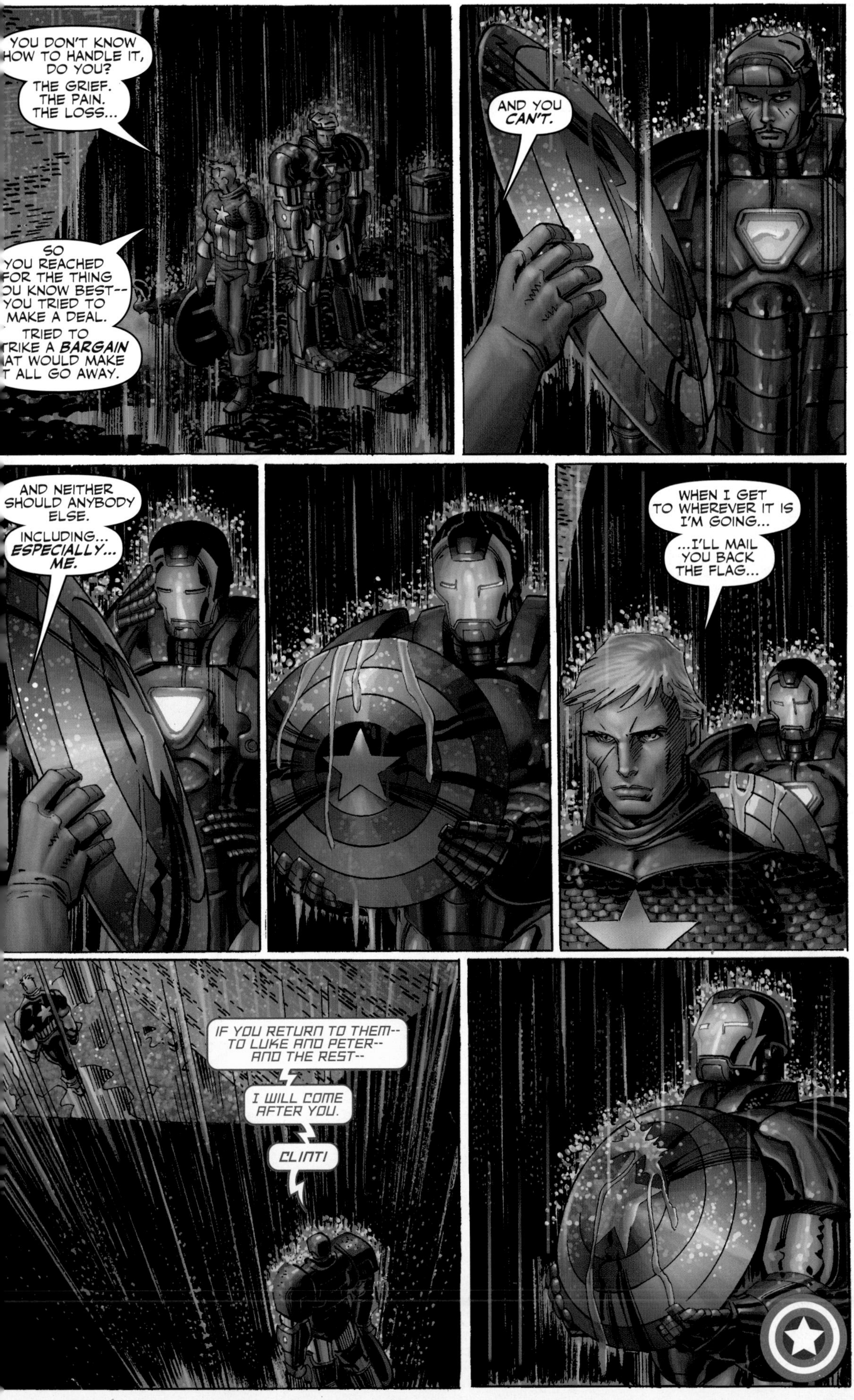
YOU DON'T KNOW HOW TO HANDLE IT, DO YOU?
THE GRIEF. THE PAIN. THE LOSS...
SO YOU REACHED FOR THE THING OU KNOW BEST-- YOU TRIED TO MAKE A DEAL.
TRIED TO TRIKE A BARGAIN AT WOULD MAKE T ALL GO AWAY.
AND YOU CAN'T.
AND NEITHER SHOULD ANYBODY ELSE.
INCLUDING... ESPECIALLY... ME.
WHEN I GET TO WHEREVER IT IS I'M GOING...
...I'LL MAIL YOU BACK THE FLAG...
IF YOU RETURN TO THEM-- TO LUKE AND PETER-- AND THE REST--
I WILL COME AFTER YOU.
CLINT!

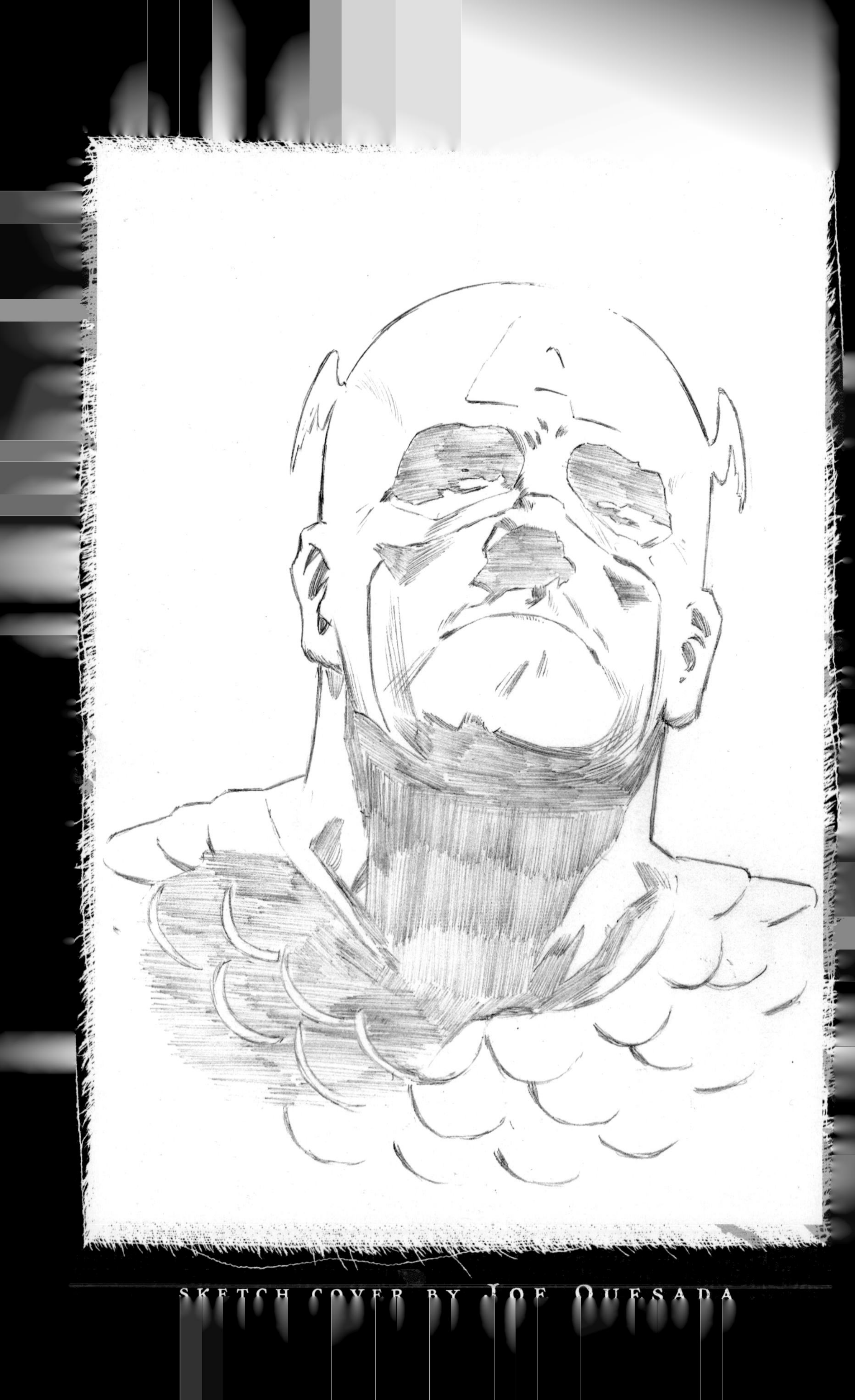

SKETCH COVER BY JOE QUESADA

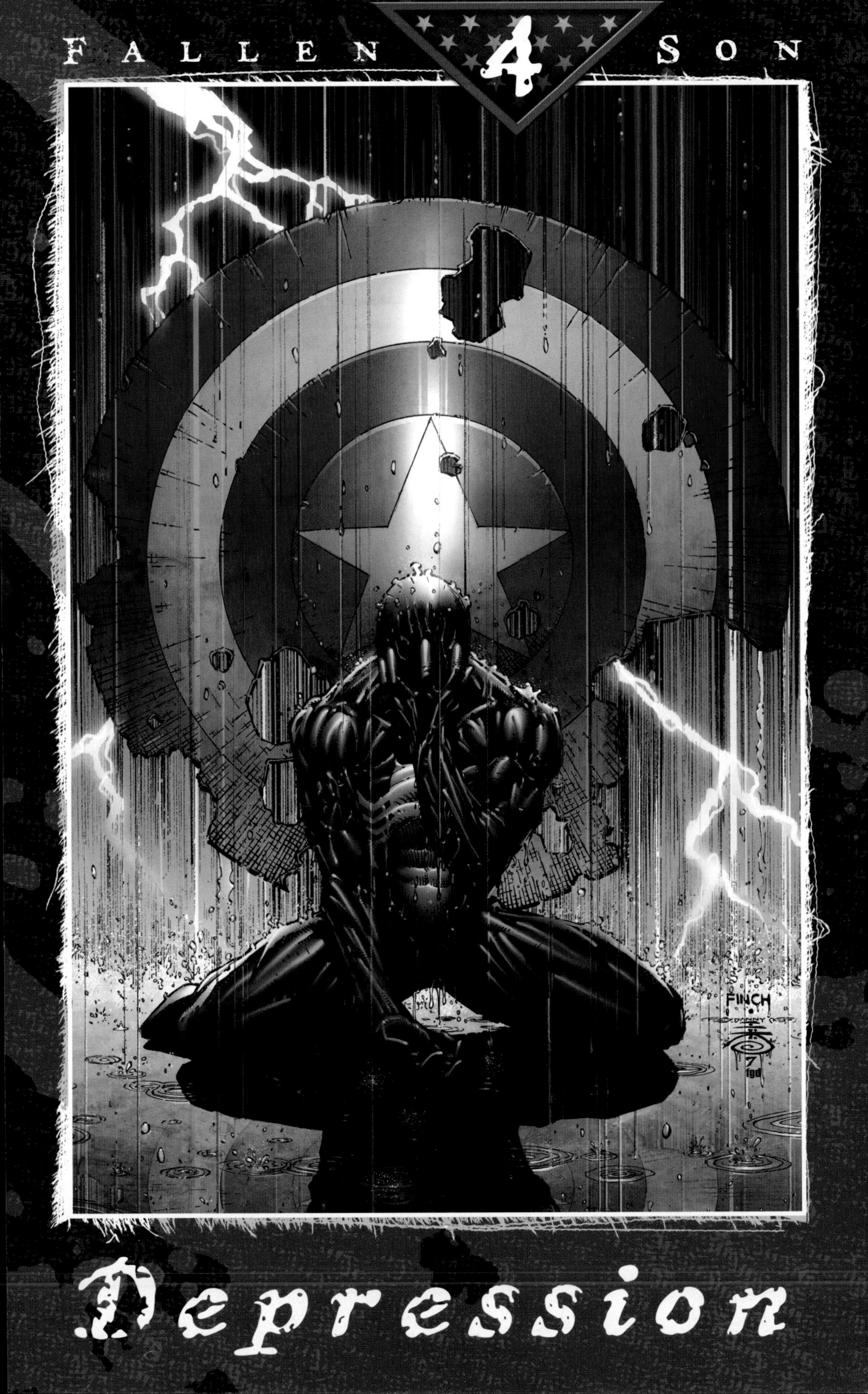
FALLEN 4 SON
FINCH
Depression

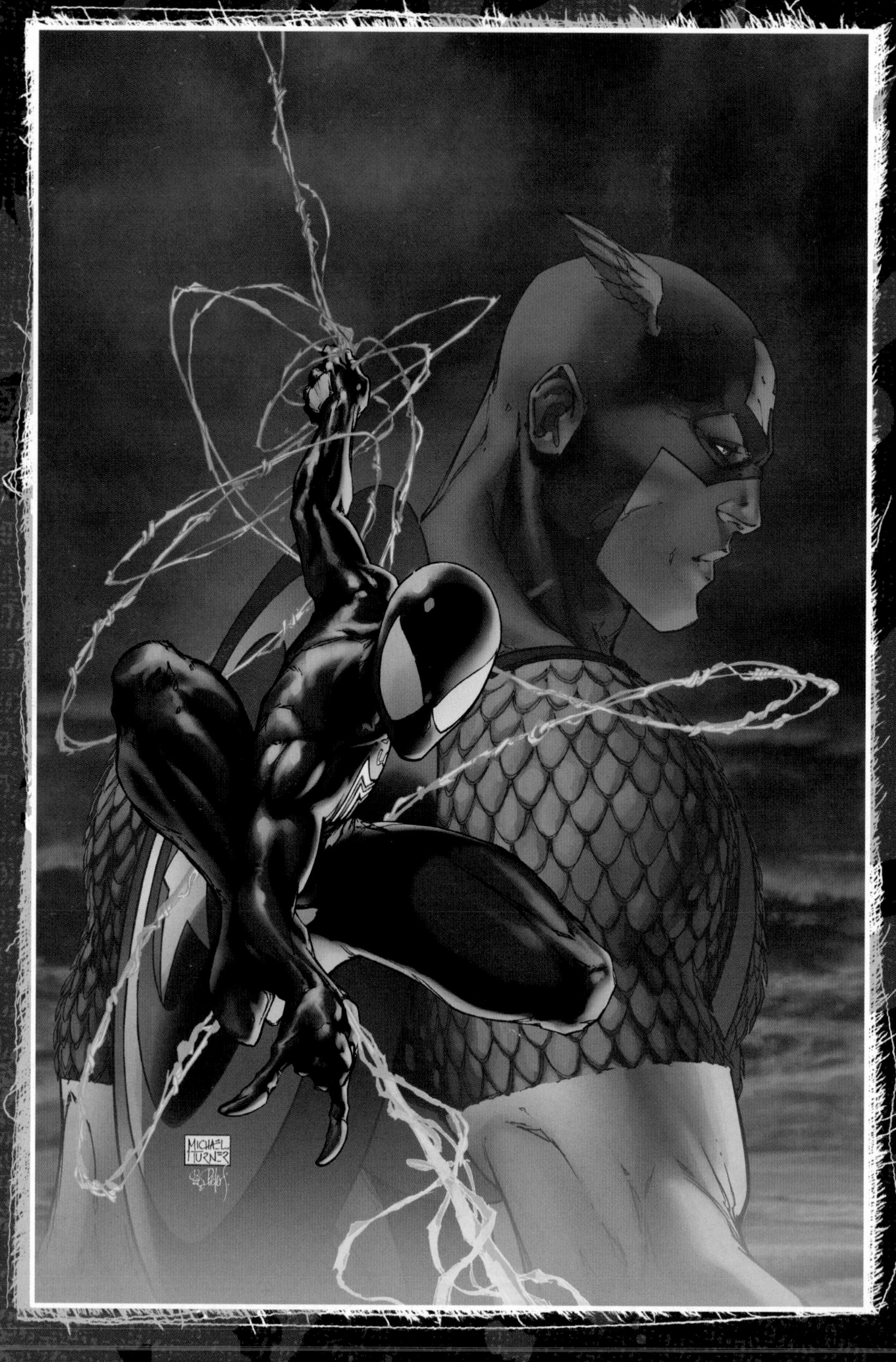
MICHAEL TURNER

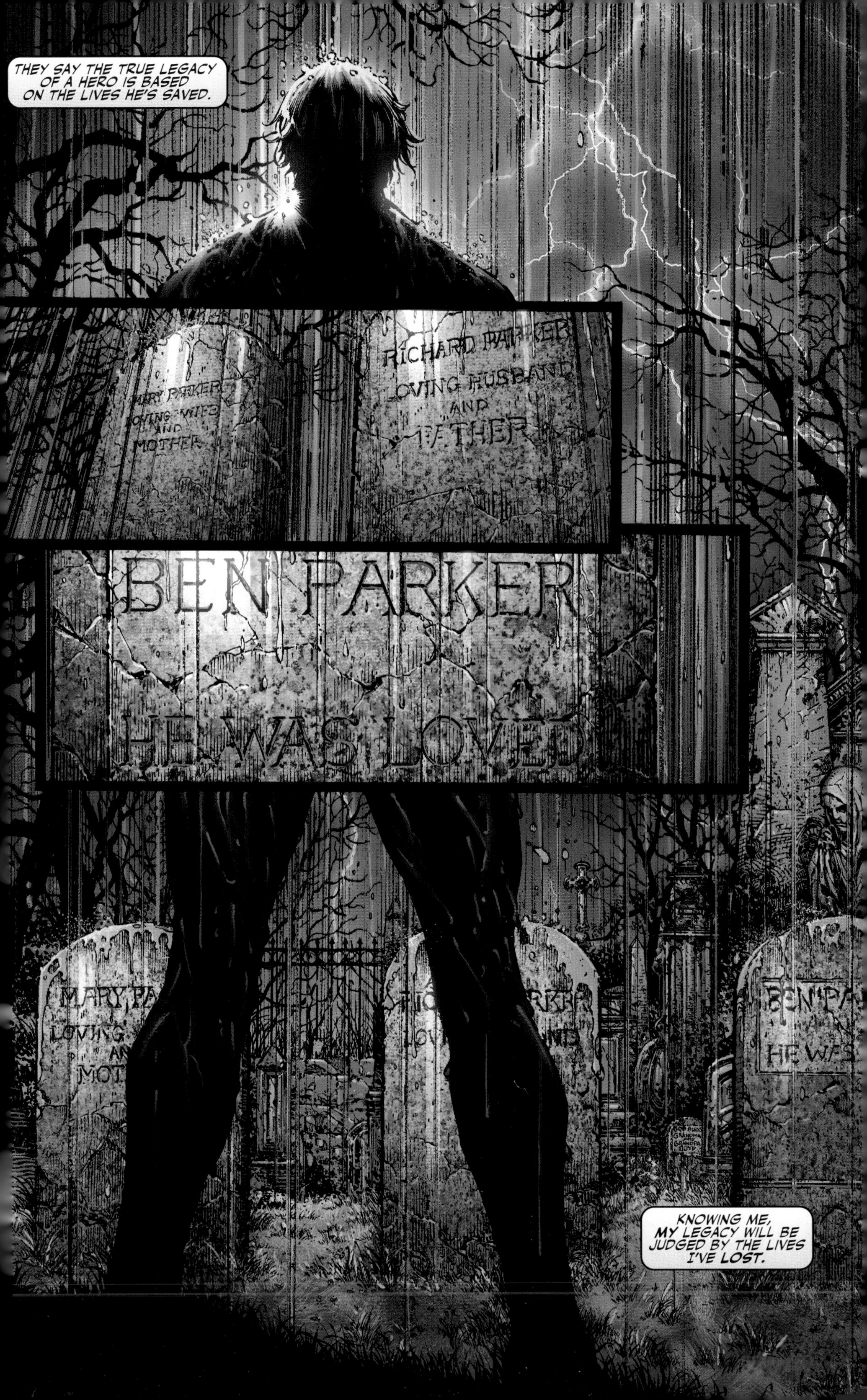
THEY SAY THE TRUE LEGACY OF A HERO IS BASED ON THE LIVES HE'S SAVED.
MARY PARKER LOVING WIFE AND MOTHER
RICHARD PARKER LOVING HUSBAND AND FATHER
BEN PARKER
HE WAS LOVED
KNOWING ME, MY LEGACY WILL BE JUDGED BY THE LIVES I'VE **LOST**.

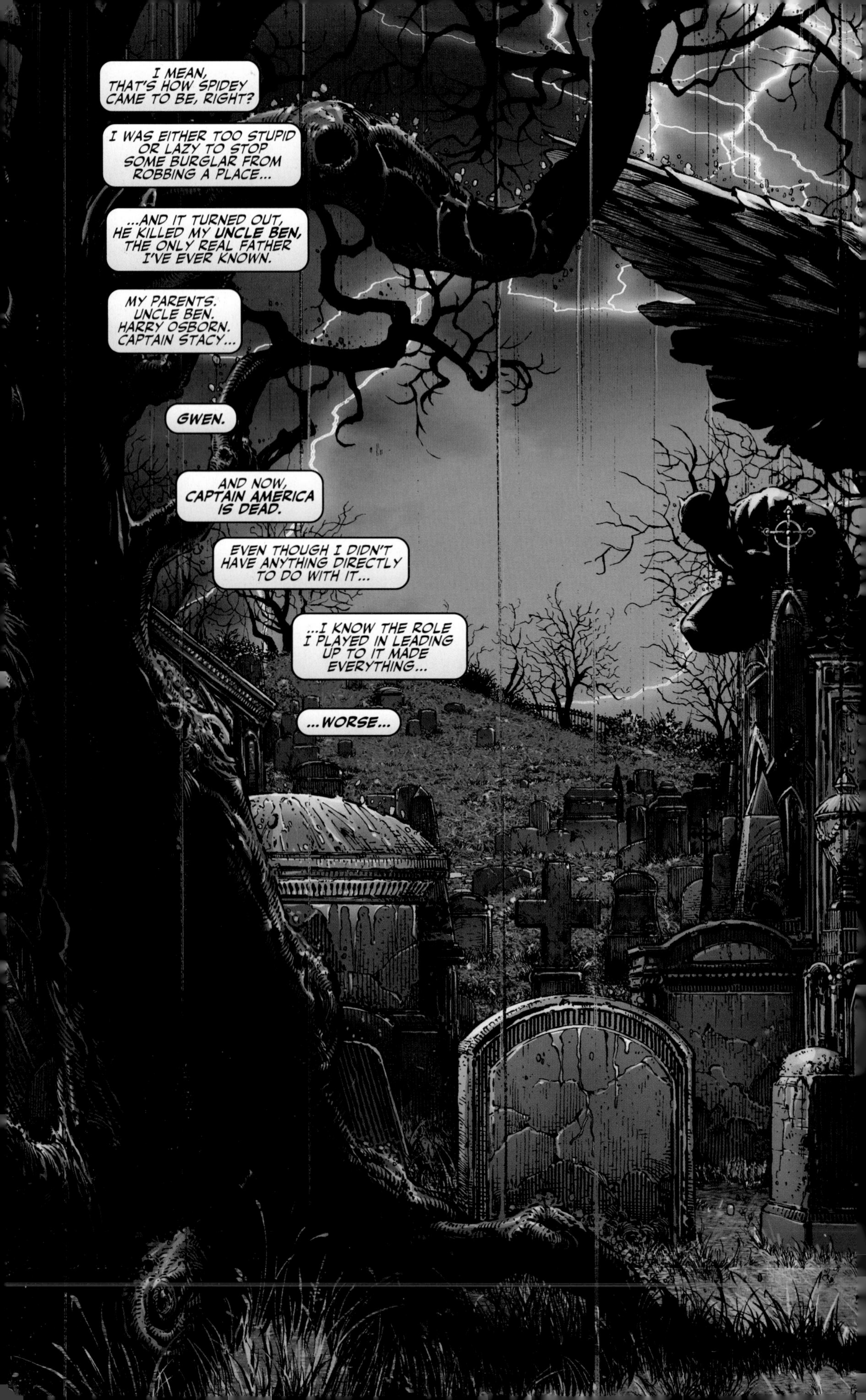
I MEAN, THAT'S HOW SPIDEY CAME TO BE, RIGHT?
I WAS EITHER TOO STUPID OR LAZY TO STOP SOME BURGLAR FROM ROBBING A PLACE...
...AND IT TURNED OUT, HE KILLED MY UNCLE BEN, THE ONLY REAL FATHER I'VE EVER KNOWN.
MY PARENTS. UNCLE BEN. HARRY OSBORN. CAPTAIN STACY...
GWEN.
AND NOW, CAPTAIN AMERICA IS DEAD.
EVEN THOUGH I DIDN'T HAVE ANYTHING DIRECTLY TO DO WITH IT...
...I KNOW THE ROLE I PLAYED IN LEADING UP TO IT MADE EVERYTHING...
...WORSE...

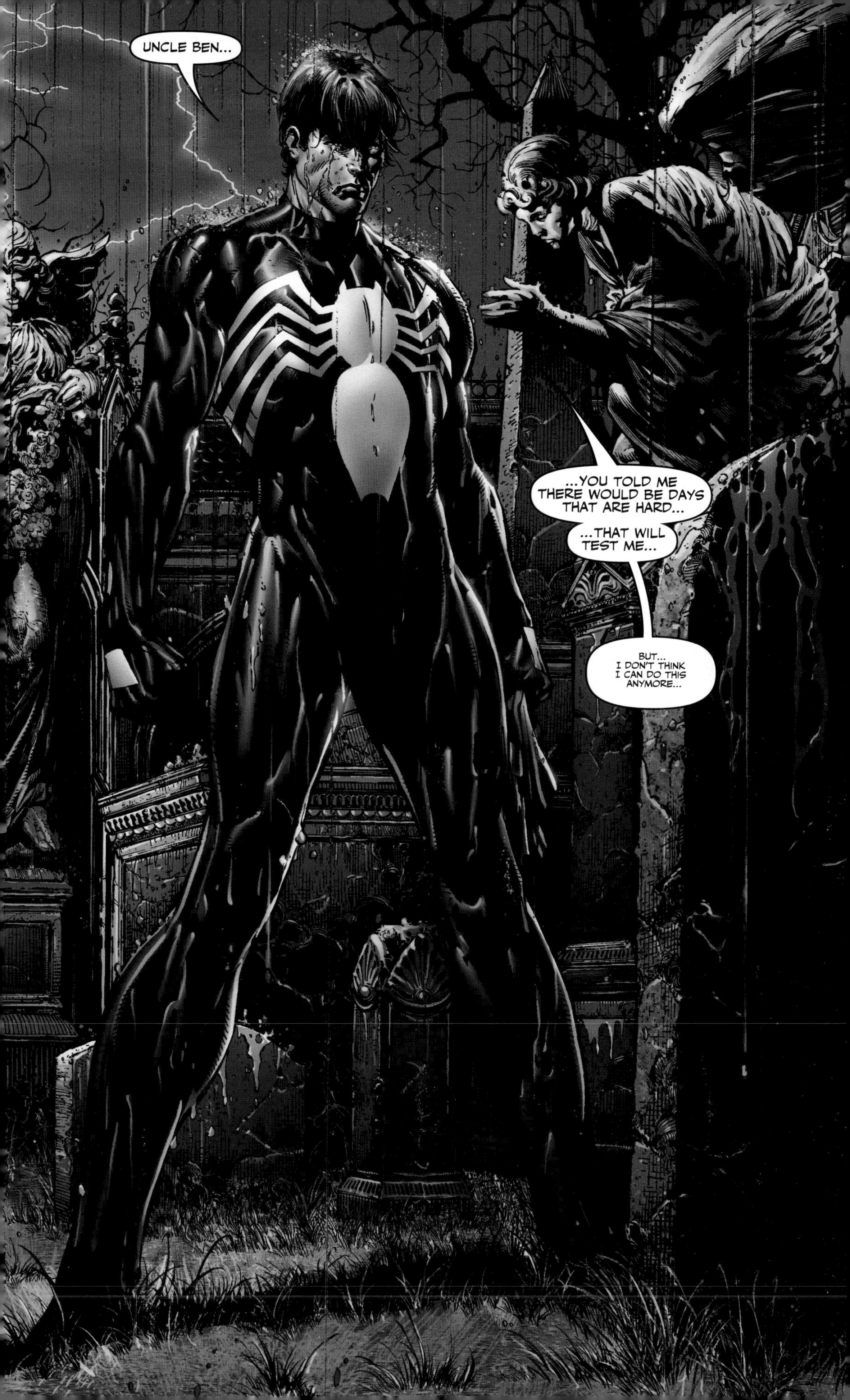
UNCLE BEN...
...YOU TOLD ME THERE WOULD BE DAYS THAT ARE HARD...
...THAT WILL TEST ME...
BUT... I DON'T THINK I CAN DO THIS ANYMORE...

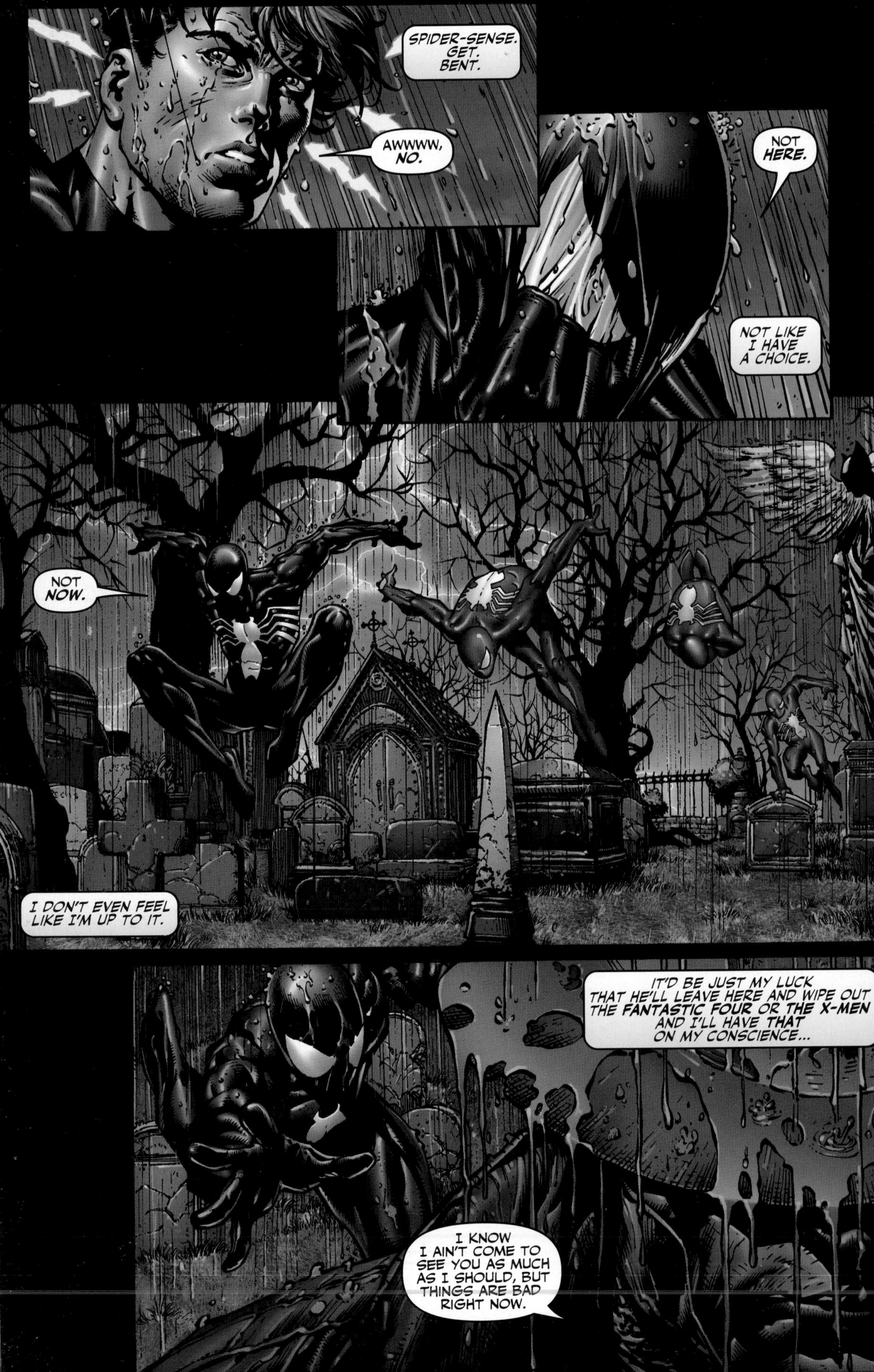
SPIDER-SENSE. GET. BENT.
AWWWW, NO.
NOT HERE.
NOT LIKE I HAVE A CHOICE.
NOT NOW.
I DON'T EVEN FEEL LIKE I'M UP TO IT.
IT'D BE JUST MY LUCK THAT HE'LL LEAVE HERE AND WIPE OUT THE FANTASTIC FOUR OR THE X-MEN AND I'LL HAVE THAT ON MY CONSCIENCE...
I KNOW I AIN'T COME TO SEE YOU AS MUCH AS I SHOULD, BUT THINGS ARE BAD RIGHT NOW.

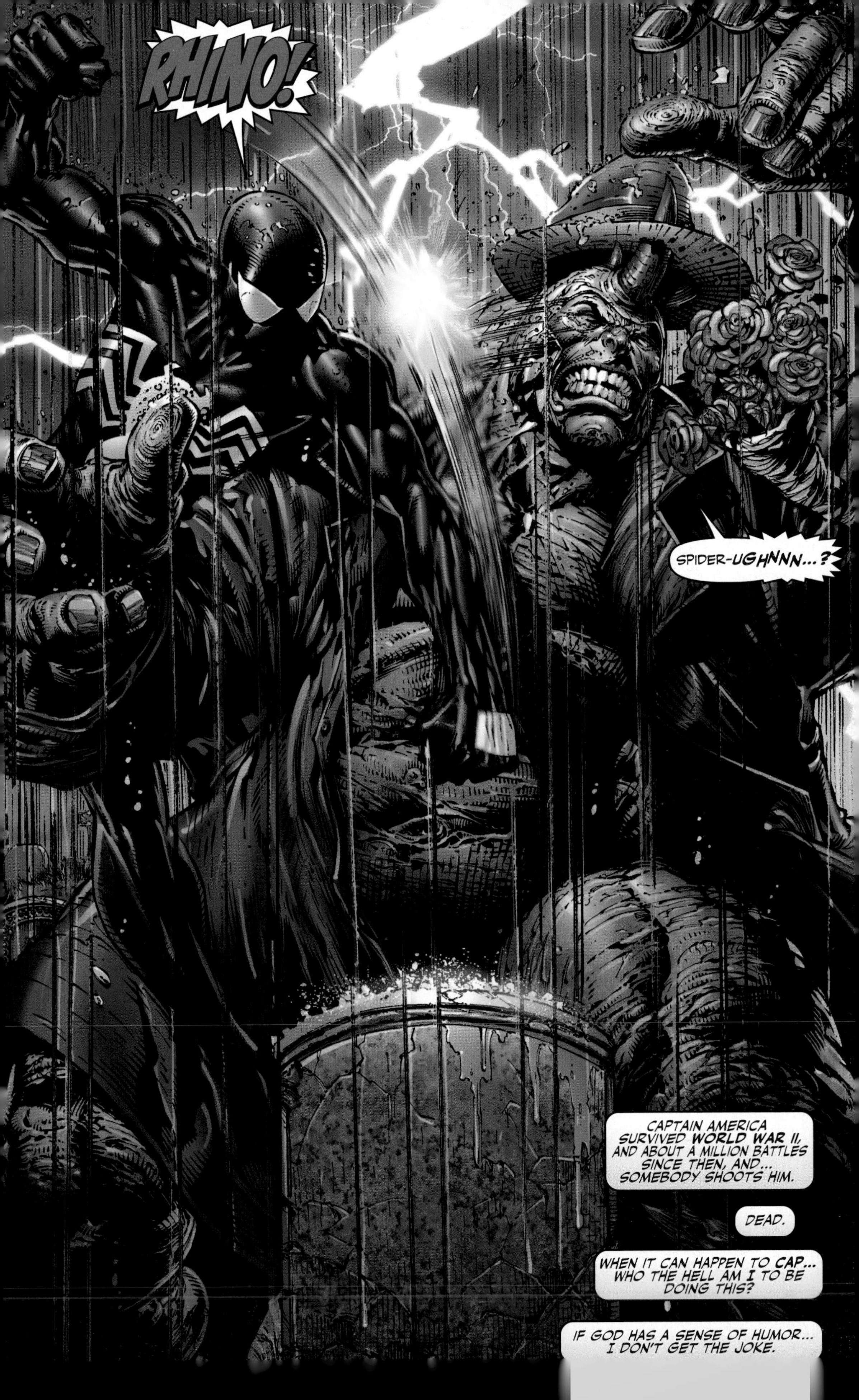
RHINO!
SPIDER-UGHNNN...?
CAPTAIN AMERICA SURVIVED WORLD WAR II, AND ABOUT A MILLION BATTLES SINCE THEN, AND... SOMEBODY SHOOTS HIM.
DEAD.
WHEN IT CAN HAPPEN TO CAP... WHO THE HELL AM I TO BE DOING THIS?
IF GOD HAS A SENSE OF HUMOR... I DON'T GET THE JOKE.

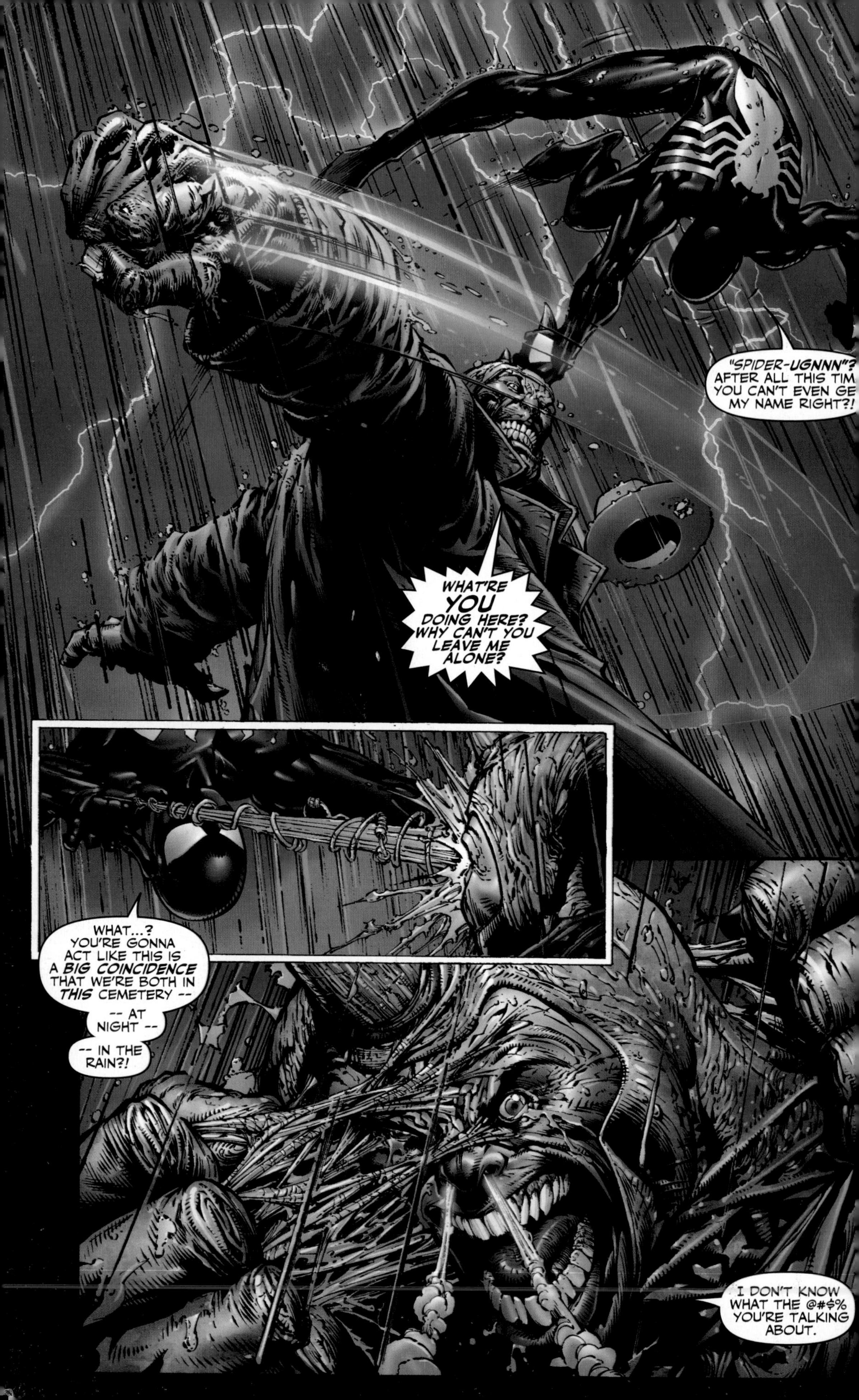
"SPIDER-UGNNN"? AFTER ALL THIS TIM YOU CAN'T EVEN GE MY NAME RIGHT?!
WHAT'RE YOU DOING HERE? WHY CAN'T YOU LEAVE ME ALONE?
WHAT...? YOU'RE GONNA ACT LIKE THIS IS A BIG COINCIDENCE THAT WE'RE BOTH IN THIS CEMETERY --
-- AT NIGHT --
-- IN THE RAIN?!
I DON'T KNOW WHAT THE @#$% YOU'RE TALKING ABOUT.

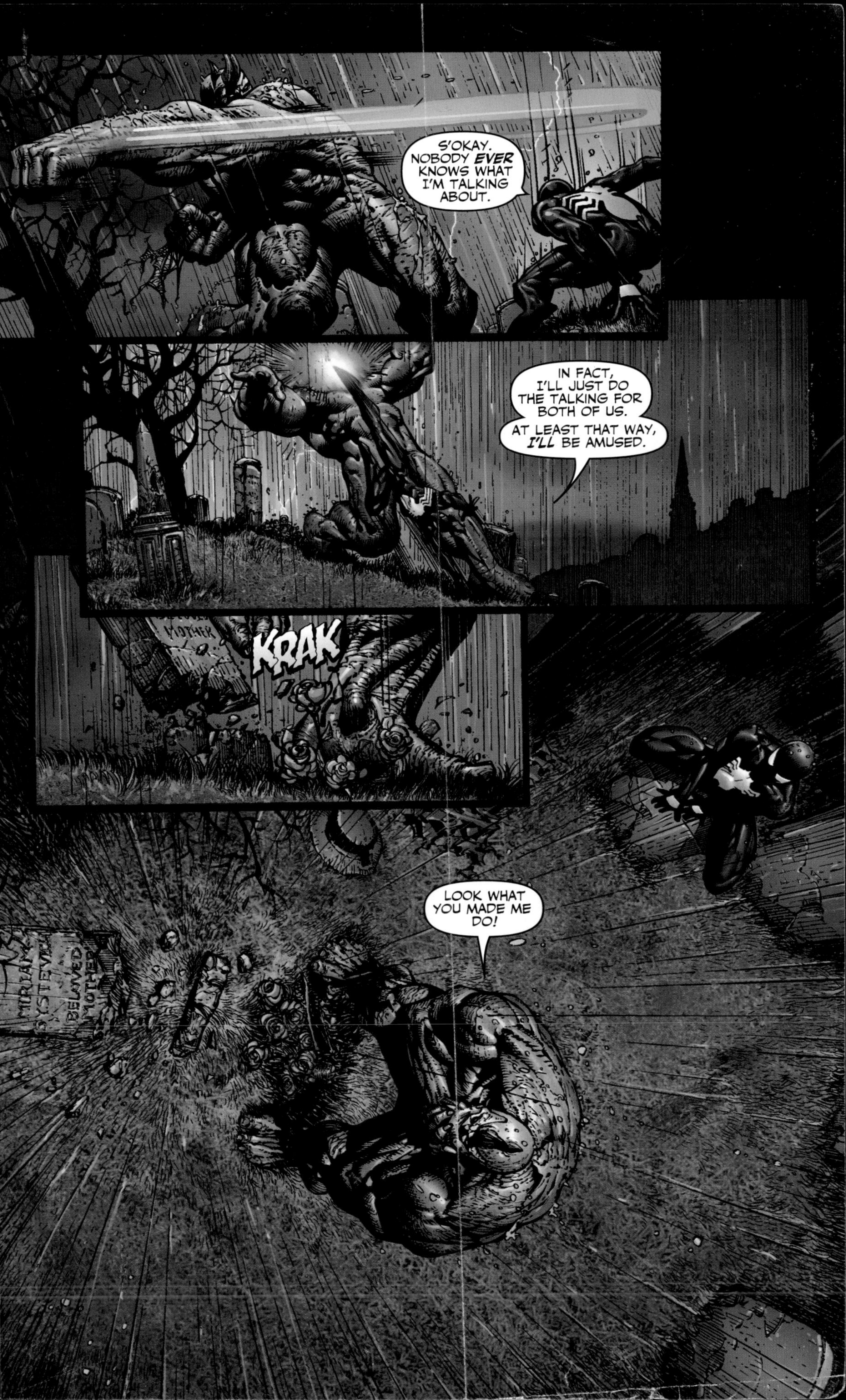
S'OKAY. NOBODY EVER KNOWS WHAT I'M TALKING ABOUT.
IN FACT, I'LL JUST DO THE TALKING FOR BOTH OF US.
AT LEAST THAT WAY, I'LL BE AMUSED.
KRAK
LOOK WHAT YOU MADE ME DO!
MIRIAM SYSTEVIC BELOVED MOTHER

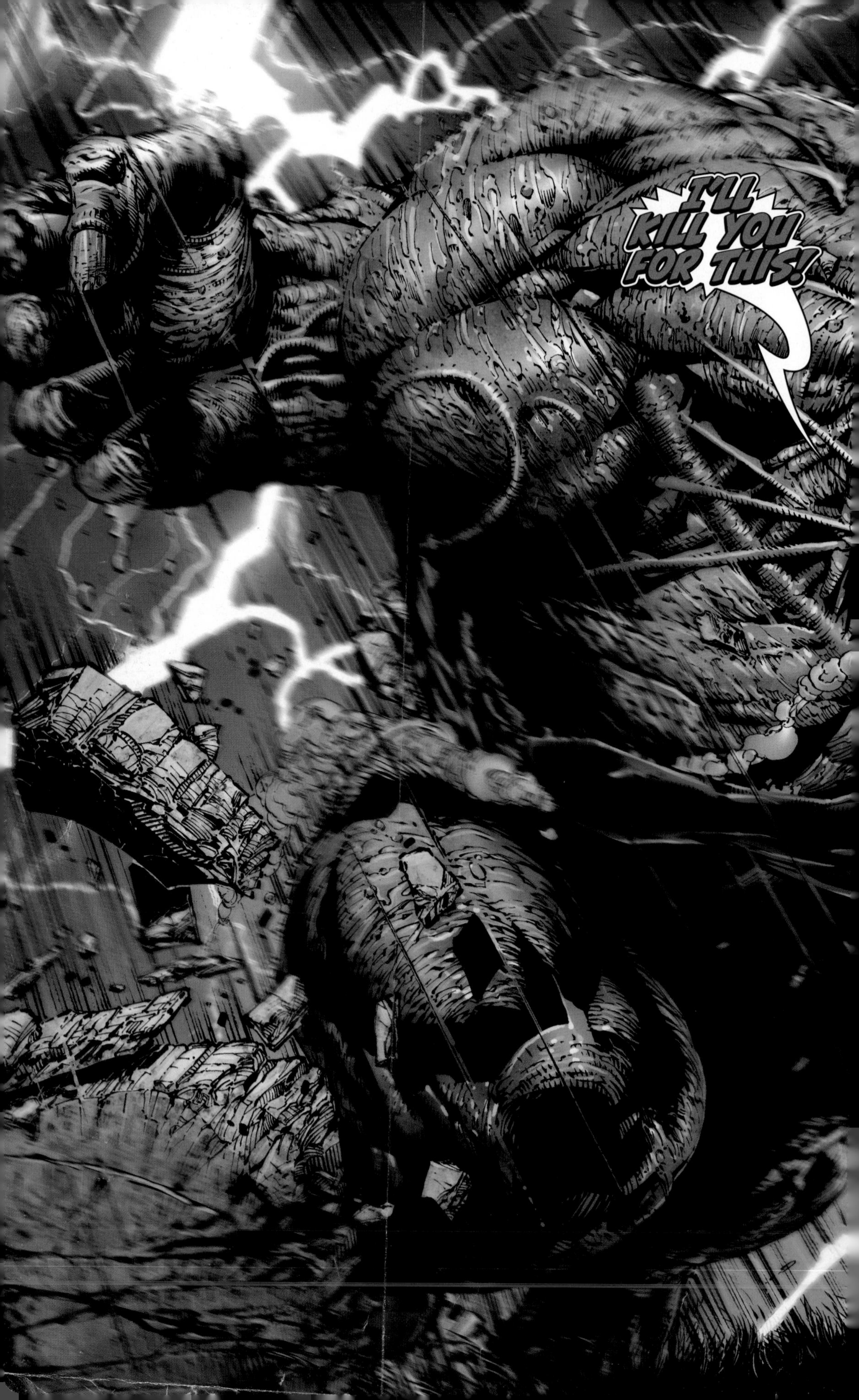
I'LL KILL YOU FOR THIS!

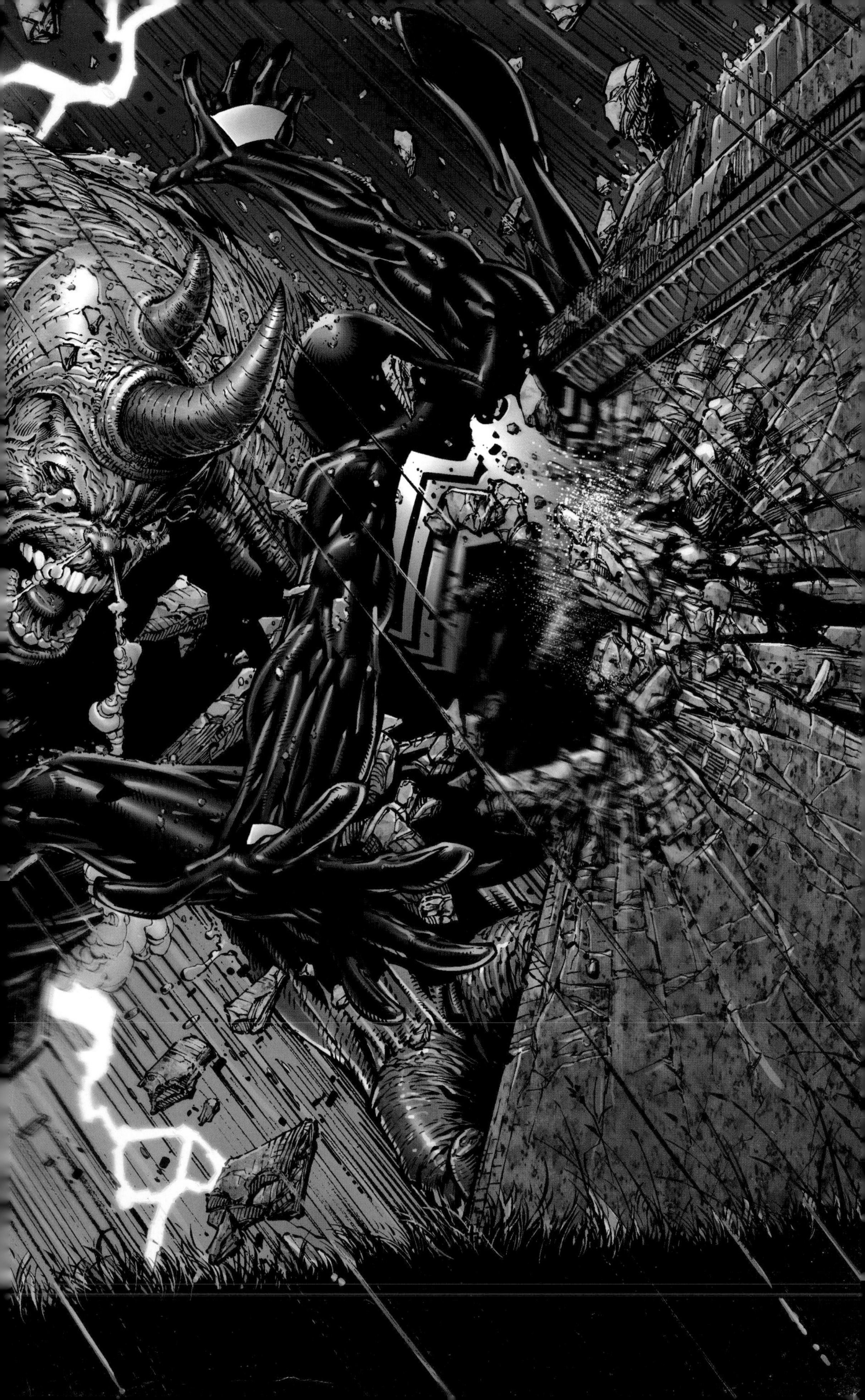

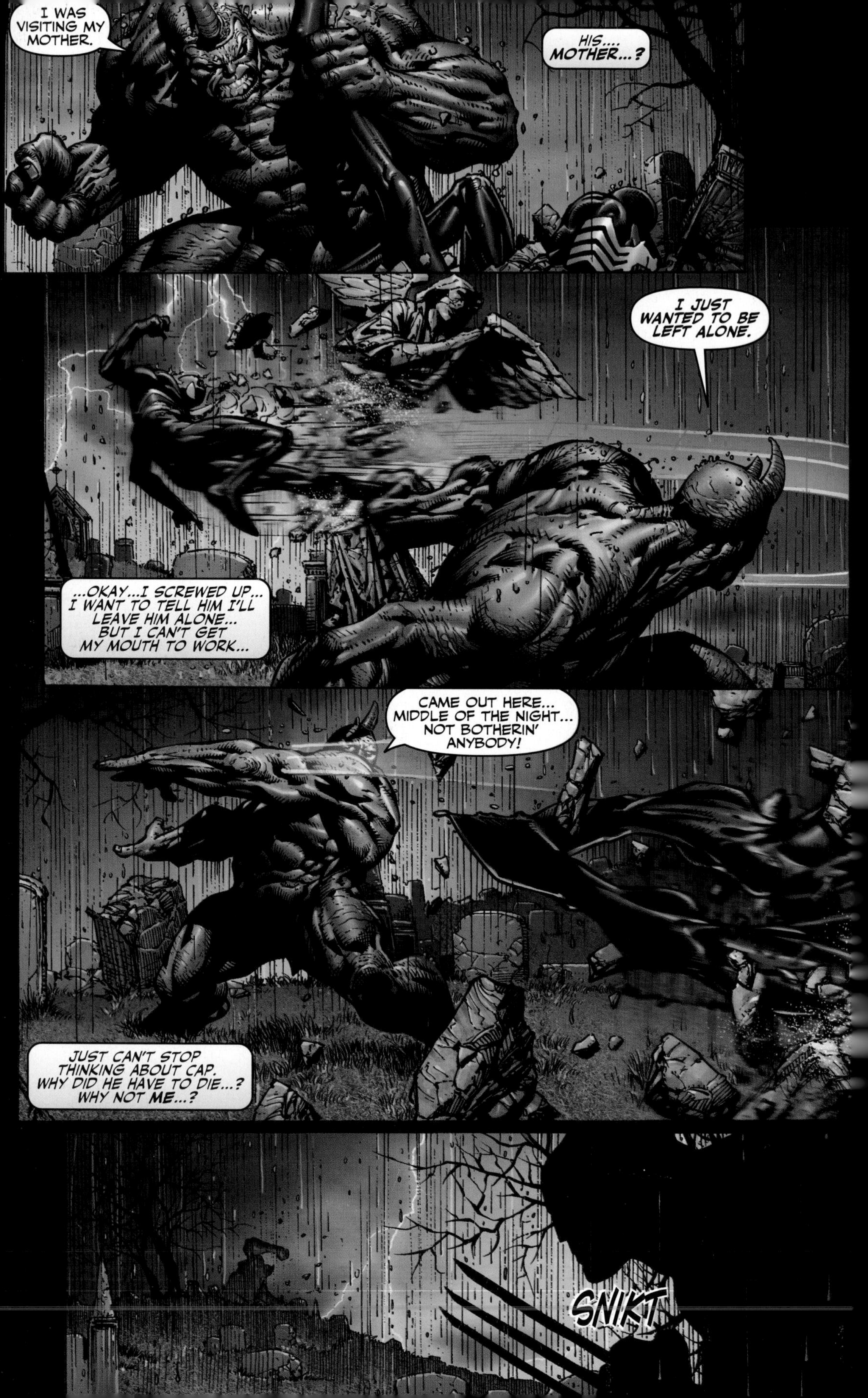
I WAS VISITING MY MOTHER.
HIS.... MOTHER...?
I JUST WANTED TO BE LEFT ALONE.
...OKAY...I SCREWED UP... I WANT TO TELL HIM I'LL LEAVE HIM ALONE... BUT I CAN'T GET MY MOUTH TO WORK...
CAME OUT HERE... MIDDLE OF THE NIGHT... NOT BOTHERIN' ANYBODY!
JUST CAN'T STOP THINKING ABOUT CAP. WHY DID HE HAVE TO DIE...? WHY NOT ME...?
SNIKT

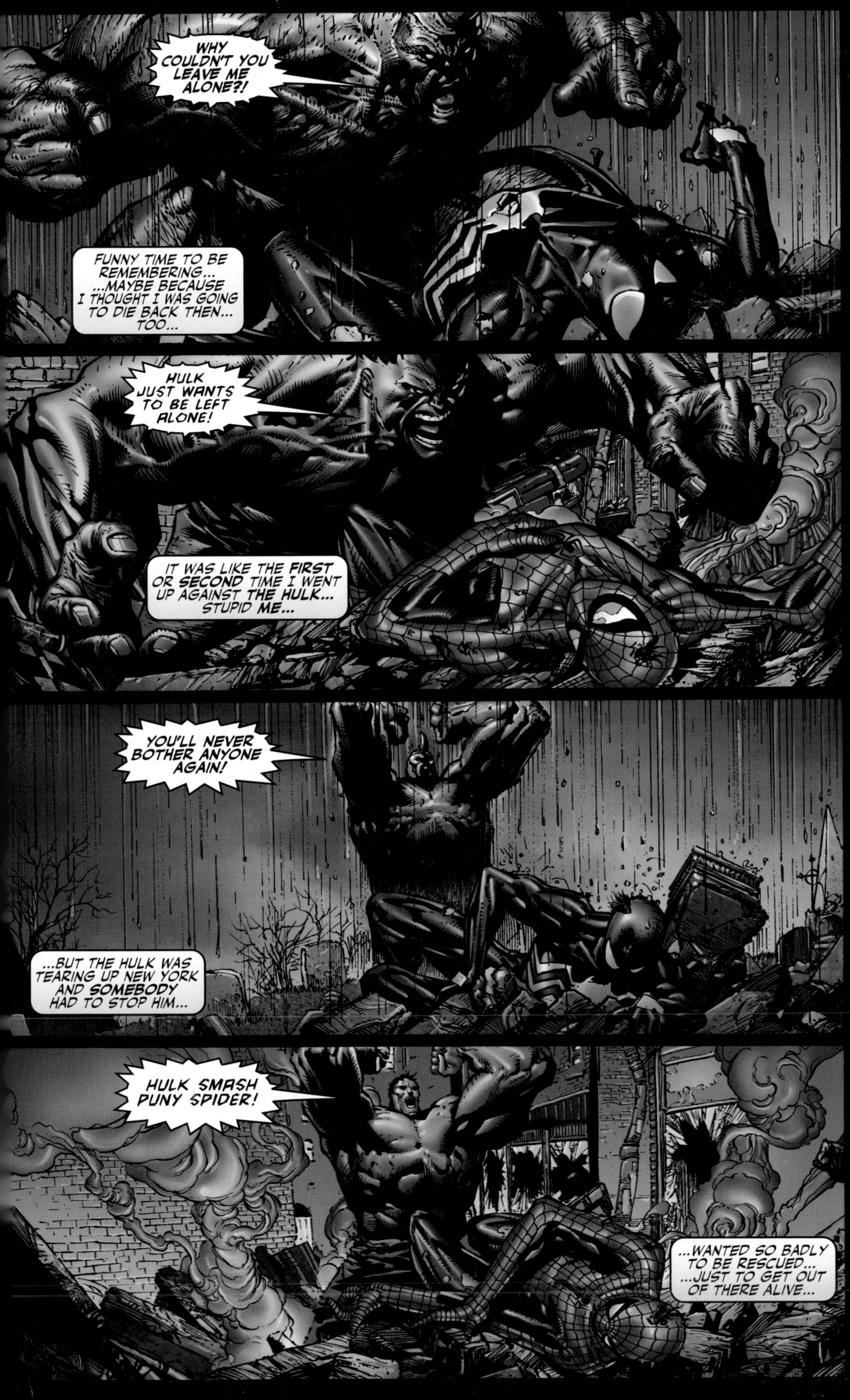
WHY COULDN'T YOU LEAVE ME ALONE?!
FUNNY TIME TO BE REMEMBERING... ...MAYBE BECAUSE I THOUGHT I WAS GOING TO DIE BACK THEN... TOO...
HULK JUST WANTS TO BE LEFT ALONE!
IT WAS LIKE THE FIRST OR SECOND TIME I WENT UP AGAINST THE HULK... STUPID ME...
YOU'LL NEVER BOTHER ANYONE AGAIN!
...BUT THE HULK WAS TEARING UP NEW YORK AND SOMEBODY HAD TO STOP HIM...
HULK SMASH PUNY SPIDER!
...WANTED SO BADLY TO BE RESCUED... ...JUST TO GET OUT OF THERE ALIVE...

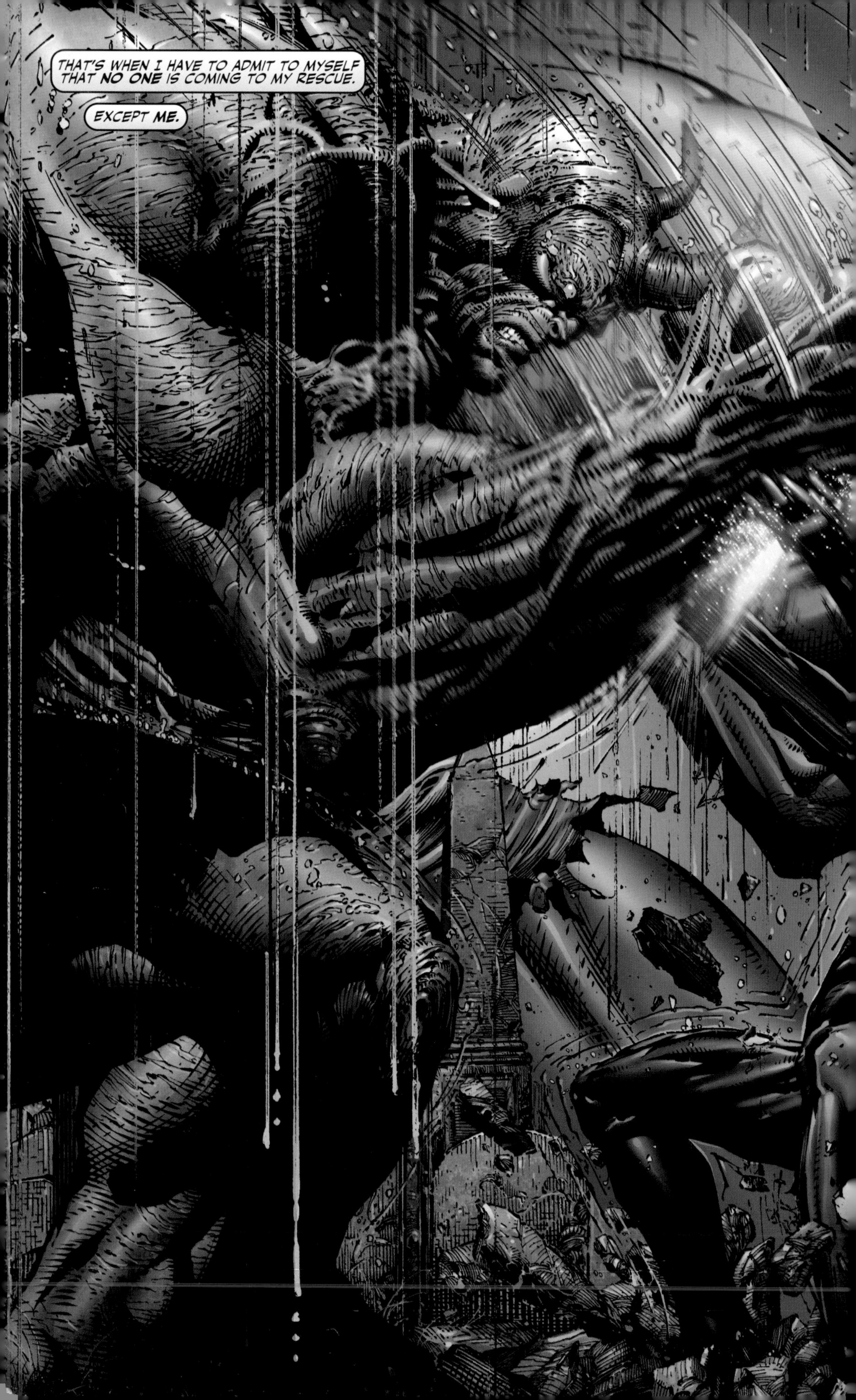
THAT'S WHEN I HAVE TO ADMIT TO MYSELF THAT NO ONE IS COMING TO MY RESCUE.
EXCEPT ME.

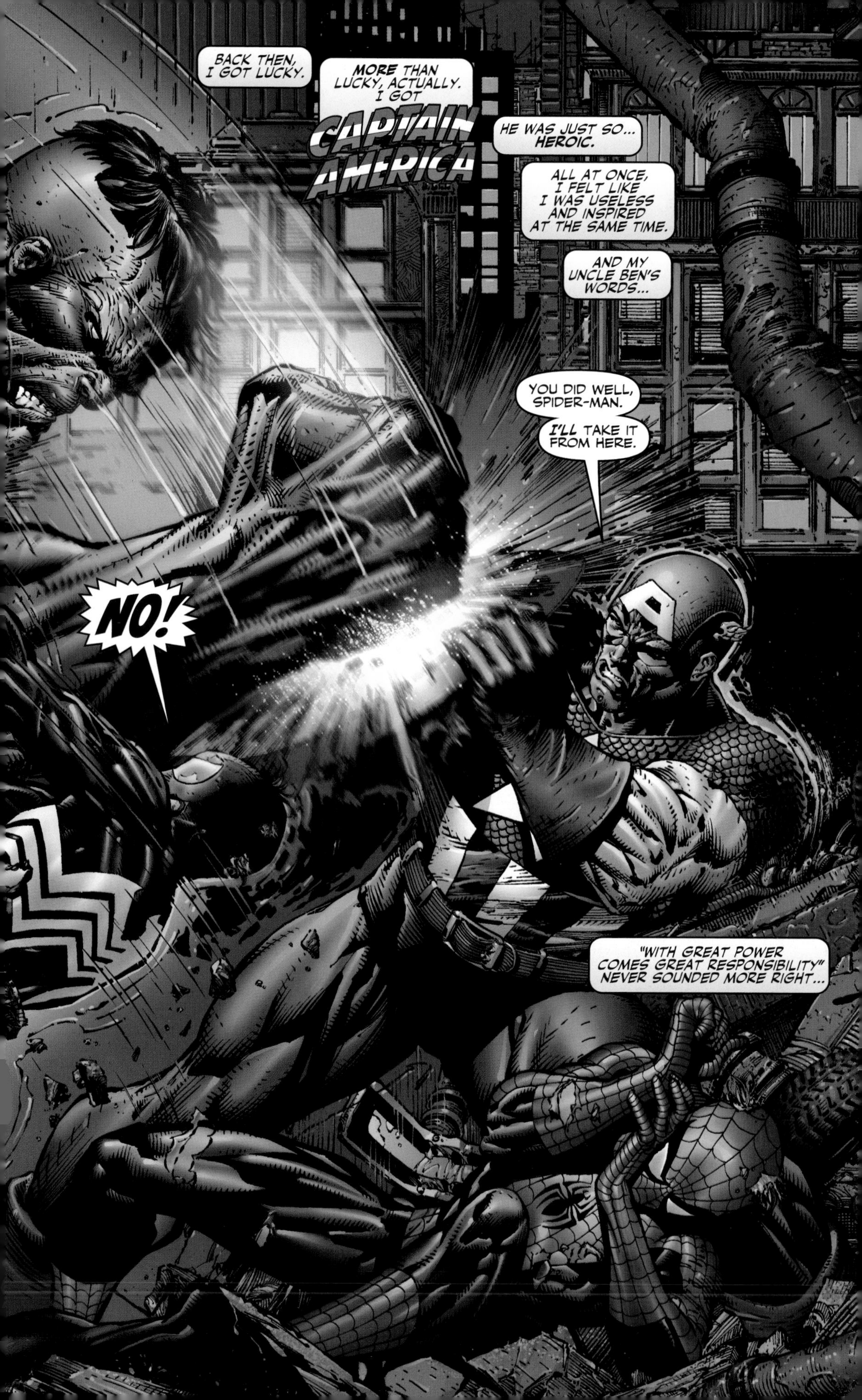
BACK THEN, I GOT LUCKY.
MORE THAN LUCKY, ACTUALLY. I GOT
CAPTAIN AMERICA
HE WAS JUST SO... HEROIC.
ALL AT ONCE, I FELT LIKE I WAS USELESS AND INSPIRED AT THE SAME TIME.
AND MY UNCLE BEN'S WORDS...
YOU DID WELL, SPIDER-MAN.
I'LL TAKE IT FROM HERE.
NO!
"WITH GREAT POWER COMES GREAT RESPONSIBILITY" NEVER SOUNDED MORE RIGHT...

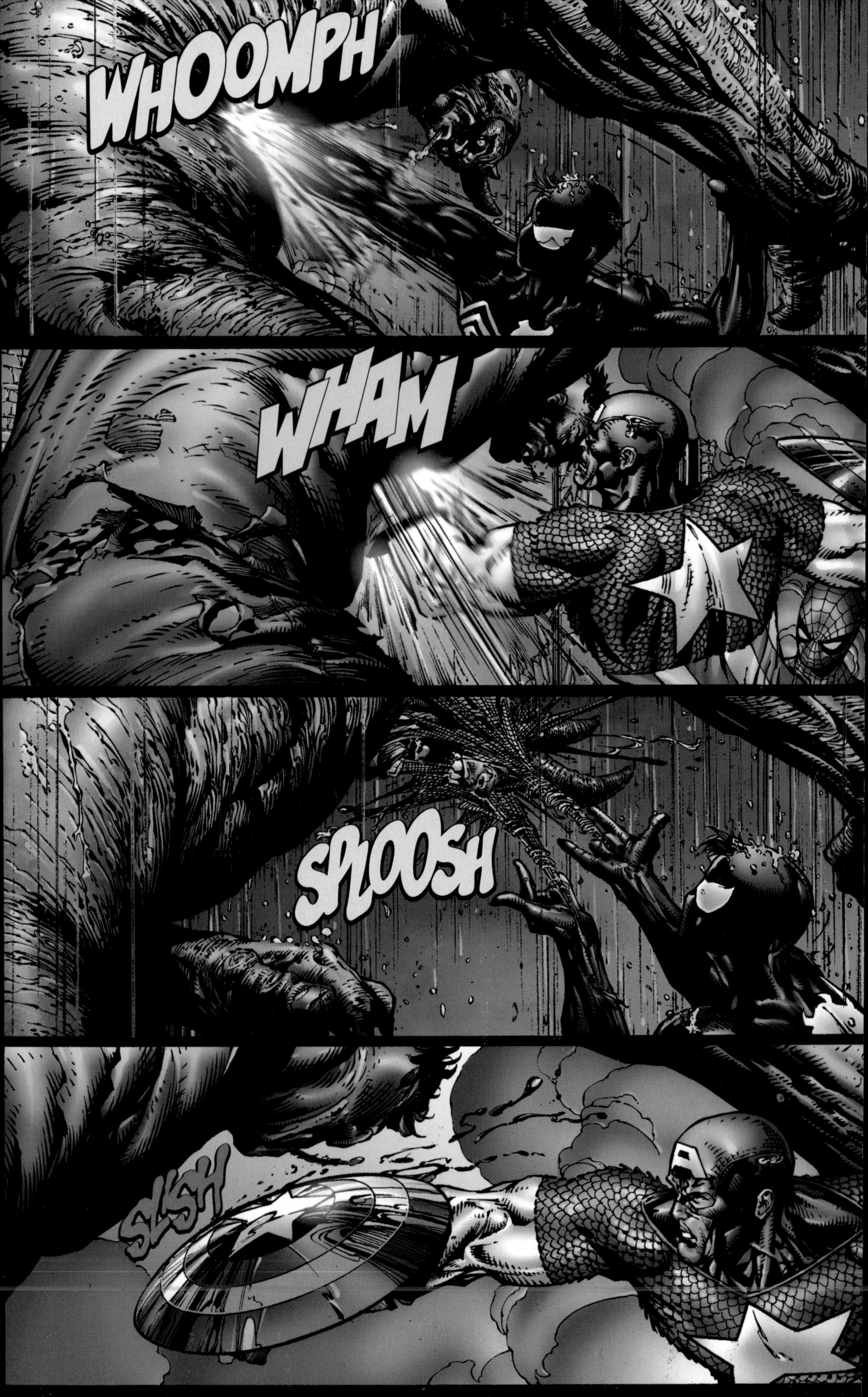
WHOOMPH
WHAM
SPLOOSH
SLISH

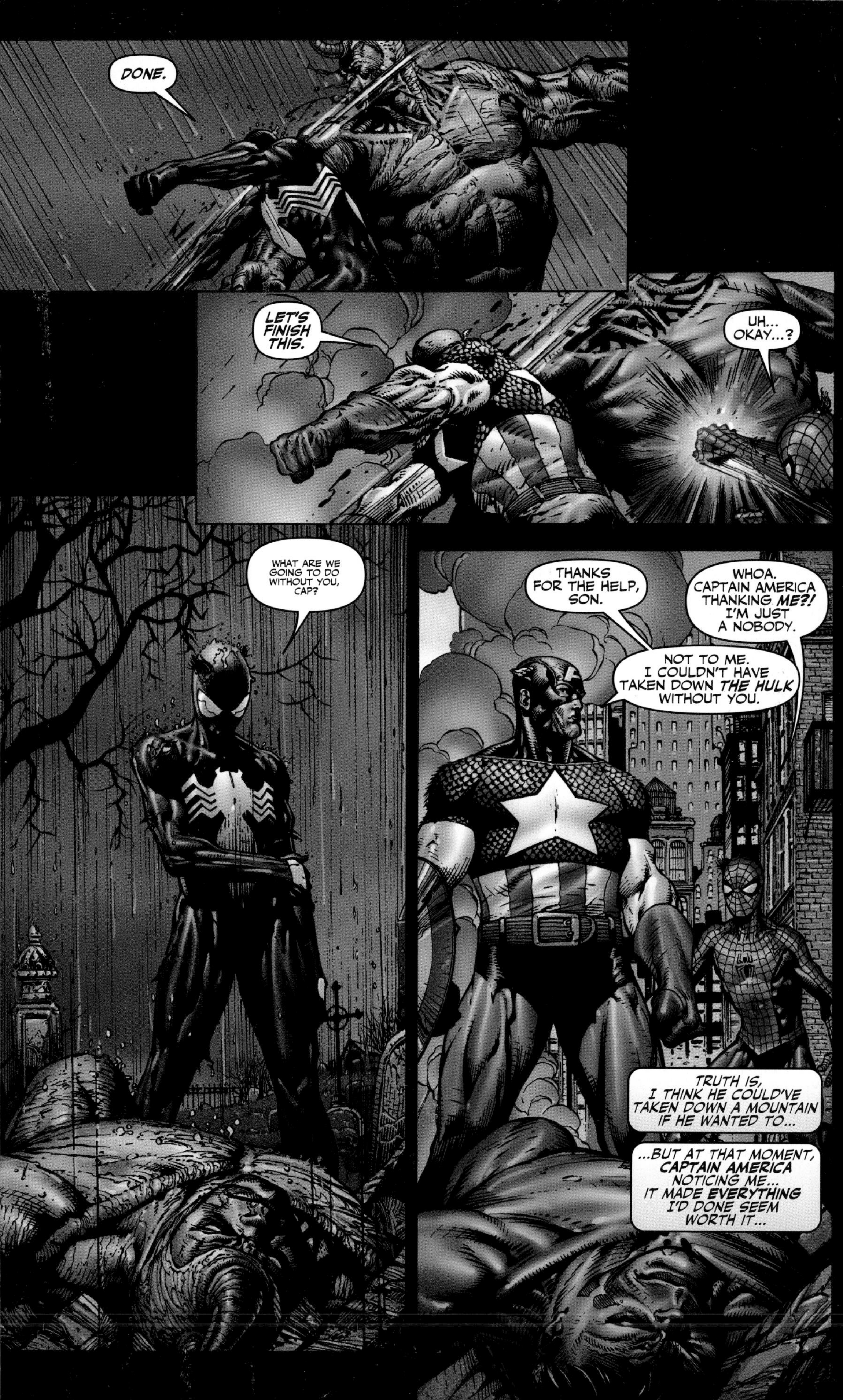
DONE.
LET'S FINISH THIS.
UH... OKAY...?
WHAT ARE WE GOING TO DO WITHOUT YOU, CAP?
THANKS FOR THE HELP, SON.
WHOA. CAPTAIN AMERICA THANKING ME?! I'M JUST A NOBODY.
NOT TO ME. I COULDN'T HAVE TAKEN DOWN THE HULK WITHOUT YOU.
TRUTH IS, I THINK HE COULD'VE TAKEN DOWN A MOUNTAIN IF HE WANTED TO...
...BUT AT THAT MOMENT, CAPTAIN AMERICA NOTICING ME... IT MADE EVERYTHING I'D DONE SEEM WORTH IT...

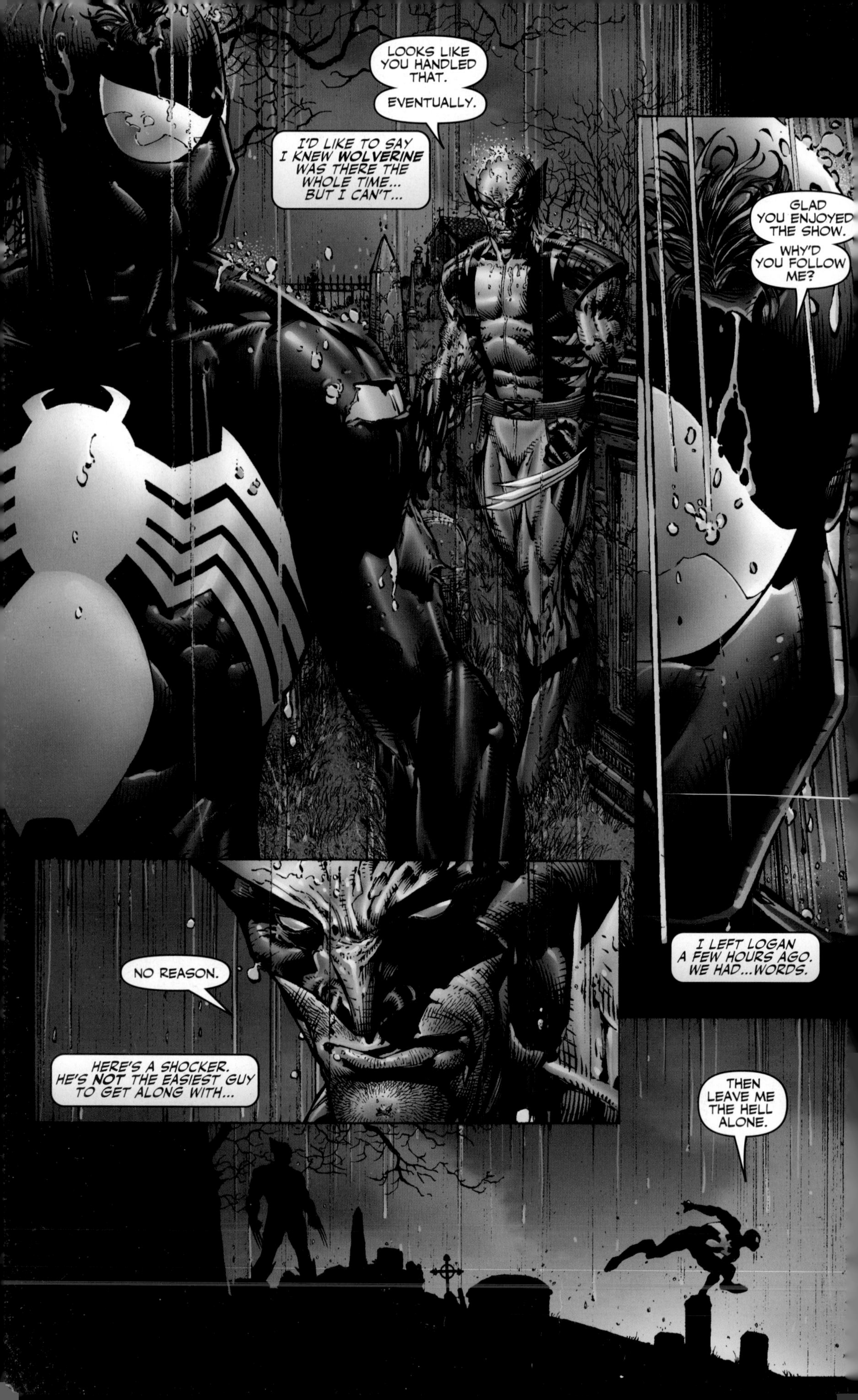
LOOKS LIKE YOU HANDLED THAT.
EVENTUALLY.
I'D LIKE TO SAY I KNEW WOLVERINE WAS THERE THE WHOLE TIME... BUT I CAN'T...
GLAD YOU ENJOYED THE SHOW.
WHY'D YOU FOLLOW ME?
NO REASON.
I LEFT LOGAN A FEW HOURS AGO. WE HAD...WORDS.
HERE'S A SHOCKER. HE'S NOT THE EASIEST GUY TO GET ALONG WITH...
THEN LEAVE ME THE HELL ALONE.

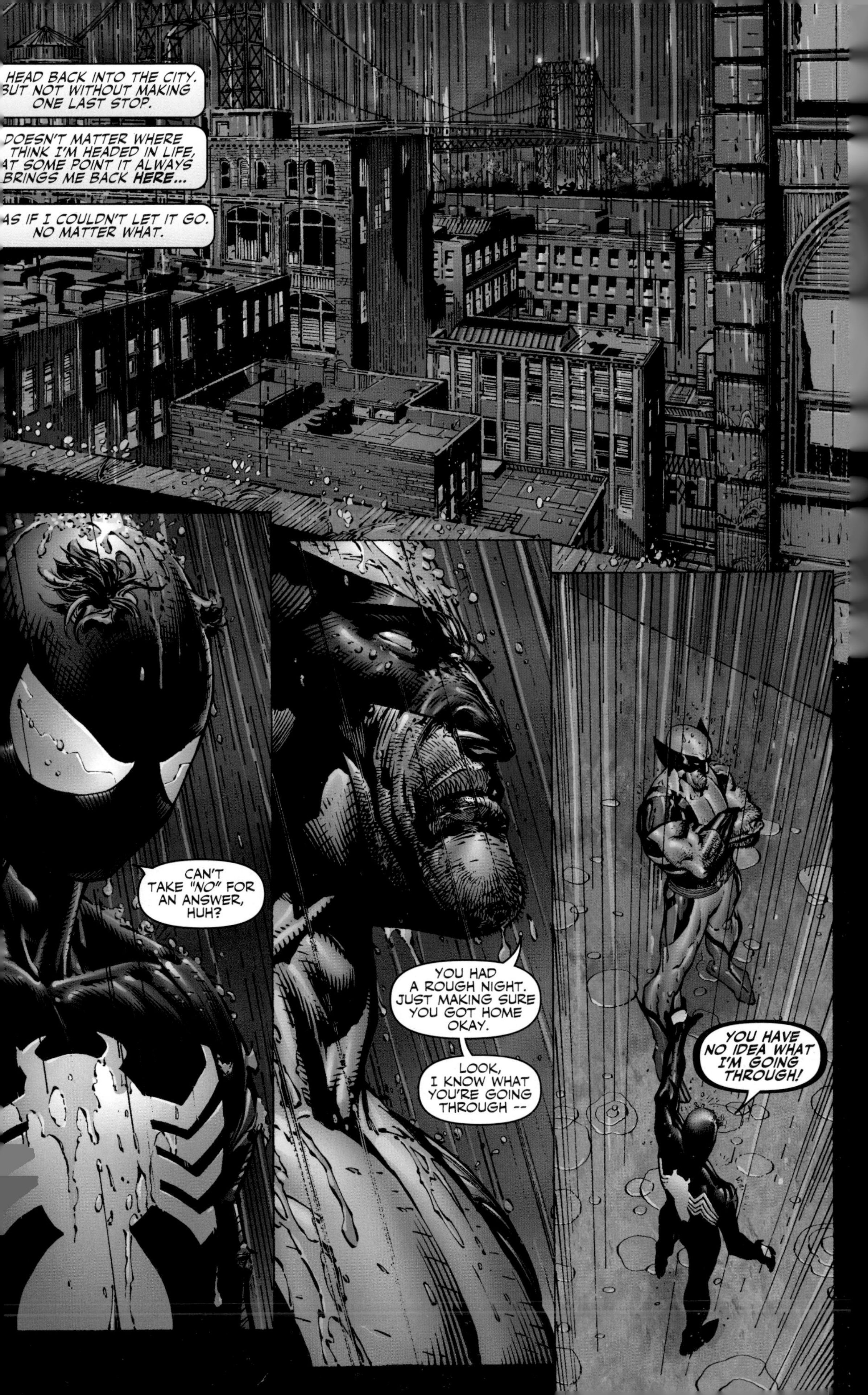
HEAD BACK INTO THE CITY. BUT NOT WITHOUT MAKING ONE LAST STOP.
DOESN'T MATTER WHERE THINK I'M HEADED IN LIFE, AT SOME POINT IT ALWAYS BRINGS ME BACK **HERE...**
AS IF I COULDN'T LET IT GO. NO MATTER WHAT.
CAN'T TAKE *"NO"* FOR AN ANSWER, HUH?
YOU HAD A ROUGH NIGHT. JUST MAKING SURE YOU GOT HOME OKAY.
LOOK, I KNOW WHAT YOU'RE GOING THROUGH --
YOU HAVE NO IDEA WHAT I'M GOING THROUGH!

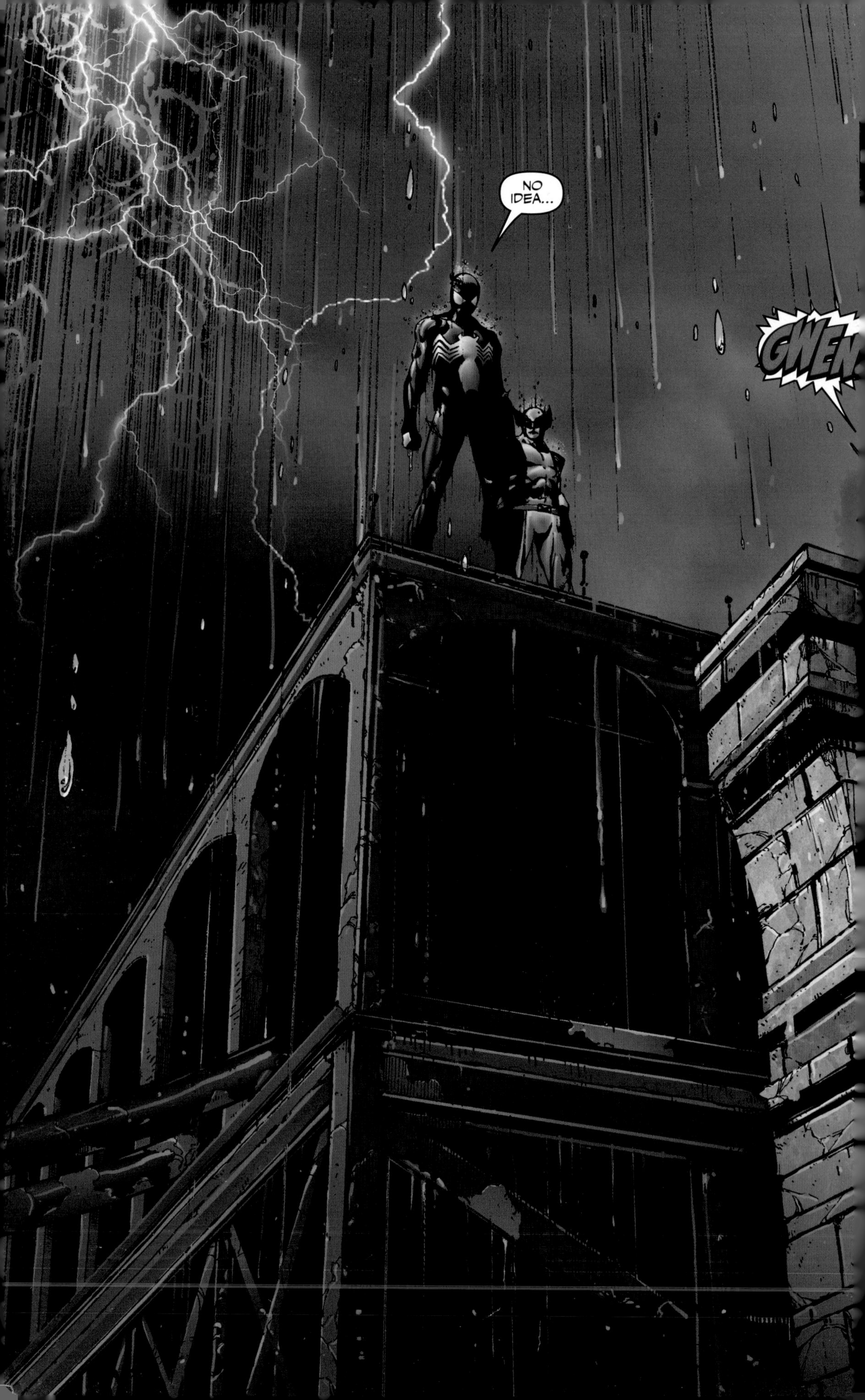
NO IDEA...
GWEN

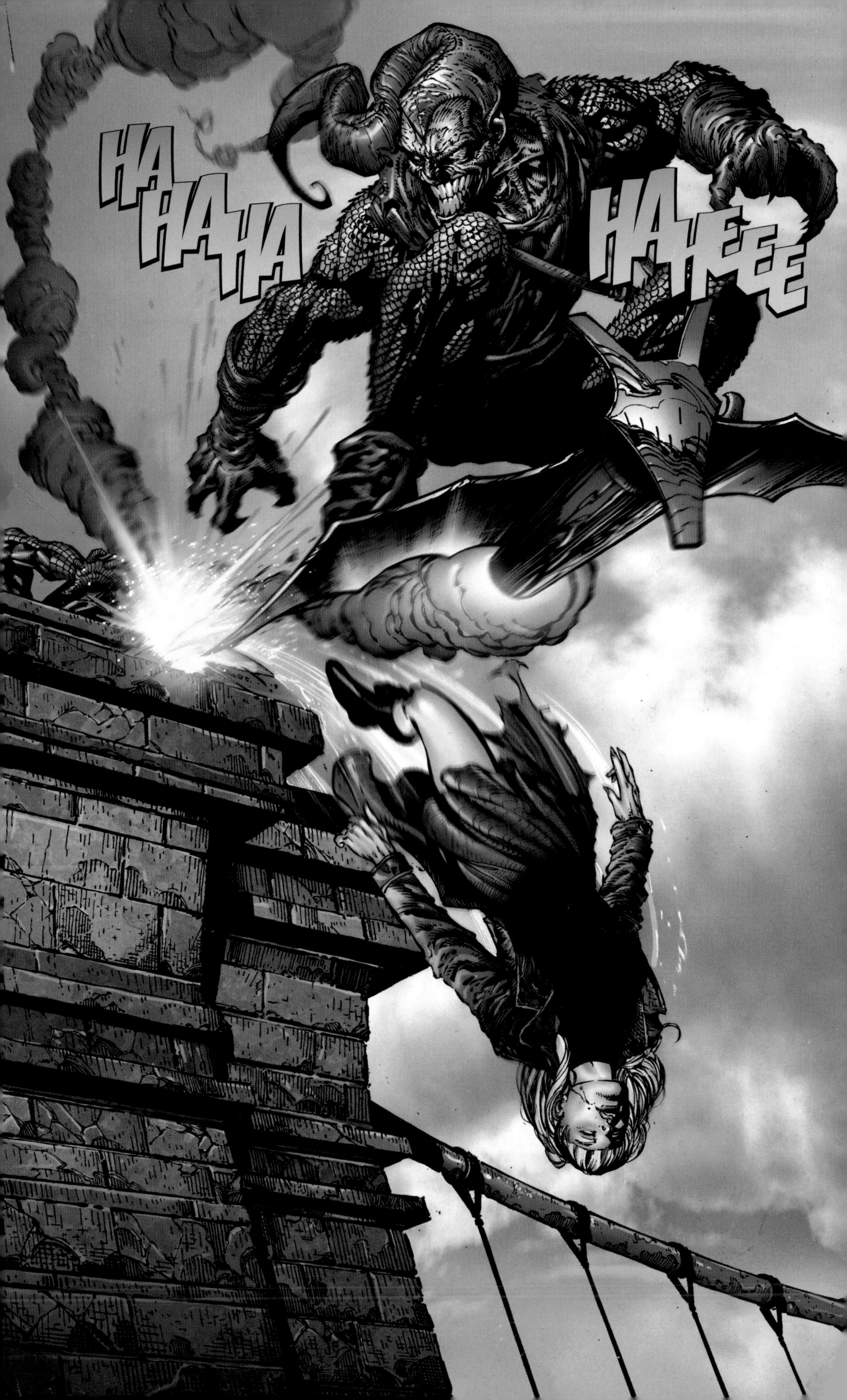
HA
HAHA
HA
HA
HAHEEE

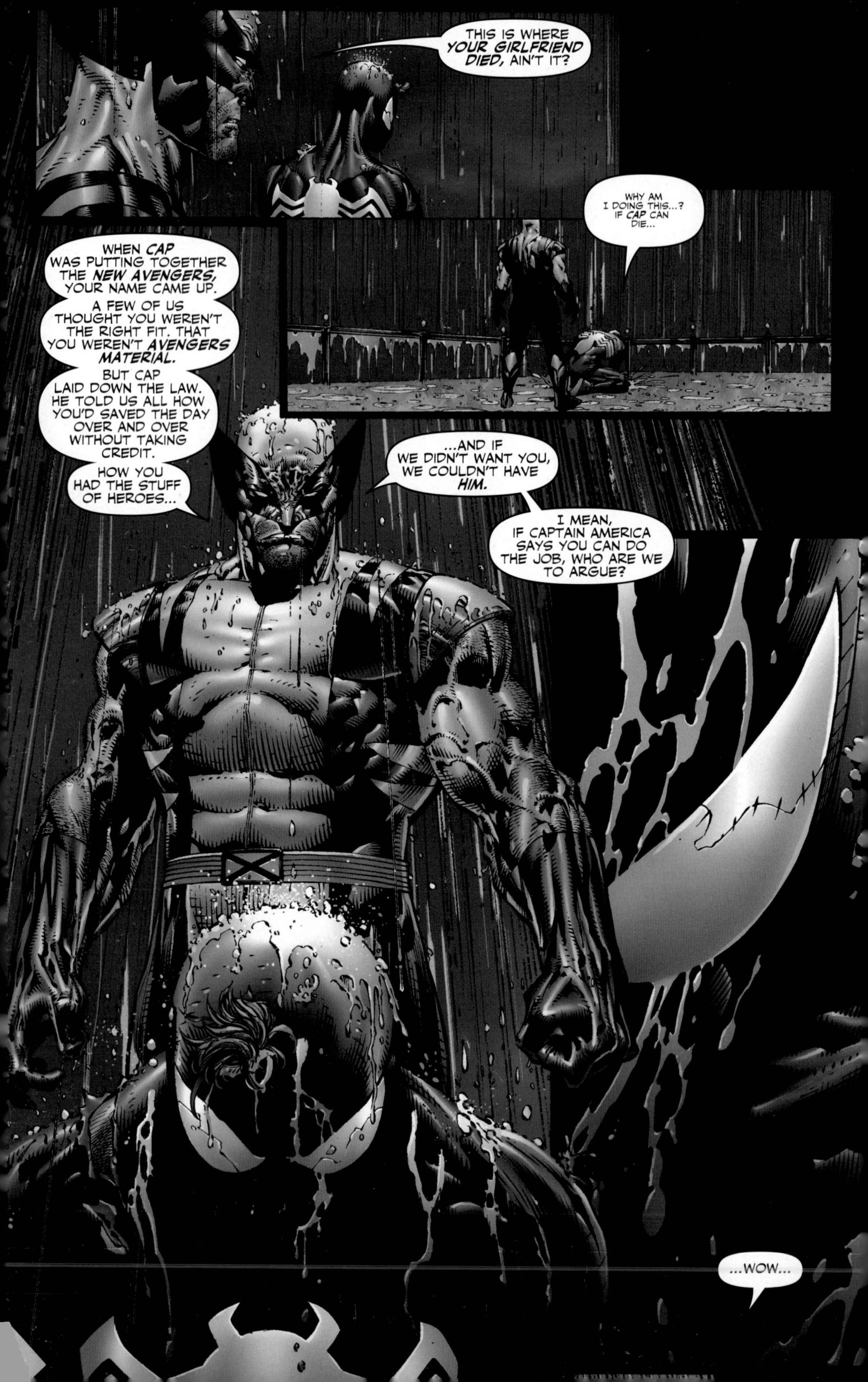

THIS IS WHERE YOUR GIRLFRIEND DIED, AIN'T IT?
WHY AM I DOING THIS...? IF CAP CAN DIE...
WHEN CAP WAS PUTTING TOGETHER THE NEW AVENGERS, YOUR NAME CAME UP.
A FEW OF US THOUGHT YOU WEREN'T THE RIGHT FIT. THAT YOU WEREN'T AVENGERS MATERIAL.
BUT CAP LAID DOWN THE LAW. HE TOLD US ALL HOW YOU'D SAVED THE DAY OVER AND OVER WITHOUT TAKING CREDIT.
HOW YOU HAD THE STUFF OF HEROES...
...AND IF WE DIDN'T WANT YOU, WE COULDN'T HAVE HIM.
I MEAN, IF CAPTAIN AMERICA SAYS YOU CAN DO THE JOB, WHO ARE WE TO ARGUE?
...WOW...

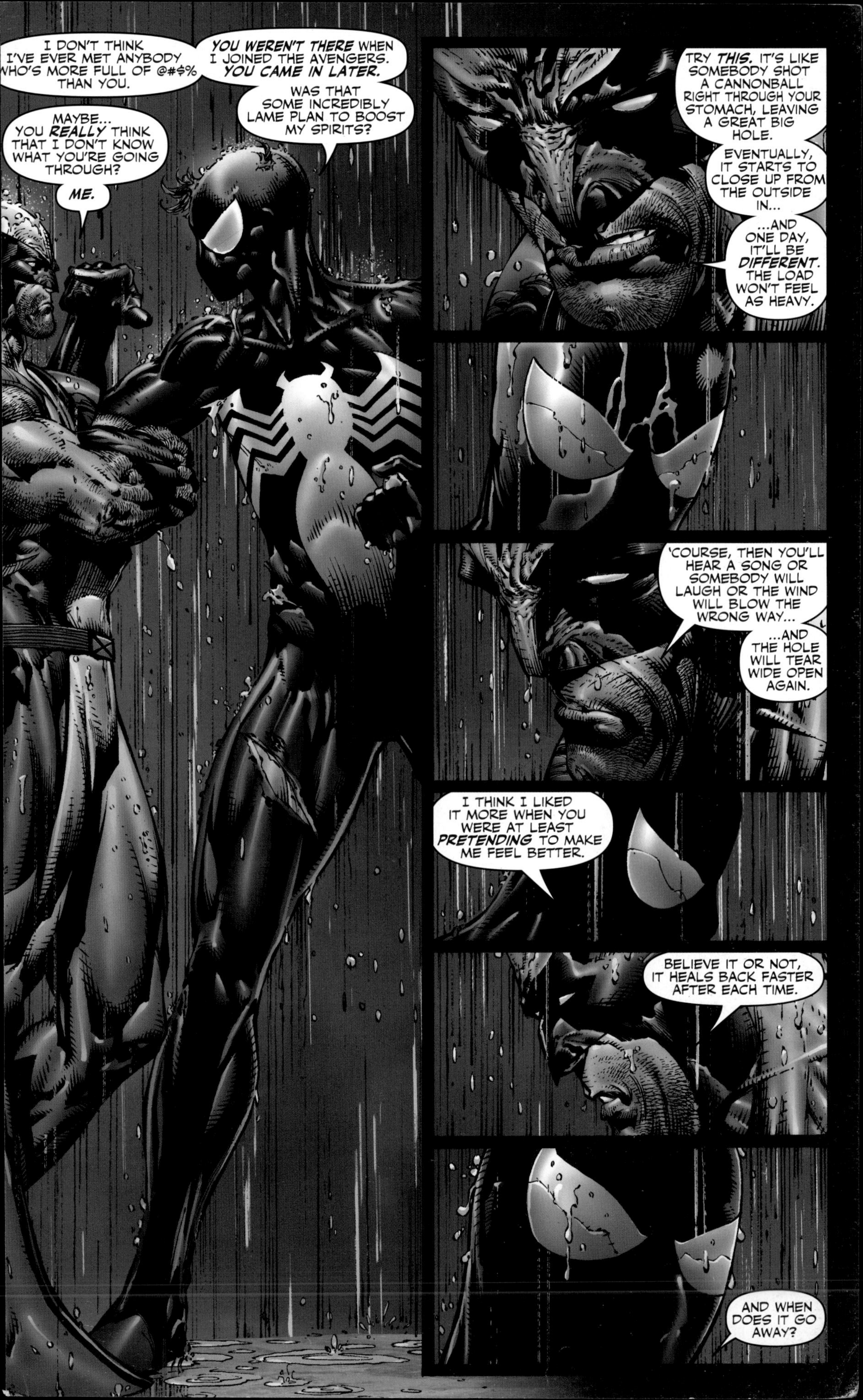
I DON'T THINK I'VE EVER MET ANYBODY WHO'S MORE FULL OF @#$% THAN YOU.
YOU WEREN'T THERE WHEN I JOINED THE AVENGERS. YOU CAME IN LATER.
WAS THAT SOME INCREDIBLY LAME PLAN TO BOOST MY SPIRITS?
MAYBE... YOU REALLY THINK THAT I DON'T KNOW WHAT YOU'RE GOING THROUGH?
ME.
TRY THIS. IT'S LIKE SOMEBODY SHOT A CANNONBALL RIGHT THROUGH YOUR STOMACH, LEAVING A GREAT BIG HOLE.
EVENTUALLY, IT STARTS TO CLOSE UP FROM THE OUTSIDE IN...
...AND ONE DAY, IT'LL BE DIFFERENT. THE LOAD WON'T FEEL AS HEAVY.
'COURSE, THEN YOU'LL HEAR A SONG OR SOMEBODY WILL LAUGH OR THE WIND WILL BLOW THE WRONG WAY...
...AND THE HOLE WILL TEAR WIDE OPEN AGAIN.
I THINK I LIKED IT MORE WHEN YOU WERE AT LEAST PRETENDING TO MAKE ME FEEL BETTER.
BELIEVE IT OR NOT, IT HEALS BACK FASTER AFTER EACH TIME.
AND WHEN DOES IT GO AWAY?

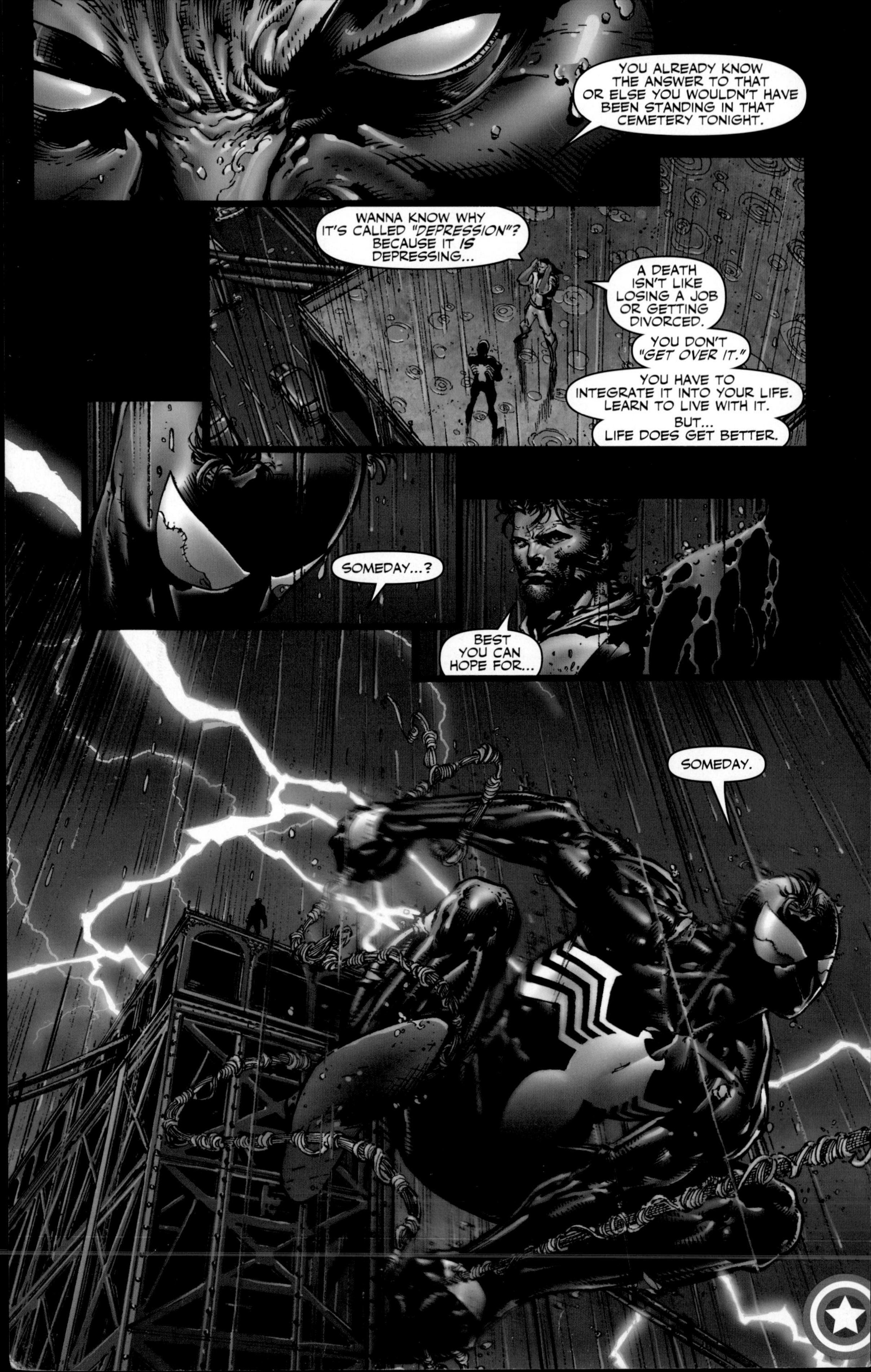
YOU ALREADY KNOW THE ANSWER TO THAT OR ELSE YOU WOULDN'T HAVE BEEN STANDING IN THAT CEMETERY TONIGHT.
WANNA KNOW WHY IT'S CALLED "*DEPRESSION*"? BECAUSE IT *IS* DEPRESSING...
A DEATH ISN'T LIKE LOSING A JOB OR GETTING DIVORCED.
YOU DON'T "*GET OVER IT.*"
YOU HAVE TO INTEGRATE IT INTO YOUR LIFE. LEARN TO LIVE WITH IT.
BUT... LIFE DOES GET BETTER.
SOMEDAY...?
BEST YOU CAN HOPE FOR...
SOMEDAY.

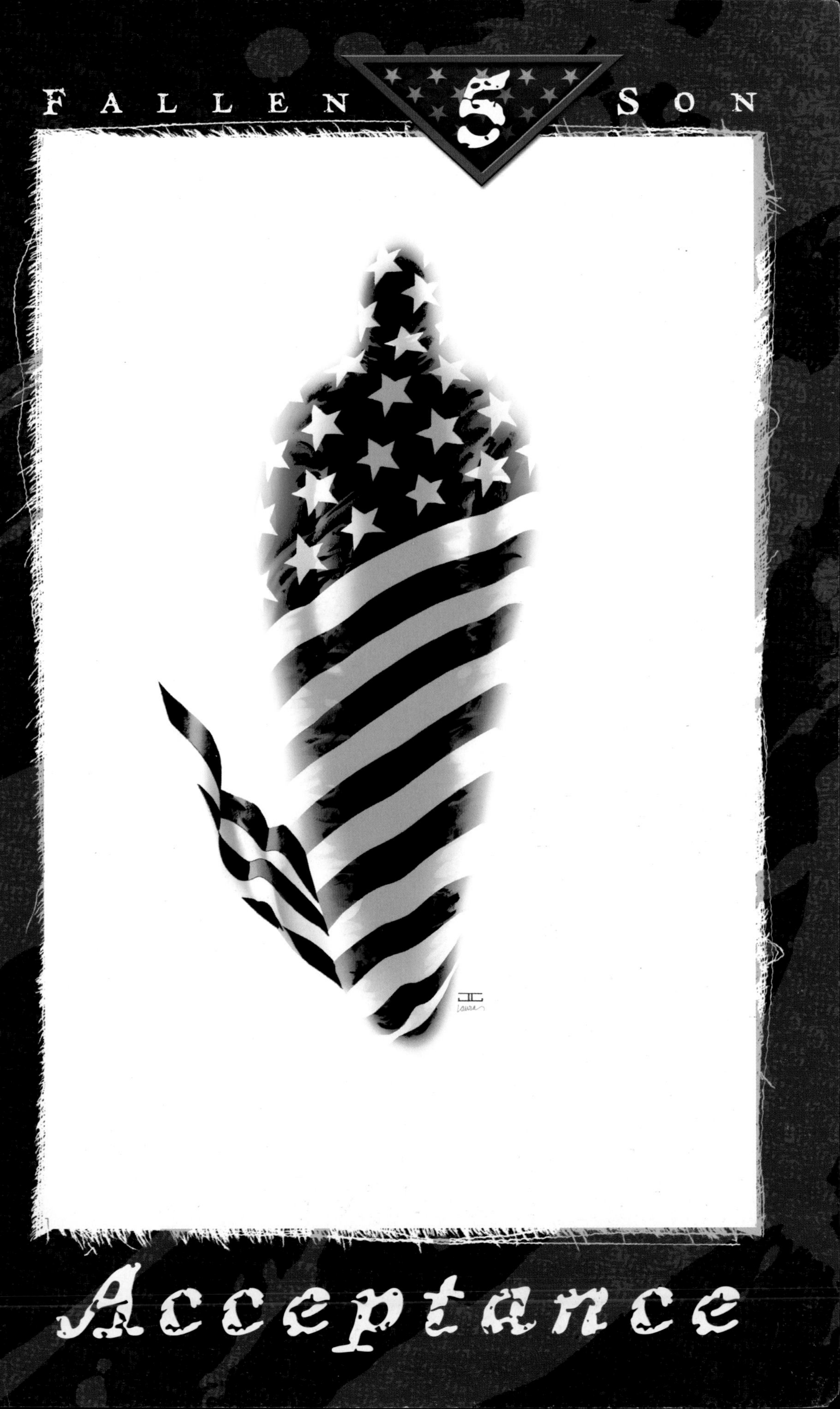
FALLEN 5 SON
Acceptance

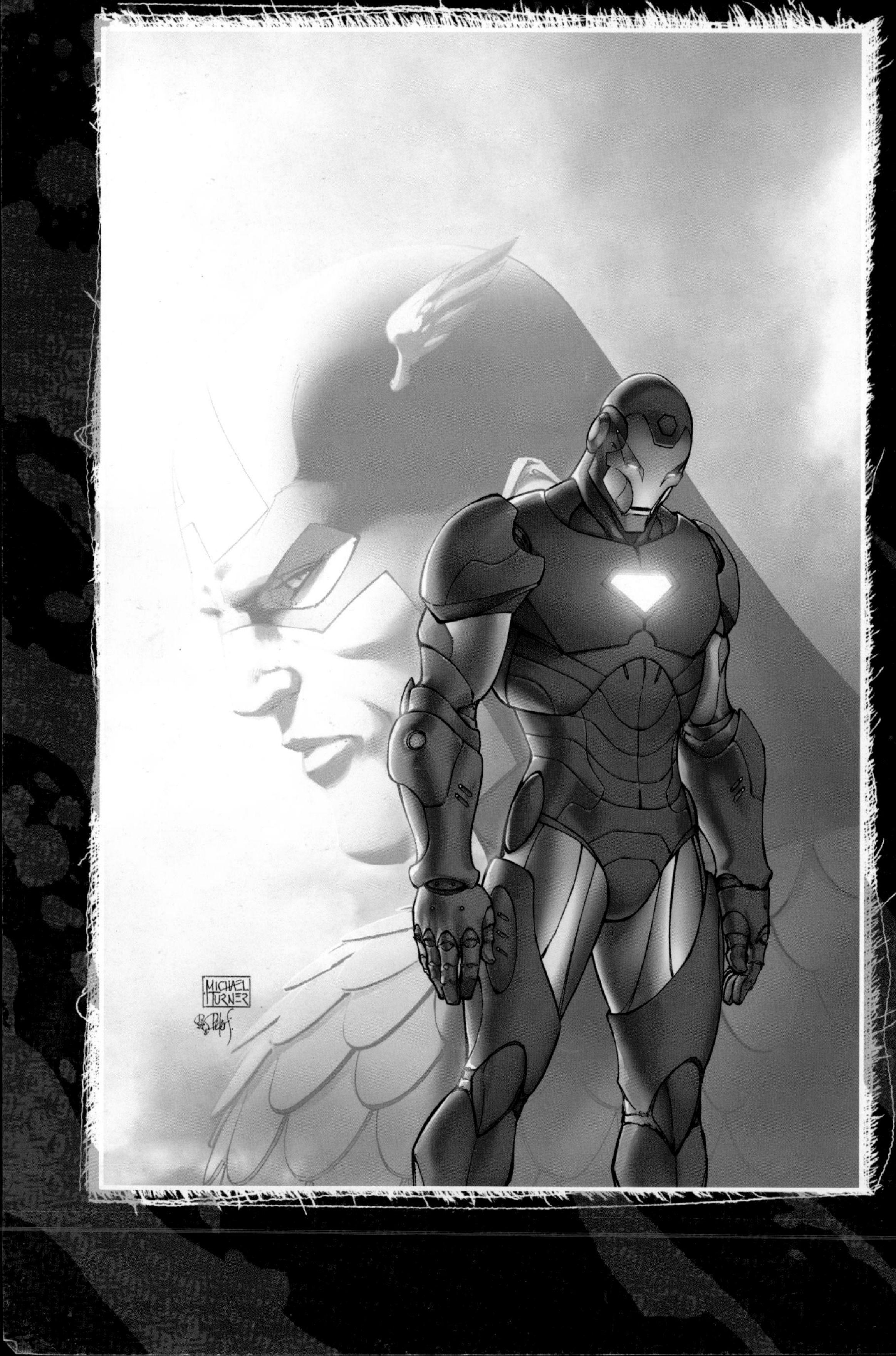
MICHAEL TURNER

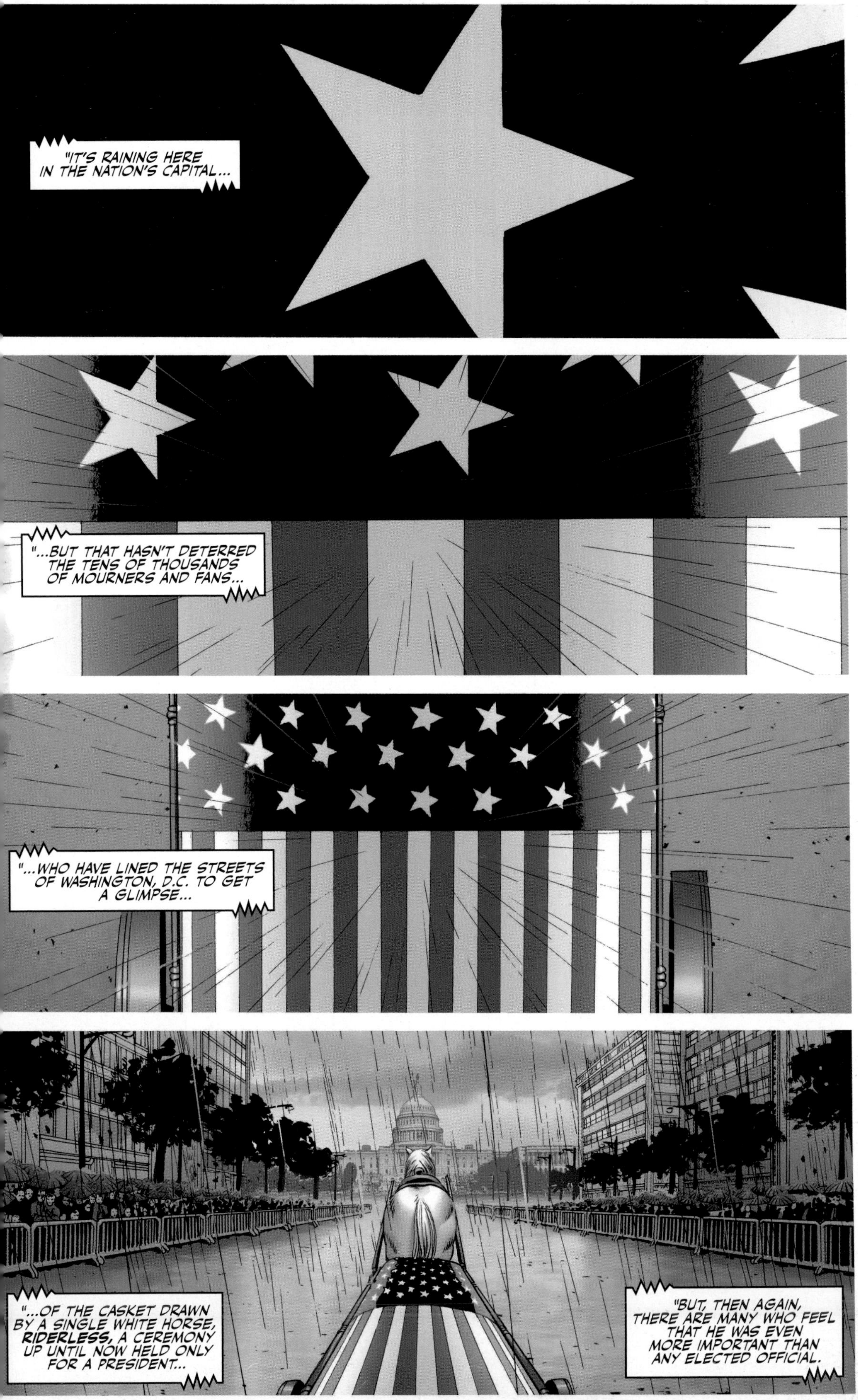

"IT'S RAINING HERE IN THE NATION'S CAPITAL...
"...BUT THAT HASN'T DETERRED THE TENS OF THOUSANDS OF MOURNERS AND FANS...
"...WHO HAVE LINED THE STREETS OF WASHINGTON, D.C. TO GET A GLIMPSE...
"...OF THE CASKET DRAWN BY A SINGLE WHITE HORSE, RIDERLESS, A CEREMONY UP UNTIL NOW HELD ONLY FOR A PRESIDENT...
"BUT, THEN AGAIN, THERE ARE MANY WHO FEEL THAT HE WAS EVEN MORE IMPORTANT THAN ANY ELECTED OFFICIAL.

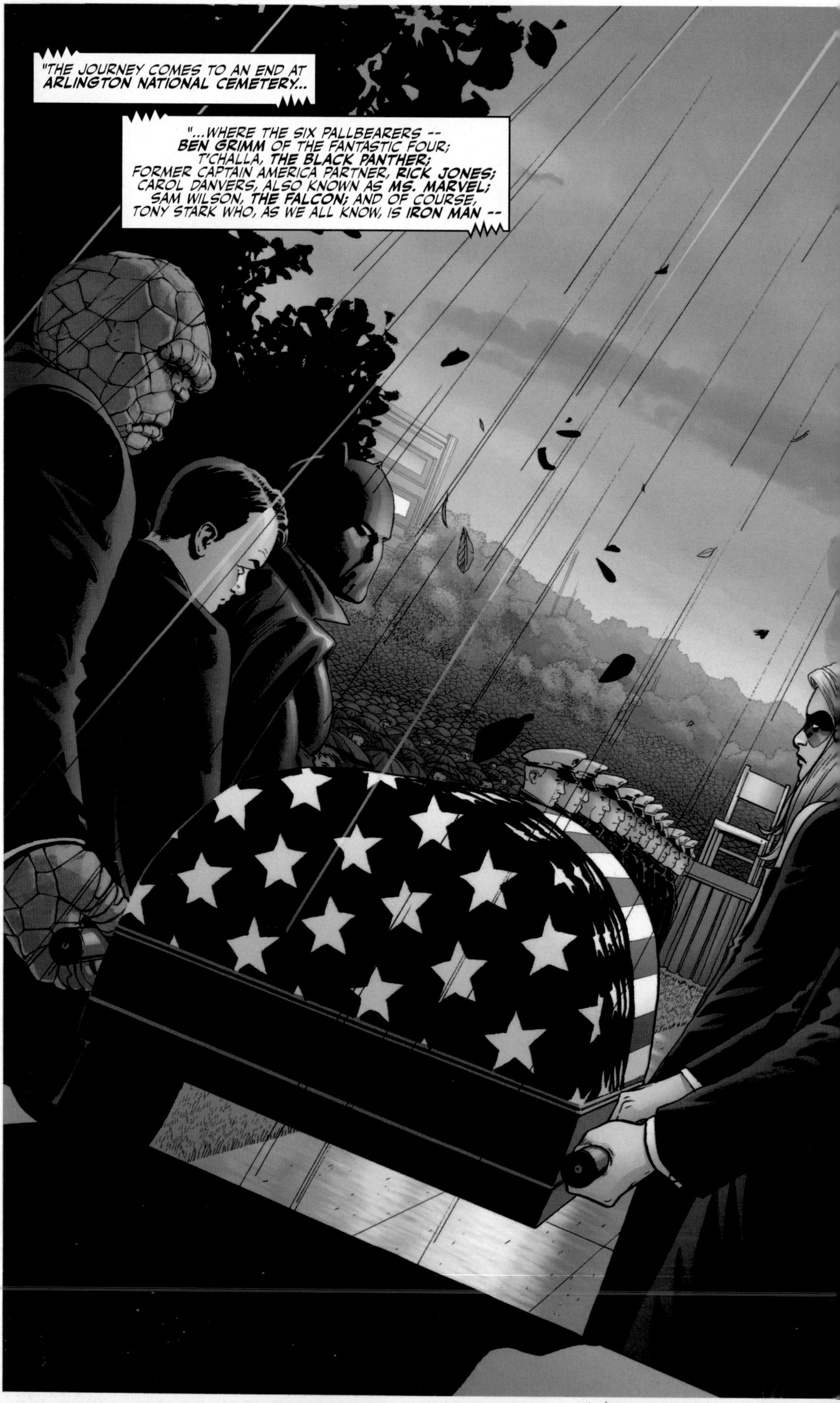
"THE JOURNEY COMES TO AN END AT ARLINGTON NATIONAL CEMETERY...
"...WHERE THE SIX PALLBEARERS -- BEN GRIMM OF THE FANTASTIC FOUR; T'CHALLA, THE BLACK PANTHER; FORMER CAPTAIN AMERICA PARTNER, RICK JONES; CAROL DANVERS, ALSO KNOWN AS MS. MARVEL; SAM WILSON, THE FALCON; AND OF COURSE, TONY STARK WHO, AS WE ALL KNOW, IS IRON MAN --

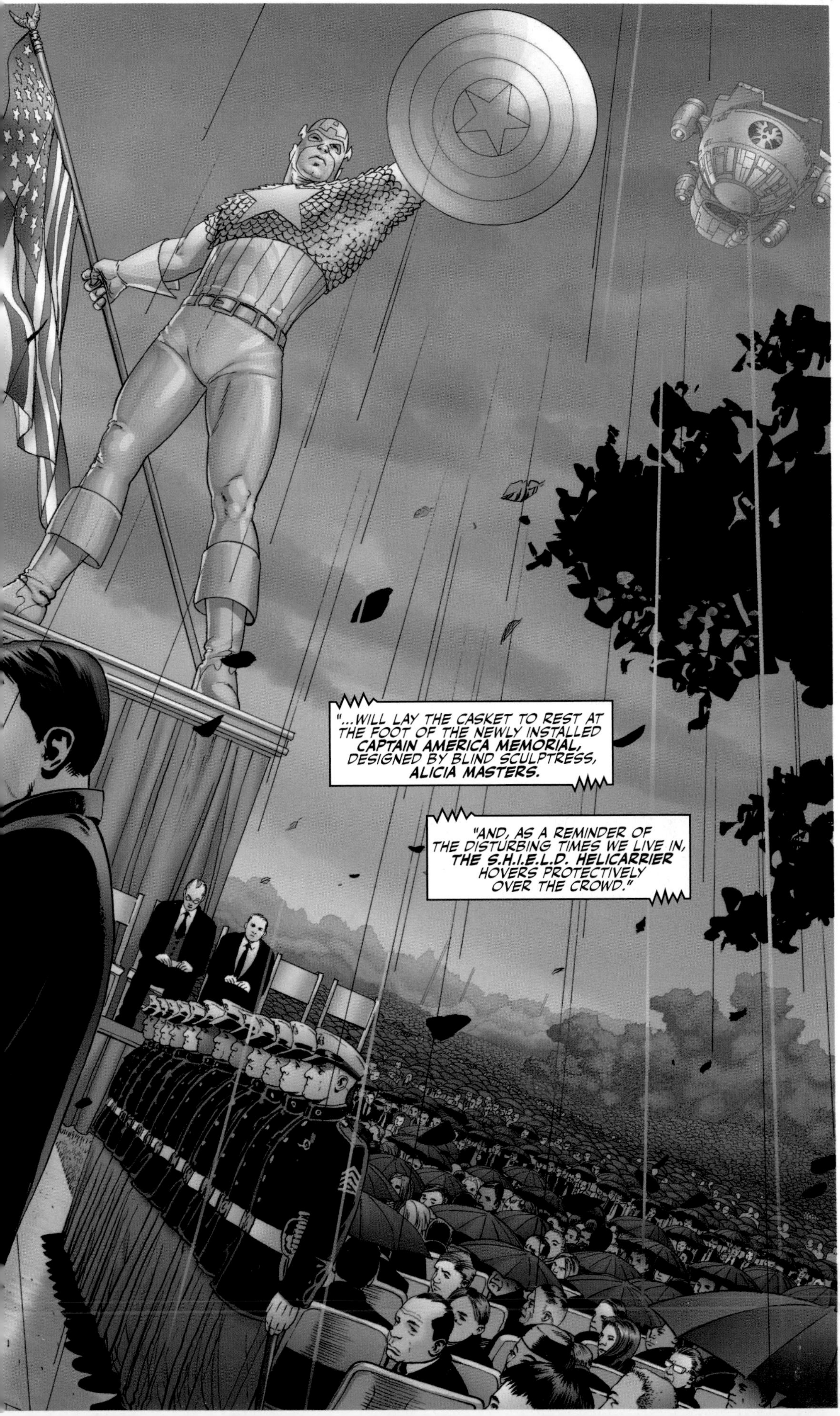
"...WILL LAY THE CASKET TO REST AT THE FOOT OF THE NEWLY INSTALLED **CAPTAIN AMERICA MEMORIAL**, DESIGNED BY BLIND SCULPTRESS, **ALICIA MASTERS**.
"AND, AS A REMINDER OF THE DISTURBING TIMES WE LIVE IN, **THE S.H.I.E.L.D. HELICARRIER** HOVERS PROTECTIVELY OVER THE CROWD."

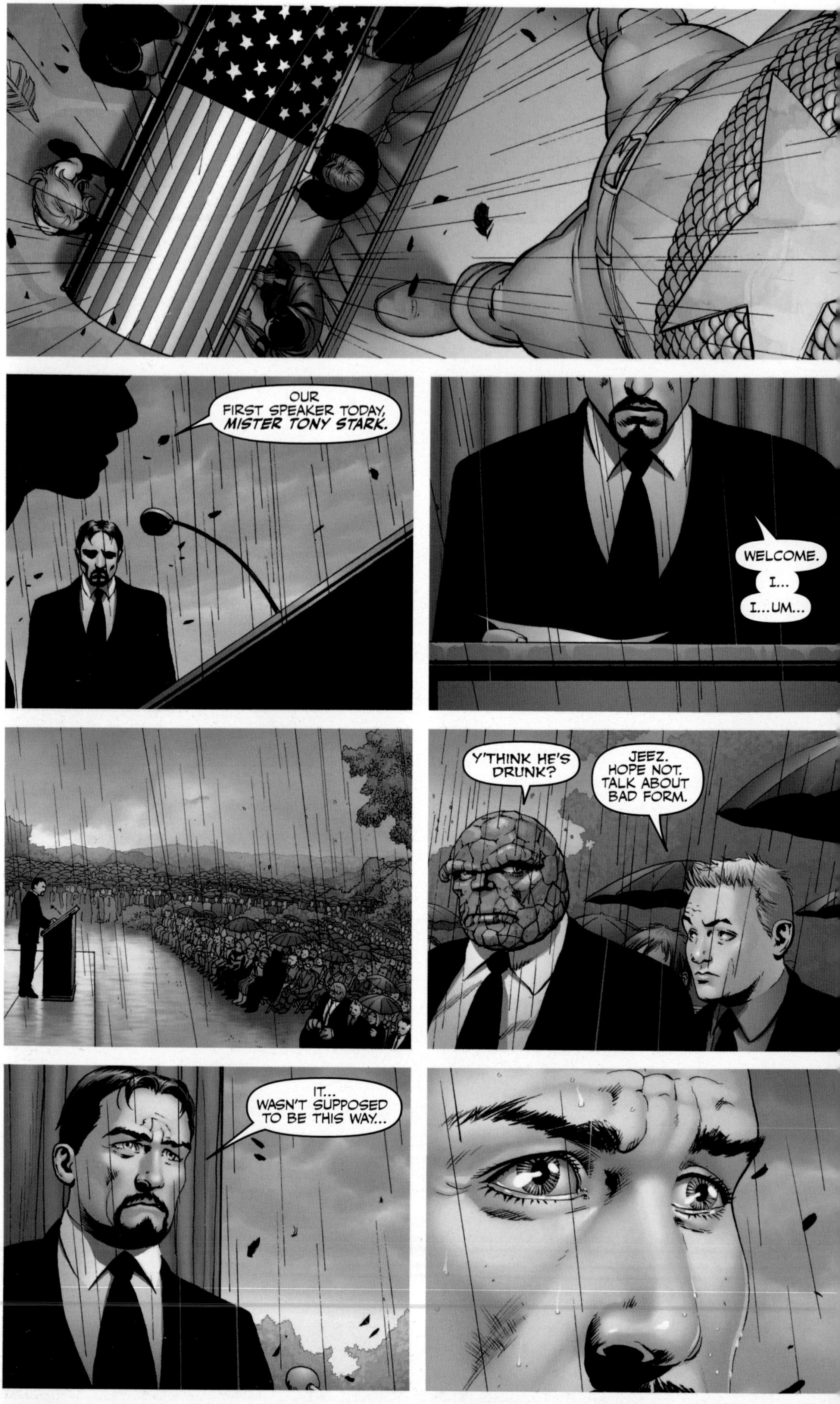
OUR FIRST SPEAKER TODAY, MISTER TONY STARK.
WELCOME. I... I...UM...
Y'THINK HE'S DRUNK?
JEEZ. HOPE NOT. TALK ABOUT BAD FORM.
IT... WASN'T SUPPOSED TO BE THIS WAY...

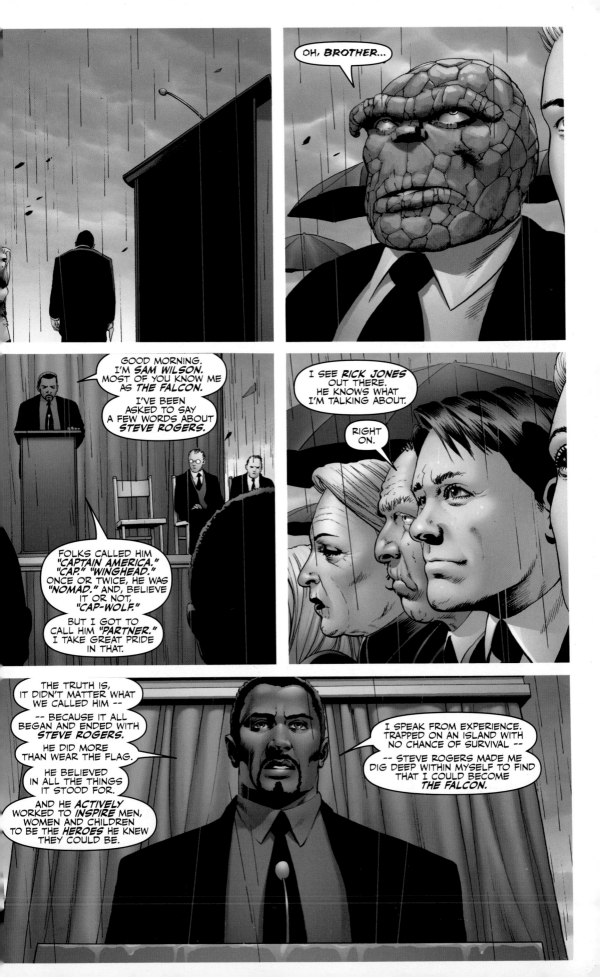

OH, *BROTHER...*

GOOD MORNING. I'M *SAM WILSON*. MOST OF YOU KNOW ME AS *THE FALCON*.

I'VE BEEN ASKED TO SAY A FEW WORDS ABOUT *STEVE ROGERS*.

FOLKS CALLED HIM *"CAPTAIN AMERICA." "CAP." "WINGHEAD."* ONCE OR TWICE, HE WAS *"NOMAD."* AND, BELIEVE IT OR NOT, *"CAP-WOLF."*

BUT I GOT TO CALL HIM *"PARTNER."* I TAKE GREAT PRIDE IN THAT.

I SEE *RICK JONES* OUT THERE. HE KNOWS WHAT I'M TALKING ABOUT.

RIGHT ON.

THE TRUTH IS, IT DIDN'T MATTER WHAT WE CALLED HIM --

-- BECAUSE IT ALL BEGAN AND ENDED WITH *STEVE ROGERS*.

HE DID MORE THAN WEAR THE FLAG.

HE BELIEVED IN ALL THE THINGS IT STOOD FOR.

AND HE *ACTIVELY* WORKED TO *INSPIRE* MEN, WOMEN AND CHILDREN TO BE THE *HEROES* HE KNEW THEY COULD BE.

I SPEAK FROM EXPERIENCE. TRAPPED ON AN ISLAND WITH NO CHANCE OF SURVIVAL --

-- STEVE ROGERS MADE ME DIG DEEP WITHIN MYSELF TO FIND THAT I COULD BECOME *THE FALCON*.

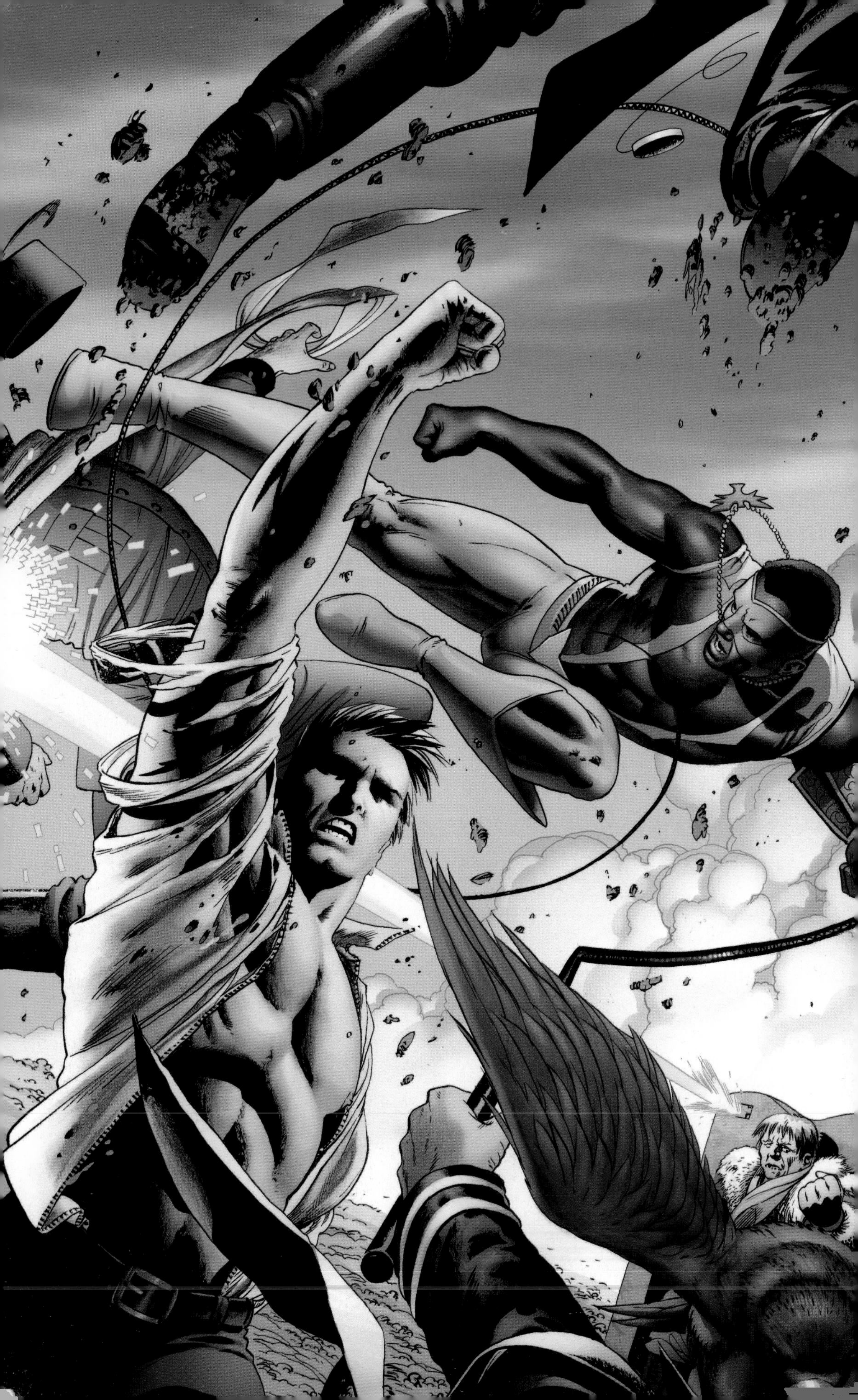

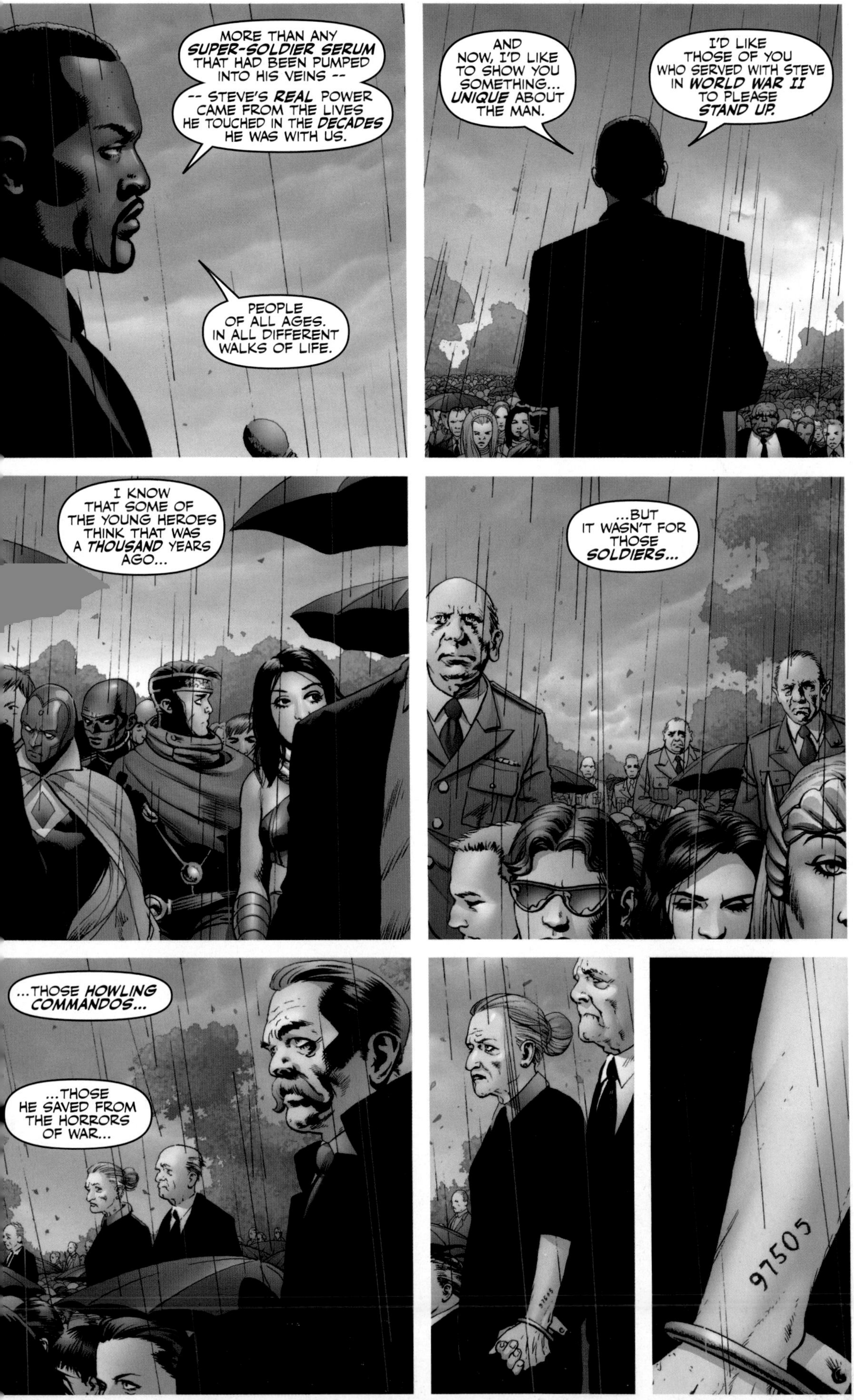
MORE THAN ANY SUPER-SOLDIER SERUM THAT HAD BEEN PUMPED INTO HIS VEINS --
-- STEVE'S REAL POWER CAME FROM THE LIVES HE TOUCHED IN THE DECADES HE WAS WITH US.
PEOPLE OF ALL AGES. IN ALL DIFFERENT WALKS OF LIFE.
AND NOW, I'D LIKE TO SHOW YOU SOMETHING... UNIQUE ABOUT THE MAN.
I'D LIKE THOSE OF YOU WHO SERVED WITH STEVE IN WORLD WAR II TO PLEASE STAND UP.
I KNOW THAT SOME OF THE YOUNG HEROES THINK THAT WAS A THOUSAND YEARS AGO...
...BUT IT WASN'T FOR THOSE SOLDIERS...
...THOSE HOWLING COMMANDOS...
...THOSE HE SAVED FROM THE HORRORS OF WAR...
97505

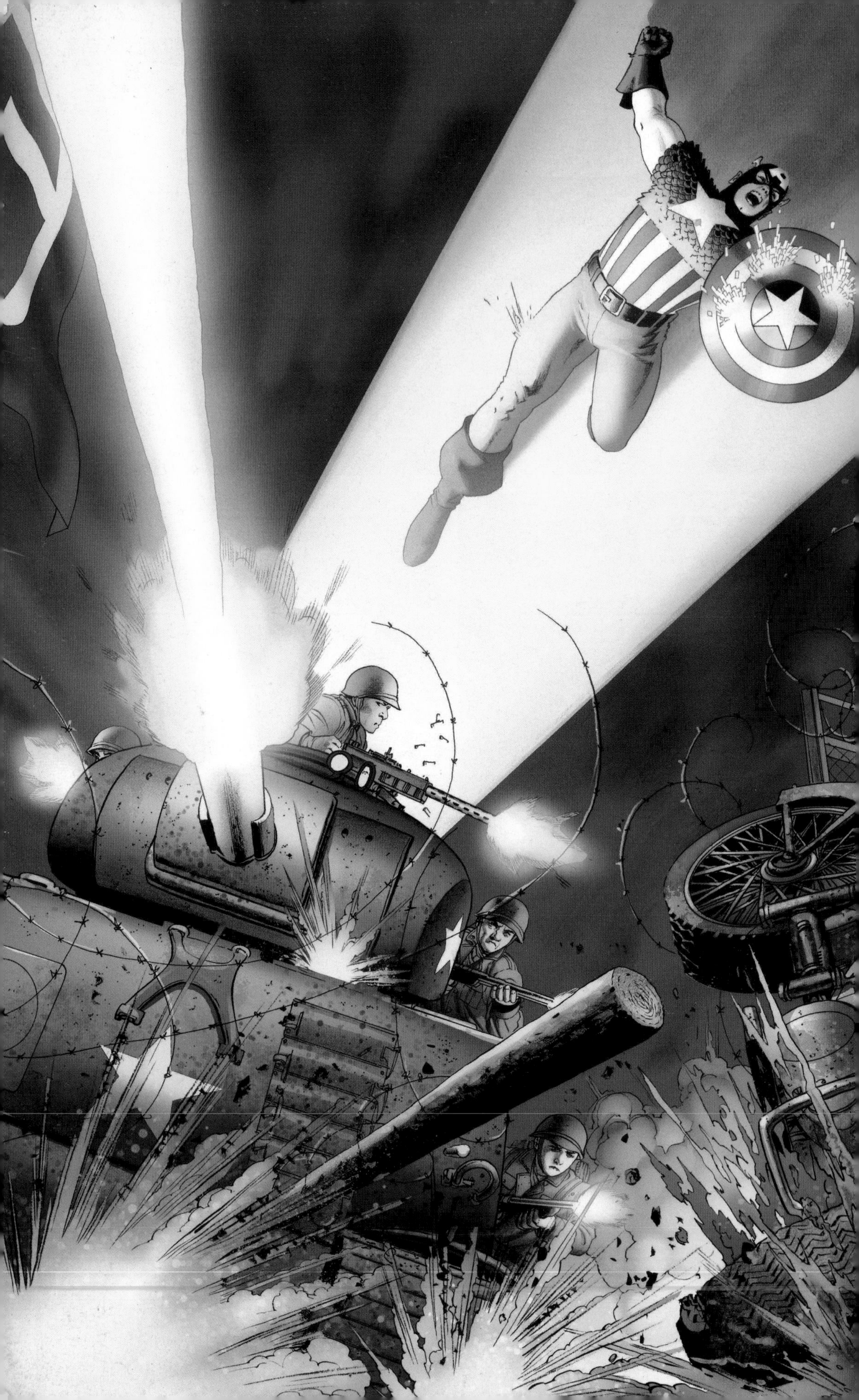

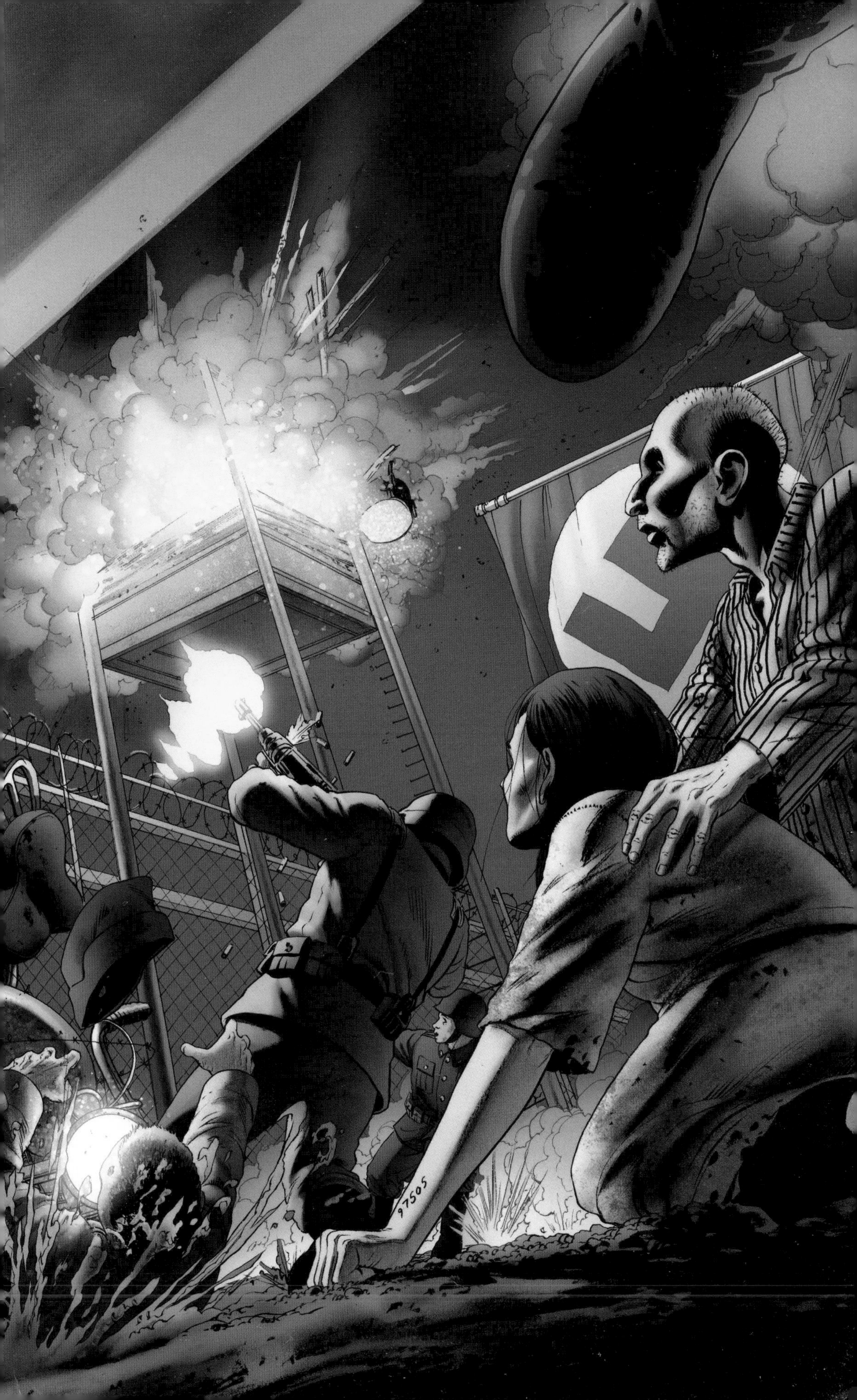
97505

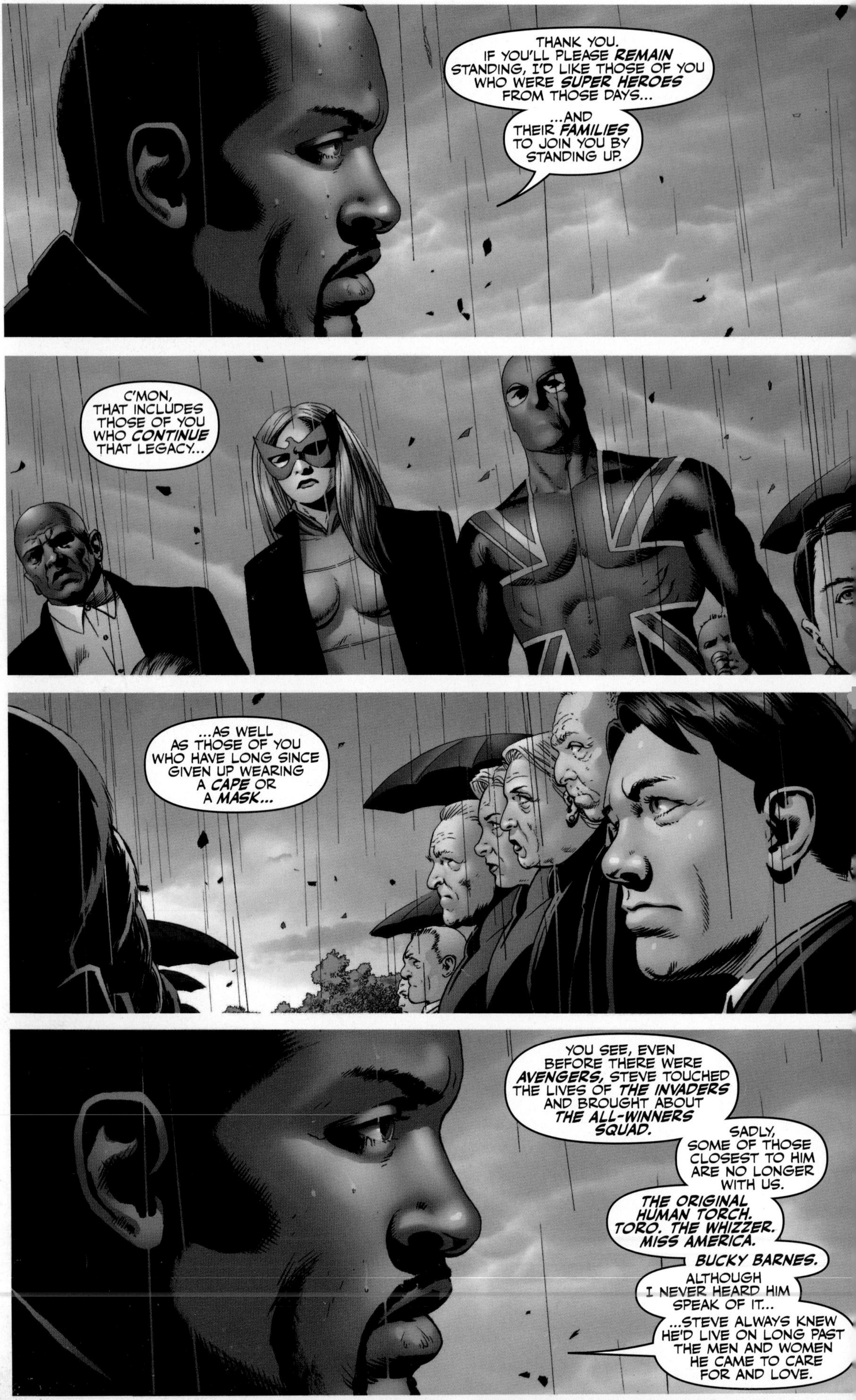
THANK YOU. IF YOU'LL PLEASE *REMAIN* STANDING, I'D LIKE THOSE OF YOU WHO WERE *SUPER HEROES* FROM THOSE DAYS...
...AND THEIR *FAMILIES* TO JOIN YOU BY STANDING UP.
C'MON, THAT INCLUDES THOSE OF YOU WHO *CONTINUE* THAT LEGACY...
...AS WELL AS THOSE OF YOU WHO HAVE LONG SINCE GIVEN UP WEARING A *CAPE* OR A *MASK*...
YOU SEE, EVEN BEFORE THERE WERE *AVENGERS*, STEVE TOUCHED THE LIVES OF *THE INVADERS* AND BROUGHT ABOUT *THE ALL-WINNERS SQUAD.*
SADLY, SOME OF THOSE CLOSEST TO HIM ARE NO LONGER WITH US.
THE ORIGINAL HUMAN TORCH. TORO. THE WHIZZER. MISS AMERICA.
BUCKY BARNES.
ALTHOUGH I NEVER HEARD HIM SPEAK OF IT...
...STEVE ALWAYS KNEW HE'D LIVE ON LONG PAST THE MEN AND WOMEN HE CAME TO CARE FOR AND LOVE.

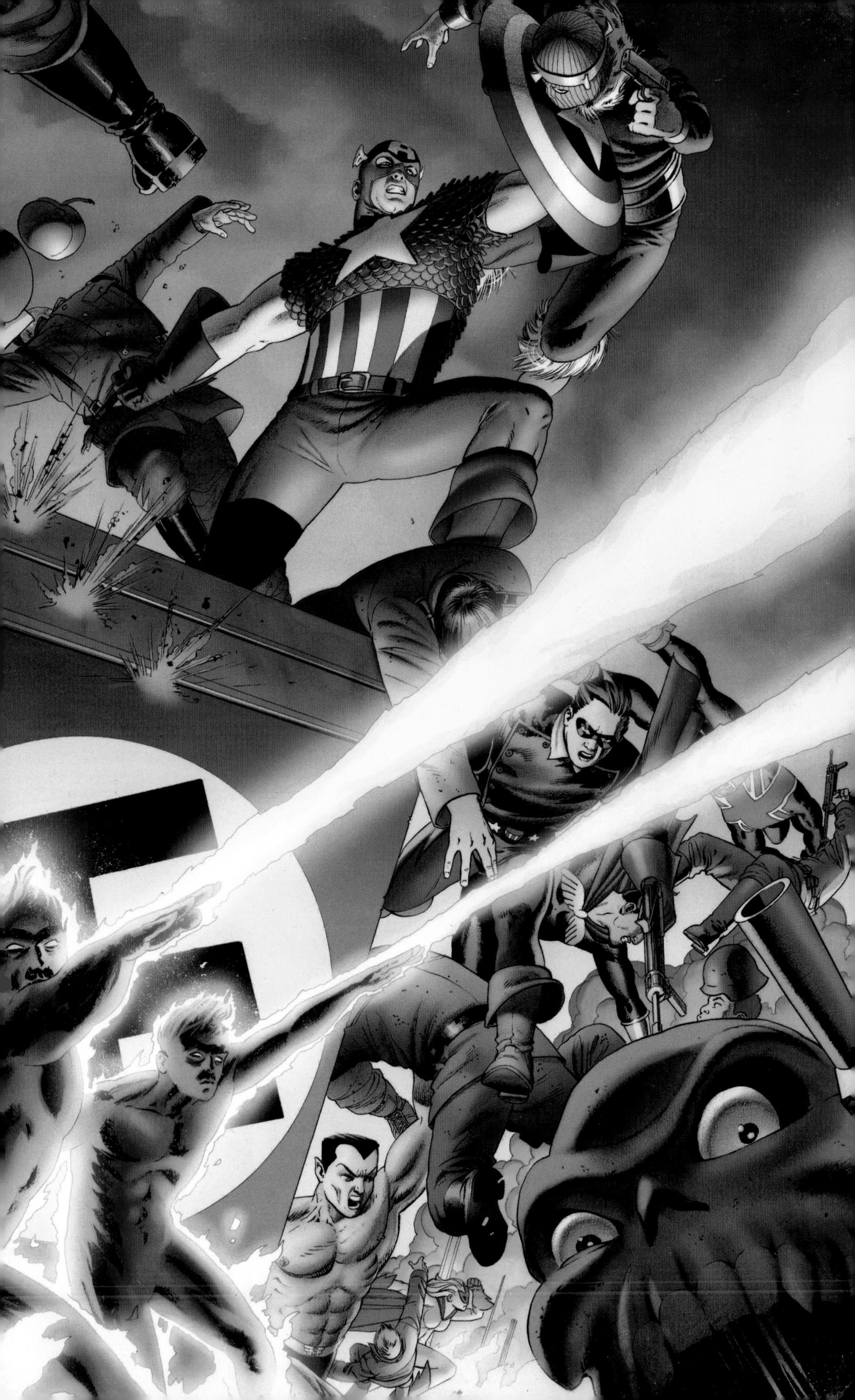

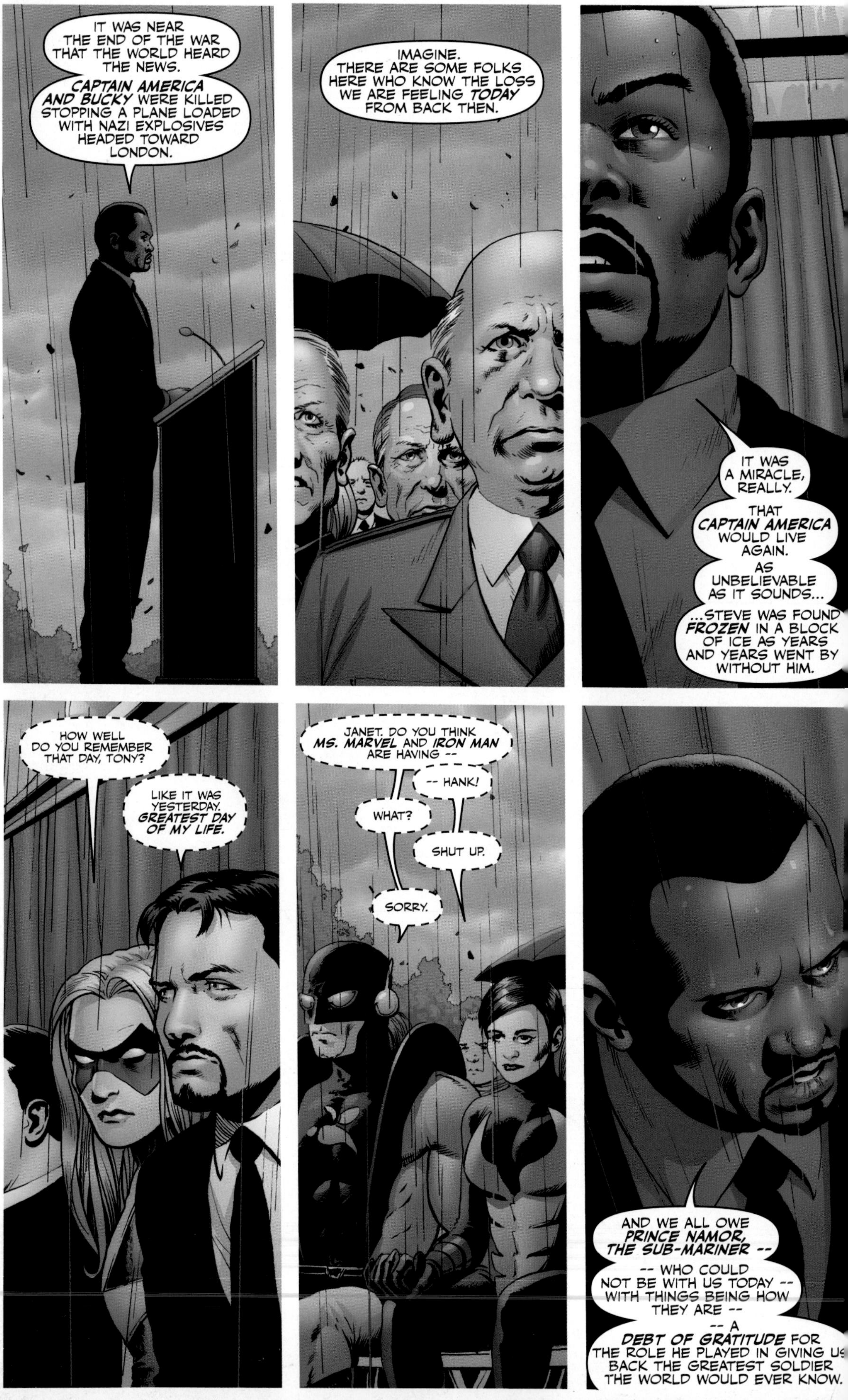
IT WAS NEAR THE END OF THE WAR THAT THE WORLD HEARD THE NEWS.
CAPTAIN AMERICA AND BUCKY WERE KILLED STOPPING A PLANE LOADED WITH NAZI EXPLOSIVES HEADED TOWARD LONDON.
IMAGINE. THERE ARE SOME FOLKS HERE WHO KNOW THE LOSS WE ARE FEELING TODAY FROM BACK THEN.
IT WAS A MIRACLE, REALLY.
THAT CAPTAIN AMERICA WOULD LIVE AGAIN.
AS UNBELIEVABLE AS IT SOUNDS...
...STEVE WAS FOUND FROZEN IN A BLOCK OF ICE AS YEARS AND YEARS WENT BY WITHOUT HIM.
HOW WELL DO YOU REMEMBER THAT DAY, TONY?
LIKE IT WAS YESTERDAY. GREATEST DAY OF MY LIFE.
JANET. DO YOU THINK MS. MARVEL AND IRON MAN ARE HAVING --
-- HANK!
WHAT?
SHUT UP.
SORRY.
AND WE ALL OWE PRINCE NAMOR, THE SUB-MARINER --
-- WHO COULD NOT BE WITH US TODAY -- WITH THINGS BEING HOW THEY ARE --
-- A DEBT OF GRATITUDE FOR THE ROLE HE PLAYED IN GIVING US BACK THE GREATEST SOLDIER THE WORLD WOULD EVER KNOW.

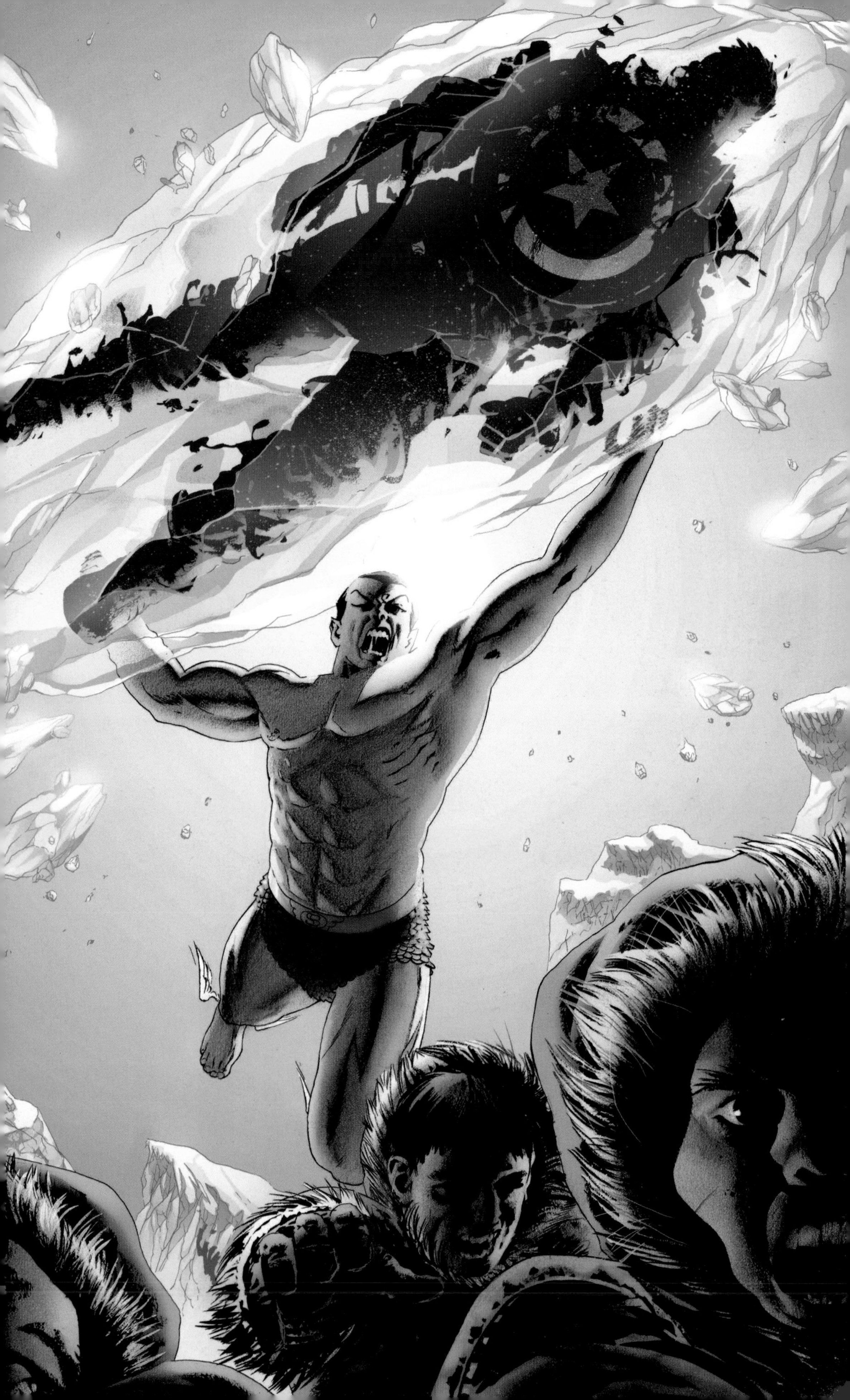

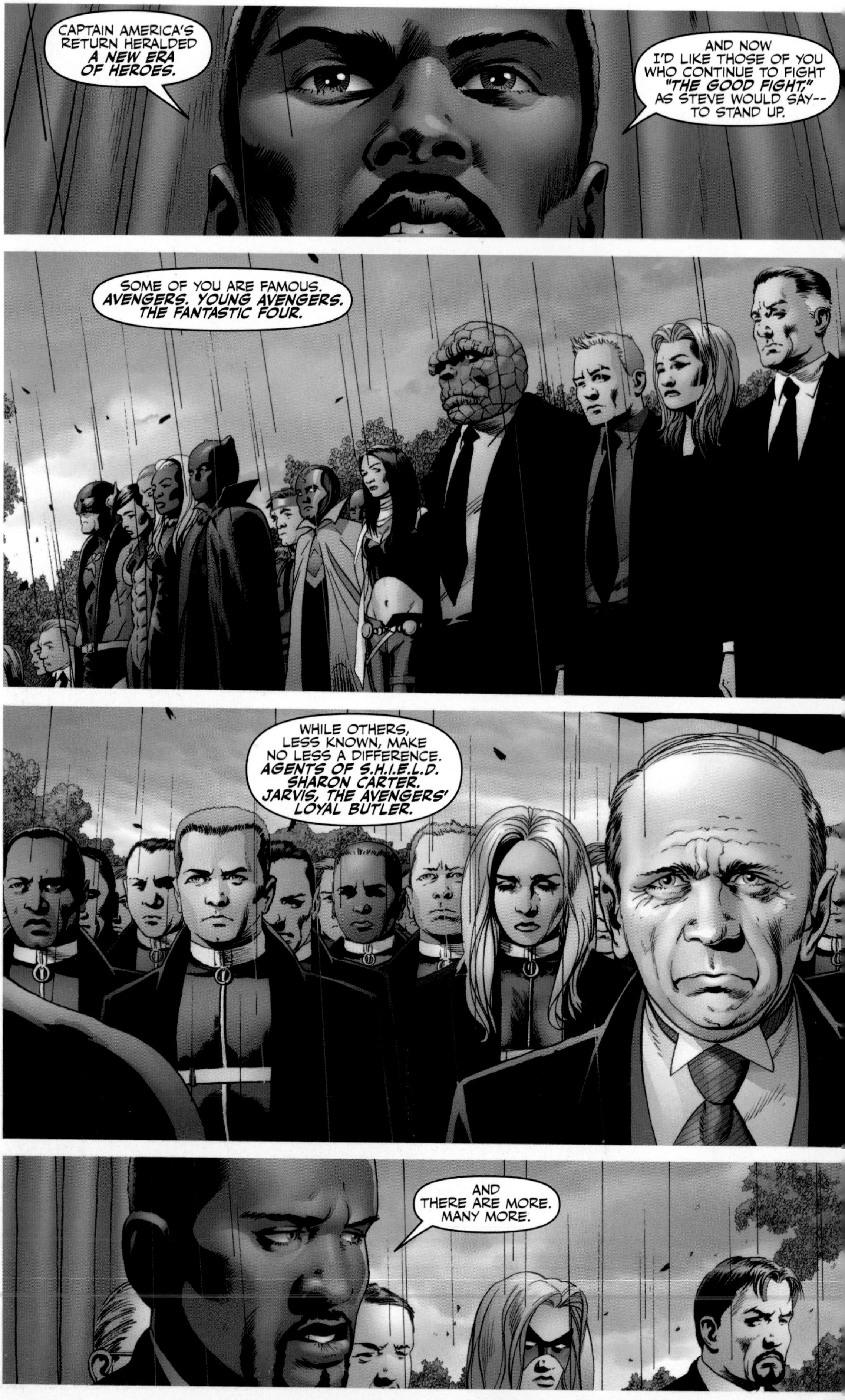
CAPTAIN AMERICA'S RETURN HERALDED *A NEW ERA OF HEROES.*
AND NOW I'D LIKE THOSE OF YOU WHO CONTINUE TO FIGHT *"THE GOOD FIGHT,"* AS STEVE WOULD SAY-- TO STAND UP.
SOME OF YOU ARE FAMOUS. *AVENGERS. YOUNG AVENGERS. THE FANTASTIC FOUR.*
WHILE OTHERS, LESS KNOWN, MAKE NO LESS A DIFFERENCE. *AGENTS OF S.H.I.E.L.D. SHARON CARTER. JARVIS, THE AVENGERS' LOYAL BUTLER.*
AND THERE ARE MORE. MANY MORE.

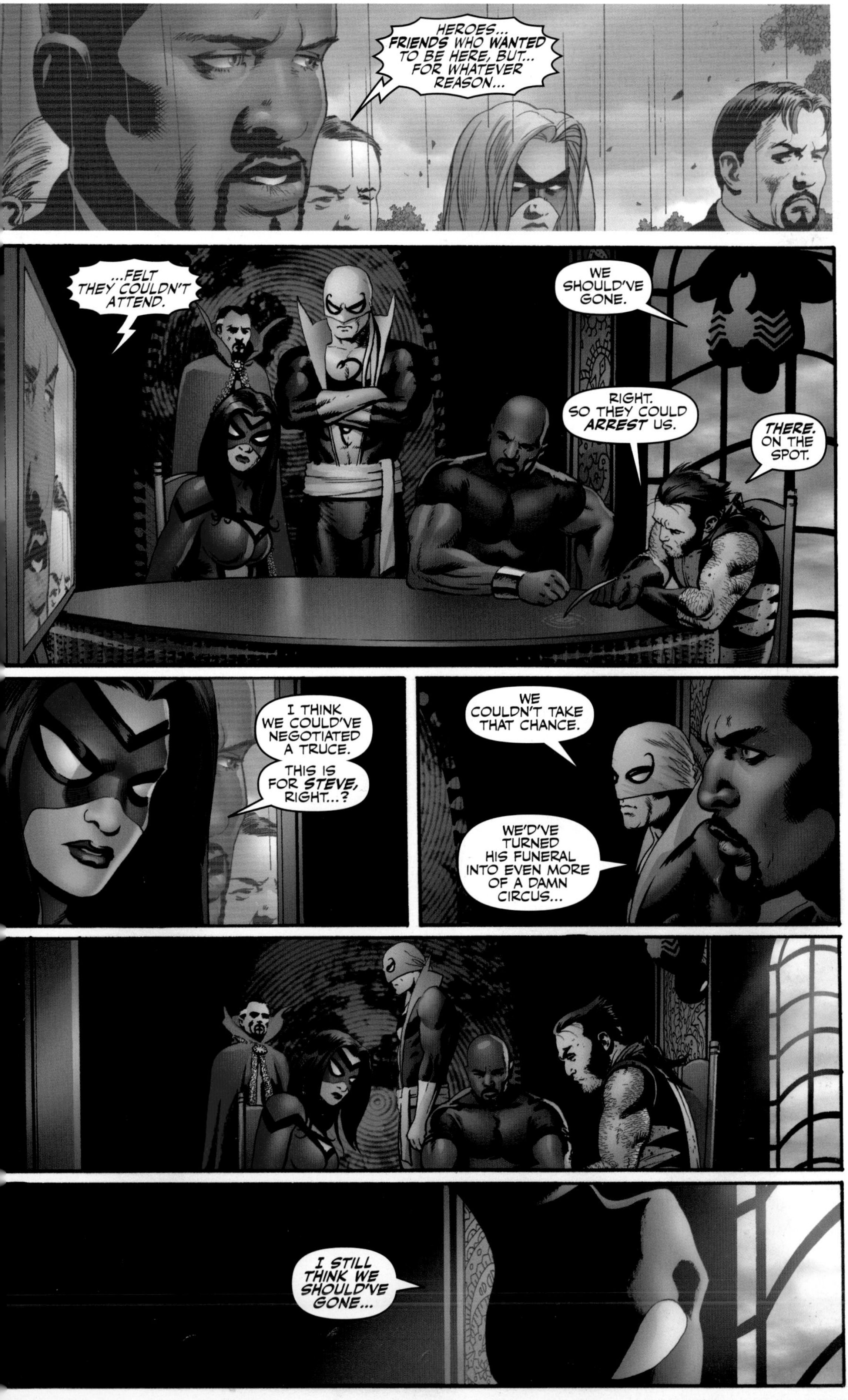
HEROES... FRIENDS WHO WANTED TO BE HERE, BUT... FOR WHATEVER REASON...
...FELT THEY COULDN'T ATTEND.
WE SHOULD'VE GONE.
RIGHT. SO THEY COULD ARREST US.
THERE. ON THE SPOT.
I THINK WE COULD'VE NEGOTIATED A TRUCE.
THIS IS FOR STEVE, RIGHT...?
WE COULDN'T TAKE THAT CHANCE.
WE'D'VE TURNED HIS FUNERAL INTO EVEN MORE OF A DAMN CIRCUS...
I STILL THINK WE SHOULD'VE GONE...

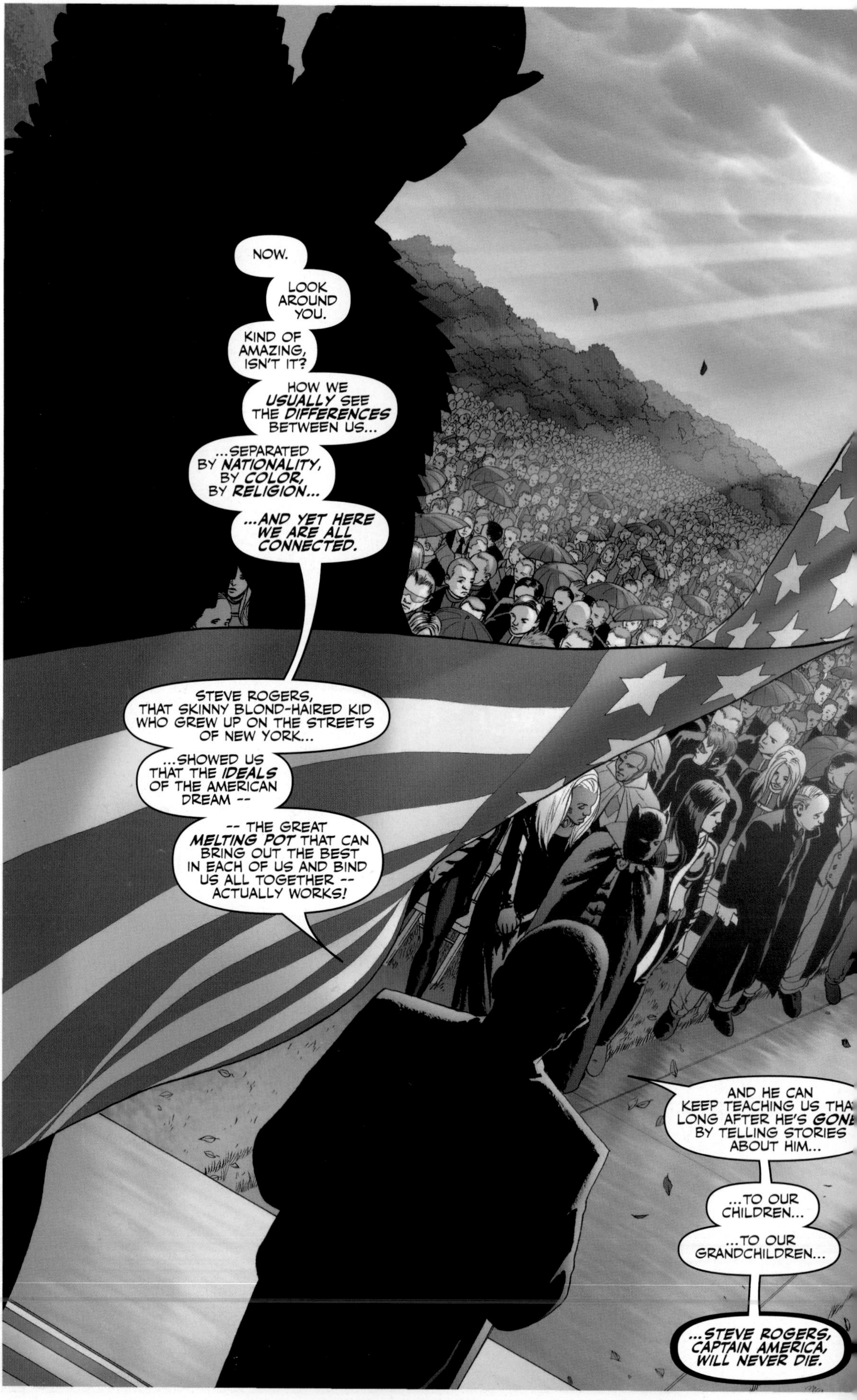

NOW.
LOOK AROUND YOU.
KIND OF AMAZING, ISN'T IT?
HOW WE *USUALLY* SEE THE *DIFFERENCES* BETWEEN US...
...SEPARATED BY *NATIONALITY,* BY *COLOR,* BY *RELIGION...*
...AND YET HERE WE ARE ALL CONNECTED.
STEVE ROGERS, THAT SKINNY BLOND-HAIRED KID WHO GREW UP ON THE STREETS OF NEW YORK...
...SHOWED US THAT THE *IDEALS* OF THE AMERICAN DREAM --
-- THE GREAT *MELTING POT* THAT CAN BRING OUT THE BEST IN EACH OF US AND BIND US ALL TOGETHER -- ACTUALLY WORKS!
AND HE CAN KEEP TEACHING US THA LONG AFTER HE'S *GON* BY TELLING STORIES ABOUT HIM...
...TO OUR CHILDREN...
...TO OUR GRANDCHILDREN...
...STEVE ROGERS, CAPTAIN AMERICA, WILL NEVER DIE.

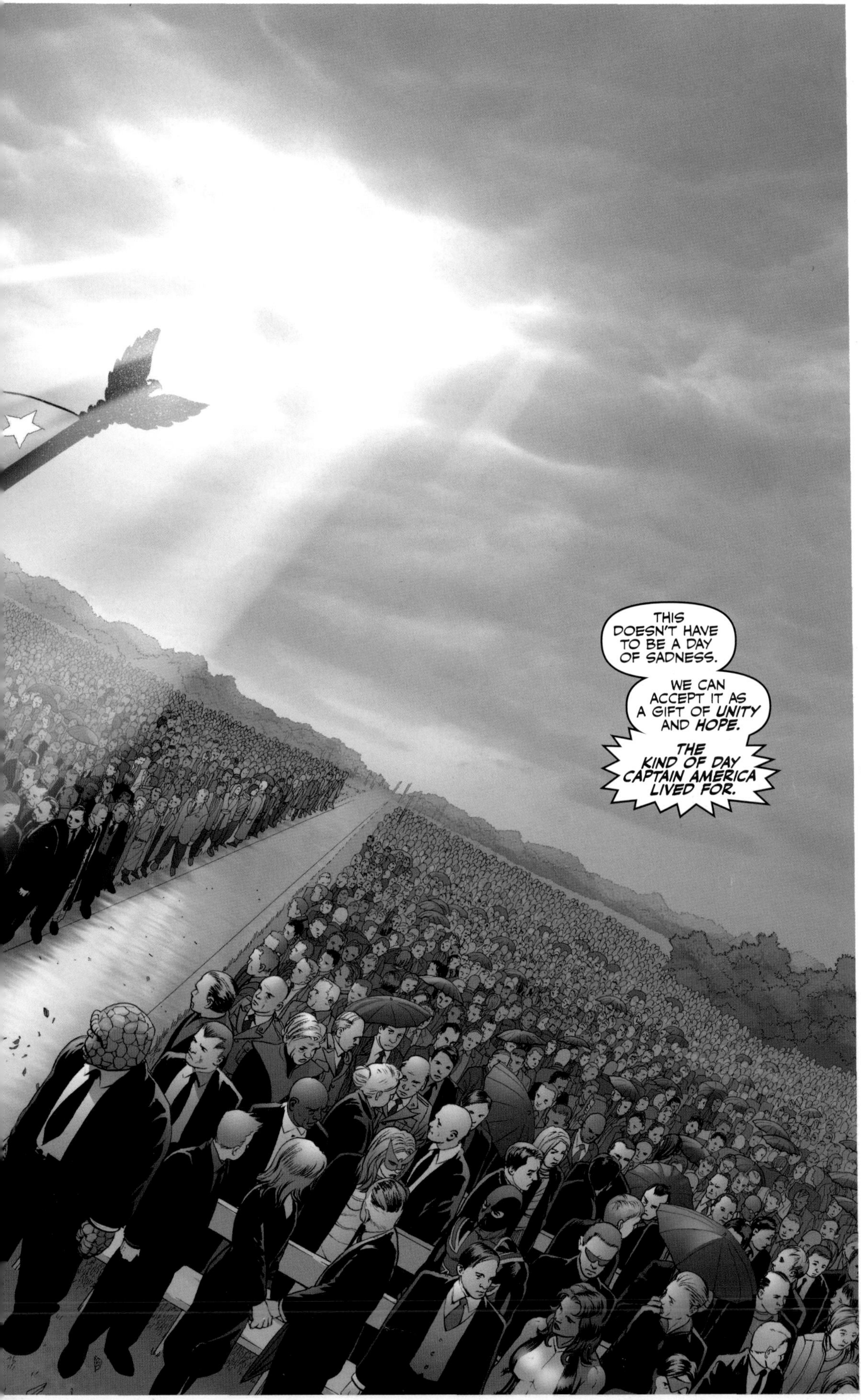
THIS DOESN'T HAVE TO BE A DAY OF SADNESS.
WE CAN ACCEPT IT AS A GIFT OF *UNITY* AND *HOPE.*
THE KIND OF DAY CAPTAIN AMERICA LIVED FOR.

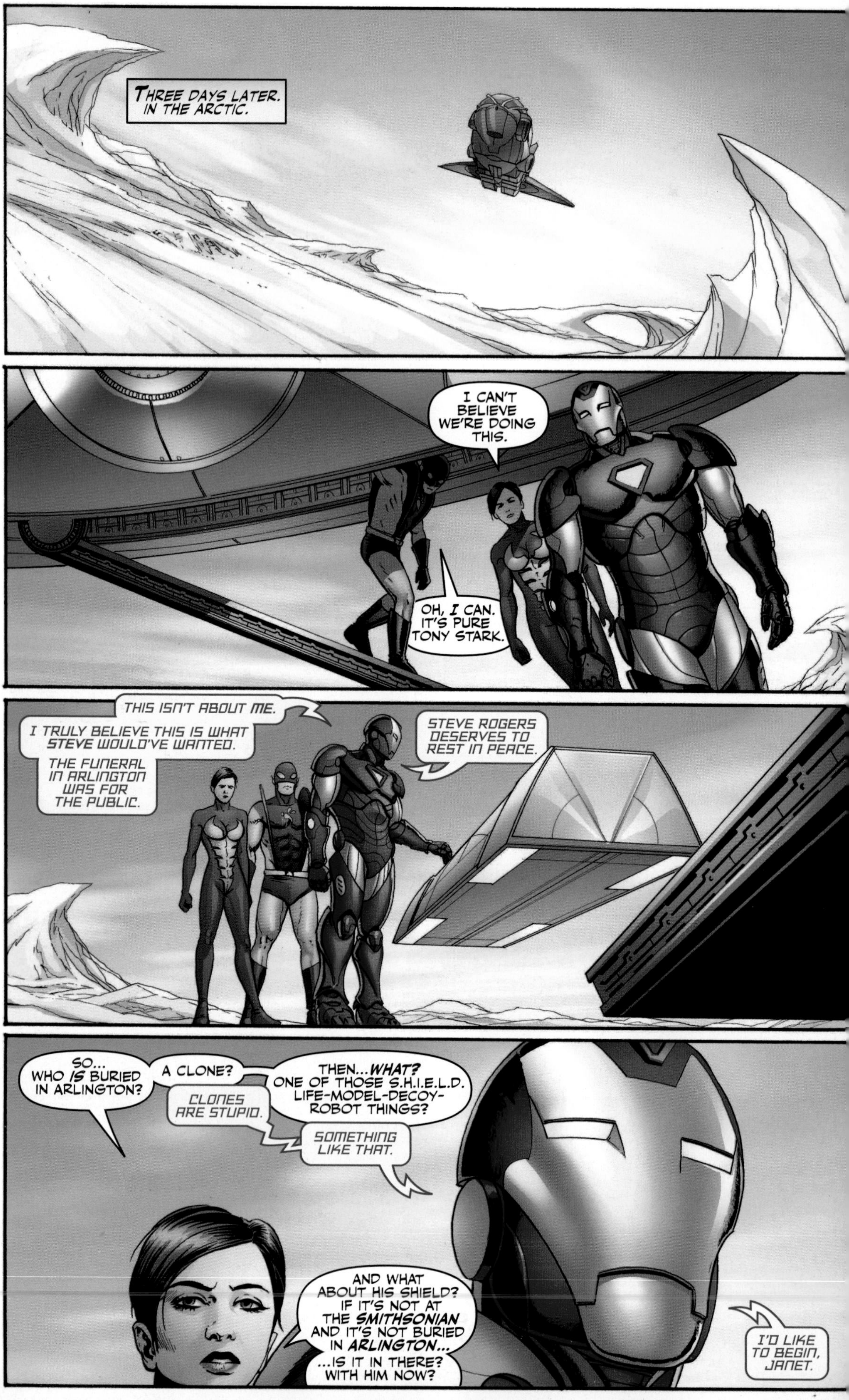
THREE DAYS LATER. IN THE ARCTIC.
I CAN'T BELIEVE WE'RE DOING THIS.
OH, I CAN. IT'S PURE TONY STARK.
THIS ISN'T ABOUT ME.
I TRULY BELIEVE THIS IS WHAT STEVE WOULD'VE WANTED.
THE FUNERAL IN ARLINGTON WAS FOR THE PUBLIC.
STEVE ROGERS DESERVES TO REST IN PEACE.
SO... WHO IS BURIED IN ARLINGTON?
A CLONE?
CLONES ARE STUPID.
THEN...WHAT? ONE OF THOSE S.H.I.E.L.D. LIFE-MODEL-DECOY-ROBOT THINGS?
SOMETHING LIKE THAT.
AND WHAT ABOUT HIS SHIELD? IF IT'S NOT AT THE SMITHSONIAN AND IT'S NOT BURIED IN ARLINGTON... ...IS IT IN THERE? WITH HIM NOW?
I'D LIKE TO BEGIN, JANET.

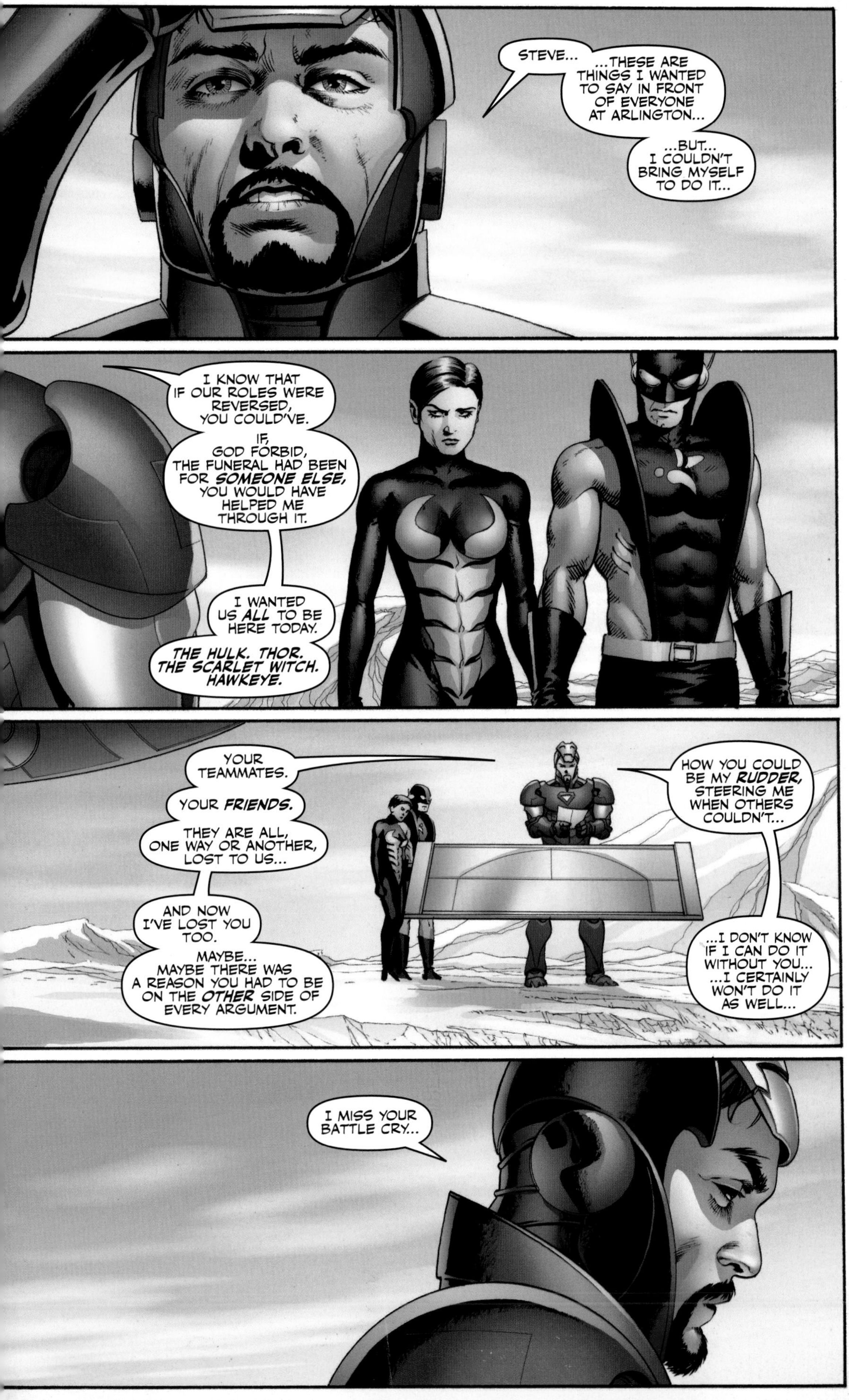
STEVE...
...THESE ARE THINGS I WANTED TO SAY IN FRONT OF EVERYONE AT ARLINGTON...
...BUT... I COULDN'T BRING MYSELF TO DO IT...
I KNOW THAT IF OUR ROLES WERE REVERSED, YOU COULD'VE.
IF, GOD FORBID, THE FUNERAL HAD BEEN FOR SOMEONE ELSE, YOU WOULD HAVE HELPED ME THROUGH IT.
I WANTED US ALL TO BE HERE TODAY.
THE HULK. THOR. THE SCARLET WITCH. HAWKEYE.
YOUR TEAMMATES.
YOUR FRIENDS.
THEY ARE ALL, ONE WAY OR ANOTHER, LOST TO US...
AND NOW I'VE LOST YOU TOO.
MAYBE... MAYBE THERE WAS A REASON YOU HAD TO BE ON THE OTHER SIDE OF EVERY ARGUMENT.
HOW YOU COULD BE MY RUDDER, STEERING ME WHEN OTHERS COULDN'T...
...I DON'T KNOW IF I CAN DO IT WITHOUT YOU... ...I CERTAINLY WON'T DO IT AS WELL...
I MISS YOUR BATTLE CRY...

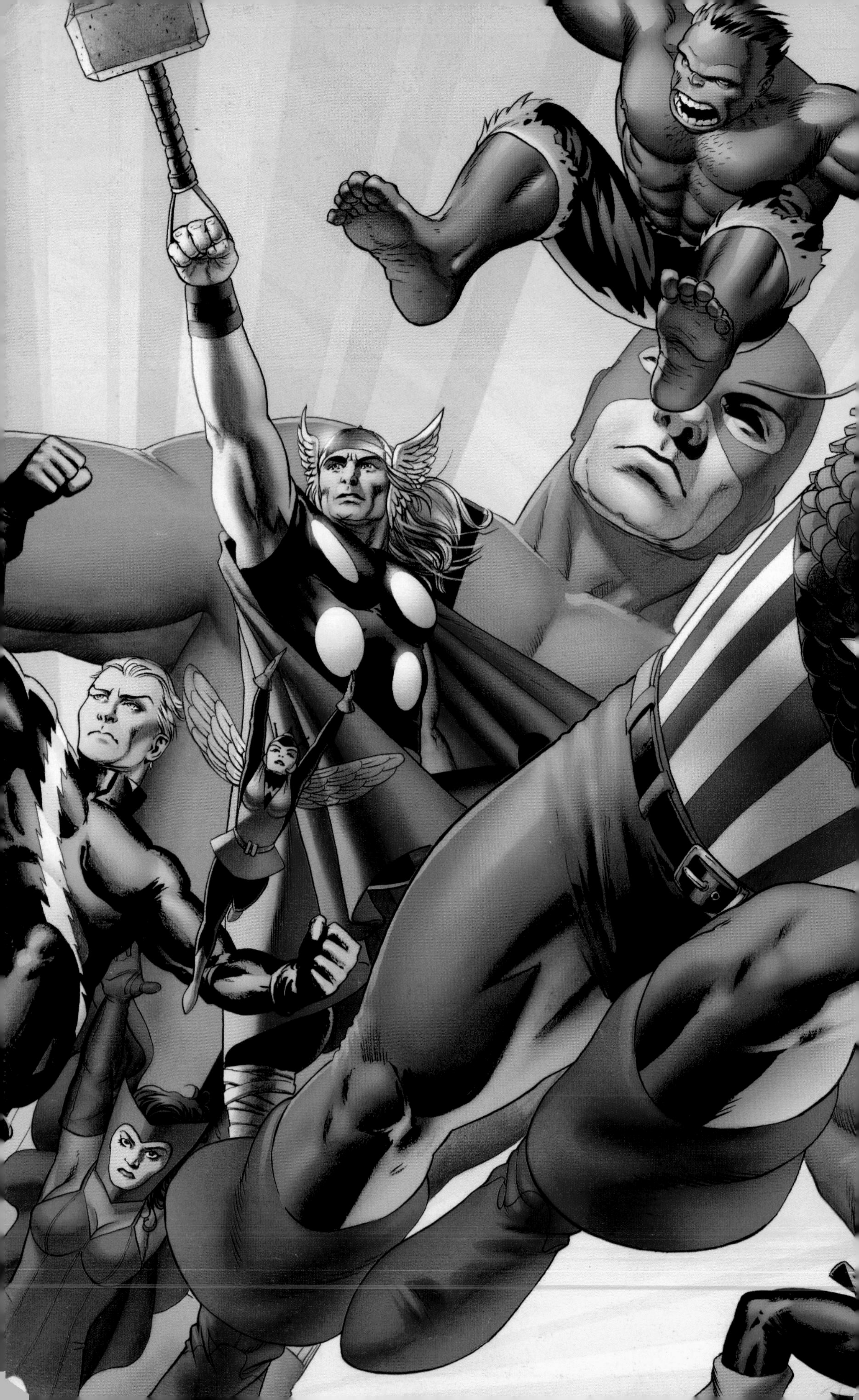

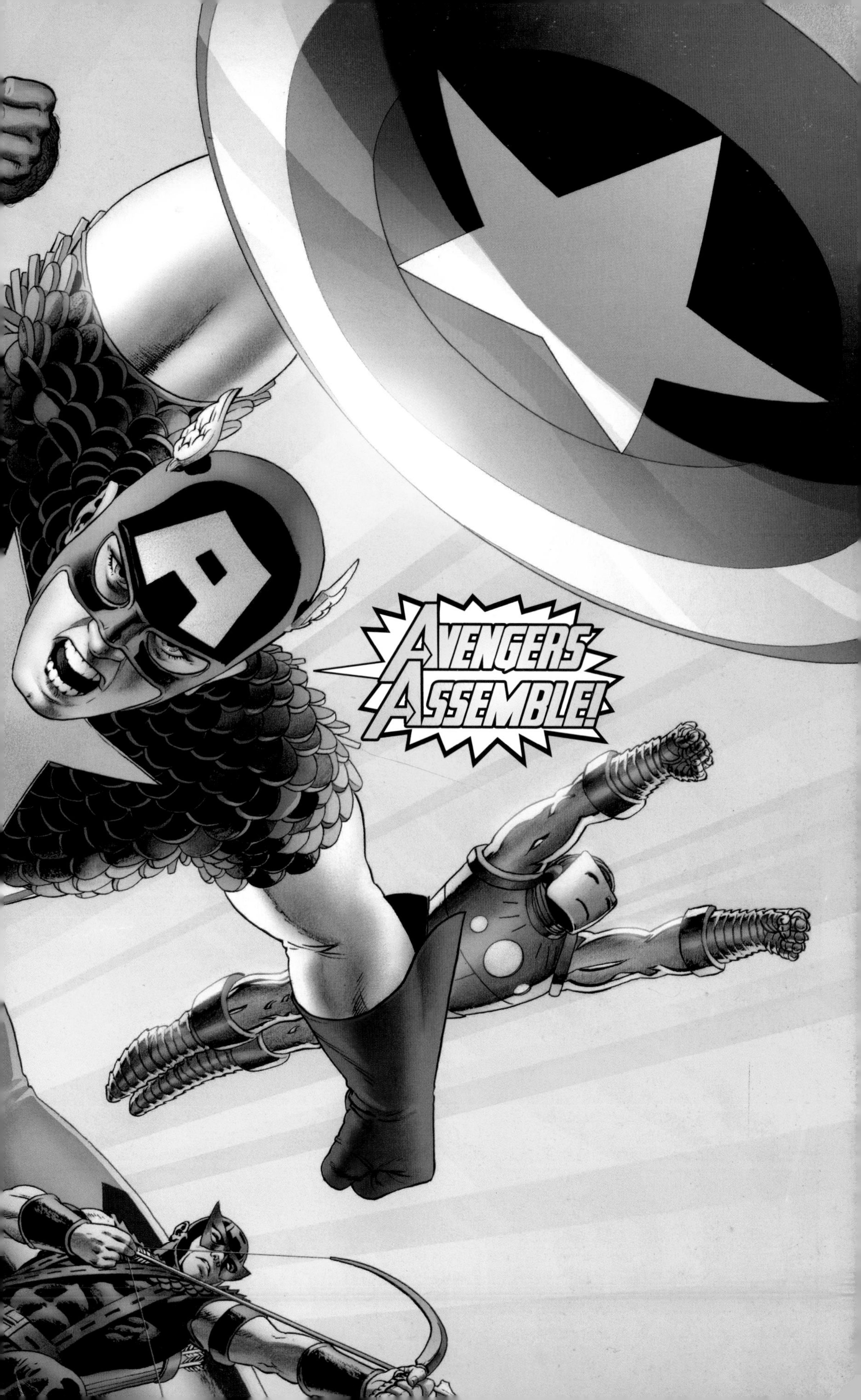
AVENGERS ASSEMBLE!

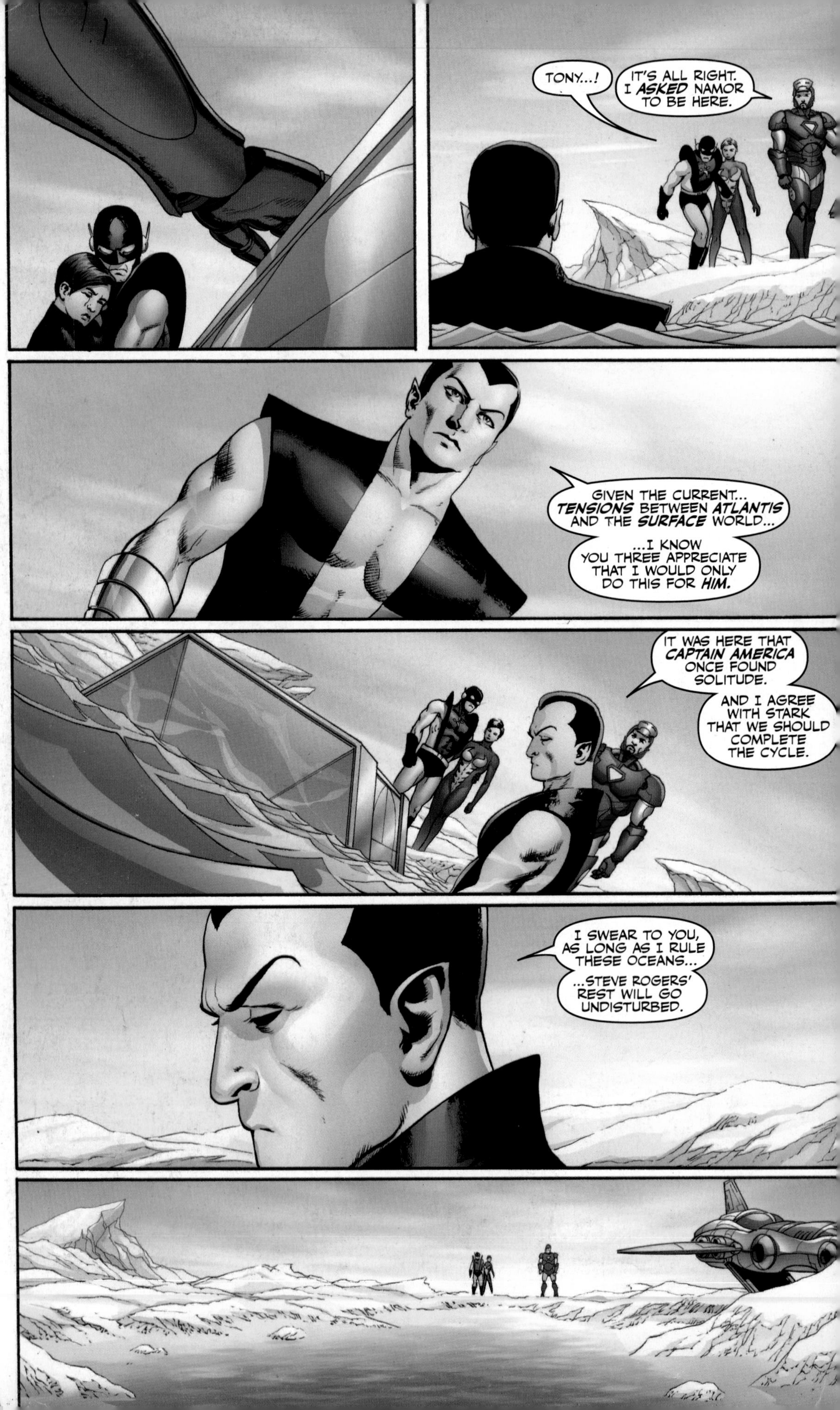
TONY...!
IT'S ALL RIGHT. I ASKED NAMOR TO BE HERE.
GIVEN THE CURRENT... TENSIONS BETWEEN ATLANTIS AND THE SURFACE WORLD...
...I KNOW YOU THREE APPRECIATE THAT I WOULD ONLY DO THIS FOR HIM.
IT WAS HERE THAT CAPTAIN AMERICA ONCE FOUND SOLITUDE.
AND I AGREE WITH STARK THAT WE SHOULD COMPLETE THE CYCLE.
I SWEAR TO YOU, AS LONG AS I RULE THESE OCEANS...
...STEVE ROGERS' REST WILL GO UNDISTURBED.

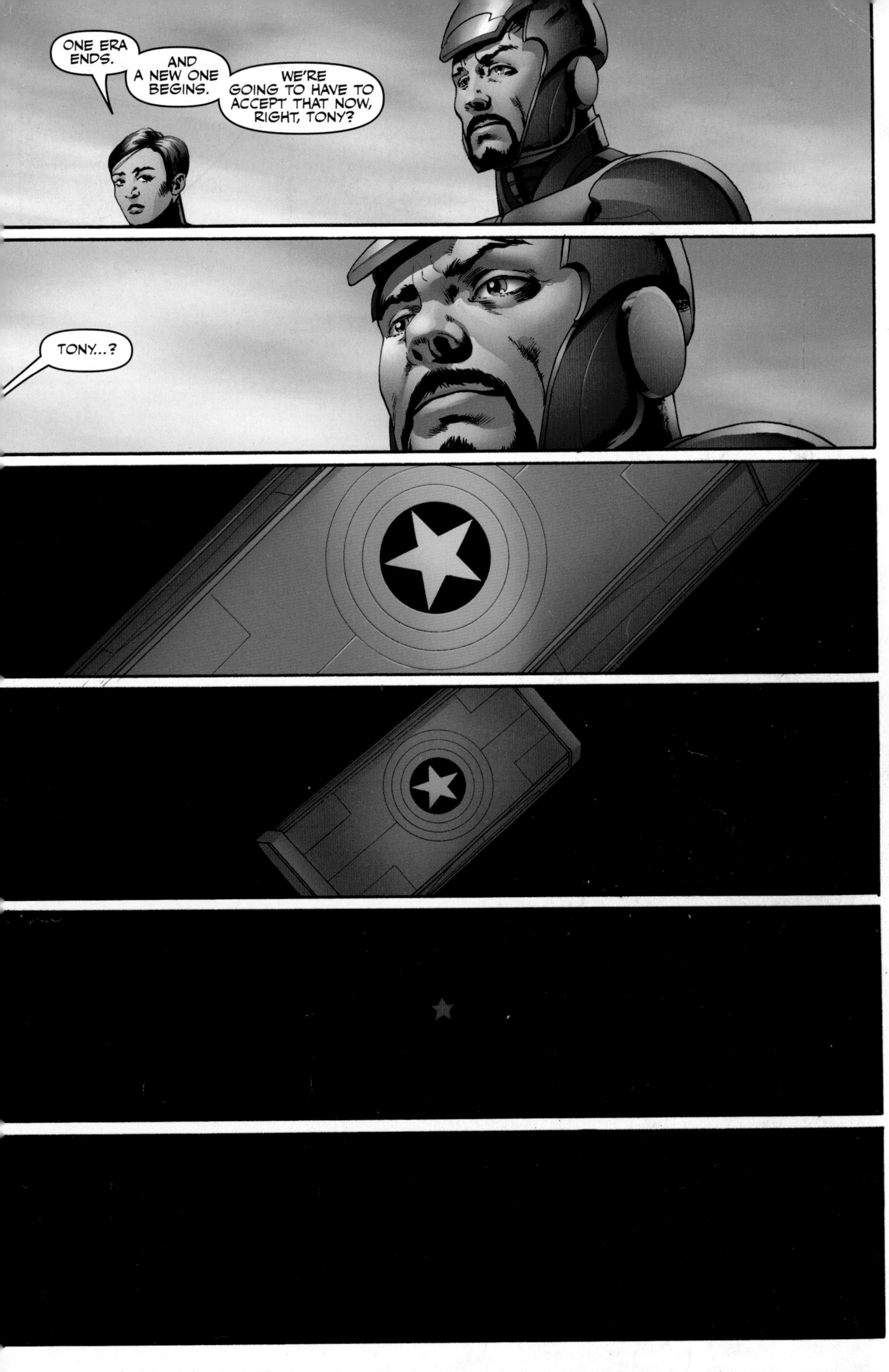
ONE ERA ENDS.
AND A NEW ONE BEGINS.
WE'RE GOING TO HAVE TO ACCEPT THAT NOW, RIGHT, TONY?
TONY...?

CAPTAIN AMERICA
★
1941~2007